BIG IN ASIA

MICHAEL BACKMAN AND CHARLOTTE BUTLER

BIG
in Asia

25 STRATEGIES FOR BUSINESS SUCCESS

Revised and updated

palgrave
macmillan

First published in hardcover 2003
First published in paperback 2004 by PALGRAVE MACMILLAN
Houndmills, Basingstoke, Hampshire RG21 6XS and
175 Fifth Avenue, New York, N.Y. 10010
Companies and representatives throughout the world

PALGRAVE MACMILLAN is the global academic imprint of the Palgrave Macmillan division of St. Martin's Press, LLC and of Palgrave Macmillan Ltd. Macmillan® is a registered trademark in the United States, United Kingdom and other countries. Palgrave is a registered trademark in the European Union and other countries.

ISBN 0–333–98511–7 hardback
ISBN 1–4039–3315–4 paperback

This book is printed on paper suitable for recycling and made from fully managed and sustained forest sources.

A catalogue record for this book is available from the British Library.

The Library of Congress has cataloged the hardcover edition: card no. 2002032672

10   9   8   7   6   5   4   3   2   1
13 12 11 10 09 08 07 06 05 04

Printed and bound in Great Britain by
Creative Print & Design (Wales), Ebbw Vale

The Chinese character that appears on the cover and which is used throughout the book is that for 'Big'.

BIG in Asia

CONTENTS

BIG in Asia

LIST OF TABLES

Preface

There was a time when all that most Asian economies ever seemed to do was to grow – and to do so rapidly. All that a company had to do to be swept along in Asia's boom was to be there. But suddenly operating in Asia seems to have grown a whole lot more complex. Political leaders such as Mahathir and Soeharto, who looked as if they would rule forever, have gone.

No longer is economic growth guaranteed and there is fear that the huge investment focus on China will starve much of the rest of Asia of vital foreign investment. China itself, revelling in its role as 'Workshop of the World' seems unstoppable – much to the horror of the US and EU where noises about uneven trade, fuelled by fears of jobs heading East, have become ever louder. But with over-heated property markets, an intrusive government, a terrible legal system and the possibility of trade sanctions, investors need to decide if China is more boom than bubble.

Another hot topic is corporate governance, still merely a spectre at the feast in most of Asia. Then there are the events that no amount of forecast could predict: things like the outbreaks of Severe Acute Respiratory Syndrome (SARS) and avian flu, and the terrorist activity of extremist groups in the region. But then, at the individual level, operating in Asia has never been easy. It is a game for insiders. And there are plenty with an interest in keeping it that way.

The ancient game of 'Tilt', as practised in Asia, is one of the most popular attractions of the competitive arena. There is no limit to the number of players and the rules are minimal, although the stakes are high. The game is played by two teams and consists of a series of moves beginning when the team going first (known as the Locals) lays down a series of obstacles across the board, thus tilting it at an angle that can vary between 45 and 90 degrees. These obstacles are stone-shaped, of different sizes and weights and variously labelled 'red tape', 'government monopoly', 'arbitrary rules', '*guanxi*' and 'special tax'.

In order to play the game, the opposing team (the Foreigners) must try to tilt the board back in the other direction by dismantling these obstacles one by one, armed with its own set of stones labelled 'choice', 'brand', 'service', 'technology transfer' and 'cash'. The game may last for some time, since if by chance the Locals use up all their stones, fresh ones may appear (regardless of the rules). Appeals to the umpire can be made but they may not be heard. He may in fact be in the employ of the Locals, but rarely will that be disclosed. It's part of the game.

Only when the final stone has been demolished is the game said to be won, with the Foreigners allowed onto the Locals' territory to collect their prize – the chance to be big – Big in Asia.

If you want to try your hand at Tilt, you'll need to be well armed. And the best choice of weapon is information. You'll also need a play – a series of strategies – to cover all manner of contingencies. You'll need to know when to advance, but also when to withdraw. This book is the unofficial guide to the game – a guide on how to be Big in Asia.

Overshooting and Undershooting on Asia – But Never Getting it Right

But why the need for such a guide, given that outsiders have been investing in Asia for the past three decades? Presumably, they should now be experts at the game. Sadly, the reality is that, with monotonous frequency, the 'Foreigners' have ended as heavy losers, wasting valuable financial and human resources on an ultimately vain attempt to build a position in the region. Why? Two of the main reasons have been poor preparation and ignorance. Too often, investment in Asia has been driven more by perceptions and less by fact. As a consequence, outsiders have tended to overshoot in the good times and undershoot in the bad. Rarely have expectations been met and rarely have returns on investments been other than poor.

These unsuccessful forays into Asia have seldom been analysed to enable companies to learn from their mistakes and build on them. Instead, the reaction often has been to cut and run, with those responsible for the investment ducking for cover or even being fired – their efforts being expunged from the corporate memory.

The history of Western involvement in the region over the last 35 years demonstrates this only too well. In the 1970s and 80s, Asia was just too far away, too poor and too 'different' to register on the company radar of hot business spots, and so was largely ignored. Some firms did make an attempt to enter Japan but, having failed to make any impact against protected local competitors, quickly withdrew to count their losses. Where Western companies did attempt to enter the region, they mostly settled for representative offices, small joint ventures to distribute their products or, at the most, set up factories.

There was little emphasis on collecting data on which to base expansion, and few companies sent out ambitious young managers to build relationships with key members of the local business and political community. Those they did send operated in splendid isolation for much of the time. Some chose to try to grow their business while others spent more time enjoying the expatriate lifestyle. In either case, any strenuous demands from corporate headquarters for information or even a significant contribution to the bottom line did not usually mark their stays. They were there to 'wave the flag' – often to each other.

Even among transnationals with a long history in Asia, such as Siemens, Unilever, Cable & Wireless, Blue Circle and British American Tobacco, the region represented only a small percentage of their portfolio. Unilever, whose presence there dated from the late nineteenth century, finally decided in 1990 to set up an East Asia Pacific group to 'make a push' to prove that regional markets could be as profitable as its traditional but saturated ones in Europe and the US. By the early 1990s it had successful operations in several countries, was having 'phenomenal success' in China and was one of the largest foreign companies operating in Japan. And yet, even then, the region generated only 7% of Unilever's total corporate sales, still too small for serious consideration when measured against the company's heavy dependence on its Western markets.

In too many companies, the importance of the region was consistently undervalued by their head offices, despite the fact that the late 1980s saw the new mantra of 'globalisation' enter the vocabulary of many Western chief executives. Unfortunately, few of them actually included Asia in this vision, or saw the gulf between theory and practice. Even companies with highly profitable operations in the region often failed to capitalise on their potential. Hong Kong Telecom, for example, was the long-established subsidiary that enabled Cable & Wireless (C&W), its parent company, to invest and lose a great deal of money on various newer, sexier businesses outside Asia over the years. But throughout that time, the Hong Kong managers often felt that their UK headquarters gave them neither the encouragement nor the appreciation which their efforts deserved. Ultimately, the head office sold off the Hong Kong operation. In companies where there was any interest in pushing forward in Asia, it was mainly due to a few Asiaphiles, who were regarded with suspicion by their more mainstream colleagues. In the higher management ranks at corporate centre, few knew anything about Asia, and fewer cared.

Then came the boom years of Asia's development in the 1990s, when the business media began to notice that the region housed some of the world's most dynamic markets, turning in growth rates of 10% annually while being home to about half the world's population. The pussy cats had become tigers and so now gaining a foothold in Asia became important.

Head offices around the world suddenly made money available to 'get established' in Asia and the money gushed in. Long neglected, dormant subsidiaries found themselves shaken up by the arrival of expatriate management teams from head office, sent to develop production, finance and marketing functions and generally galvanise them into greater performance, albeit that their efforts were usually based on little understanding of the Asian business environment.

Expectations went wild. The 'Asian miracle' was here, the 'Pacific century' was soon to arrive and to cap it all off there was China. Short cuts had to be found to compensate for the years of neglect and that meant local partners had to be found. Any would do. Due care and diligence was often thrown out the window. Transparency was not the 'Asian way' after all, and insisting on such things would seem culturally insensitive, if not downright rude. The choosers set about transforming themselves into the beggars.

Asia's economic crisis of 1997–98 brought this jamboree to an end. Many Western companies took fright, closed down their operations and withdrew from the region. Other multinationals, unable to sustain continued losses, cut their Asian budgets to the bone, perhaps leaving a lone expat manager to maintain a presence. In November 1999, a survey of Western companies attending an EIU conference in Singapore found that 55% of them had decided to refocus or consolidate their Asian-Pacific operations in anticipation of continued tough conditions. The old lack of confidence in the region had returned. Yet, since then, those same countries have been pulling out of the crisis, albeit at different speeds and as Table 0.1, which shows current per capita incomes (on a PPP basis) across the region, demonstrates, the size and growing prosperity of some Asian markets are

still providing many opportunities. (Figures for the United States, Australia
and the United Kingdom are provided for comparison purposes.)

So where are we now? It is time for a sensible approach to Asia. But
most of all it's time to learn. Information is the best antidote to risk. Ignore
stampedes, they are founded on ignorance. There is no need to rush, Asia
will still be there tomorrow. So there is time to do your homework, which
is just as well, because there is no alternative, assuming that you want to
be Big in Asia.

Table 0.1 Who's poor and who's not – the current state of play in Asia

Country or territory	GDP per capita (purchasing power parity basis, US$)	Population (millions)
Japan	28,700	127.2
Hong Kong	27,200	7.4
Singapore	25,200	4.6
South Korea	19,600	48.3
Brunei	18,600	0.36
Taiwan	18,000	22.6
Malaysia	8,800	23.1
Thailand	7,000	64.3
China	4,700	1,287.0
Philippines	4,600	84.6
Sri Lanka	3,700	19.7
Indonesia	3,100	235.0
India	2,600	1,049.7
Vietnam	2,300	81.6
Pakistan	2,000	150.7
Laos	1,800	5.9
Bangladesh	1,800	138.4
Burma (Myanmar)	1,700	42.5
Cambodia	1,600	13.1
Nepal	1,400	26.5
North Korea	1,000	22.5
East Timor	500	1.0
***	***	***
United States	36,300	290.3
Australia	26,900	19.7
United Kingdom	25,500	60.1

Source: CIA Factbook, 2004.

Information is Power

Becoming Powerful

Information is power – it reduces risk. Most Western managers know this, and can quote Sun Tzu's maxim about the need to 'know your enemy' by heart. Yet many investors and multinationals entering the Asian business arena economise on this most essential of business inputs, and sow the seeds of failure from the start. Dazzled by the market statistics – a billion consumers in China, two hundred million in Indonesia – too often they have walked blindly into a joint venture or strategic alliance with only a minimum knowledge of the prevailing operating and cultural norms, handicapping themselves from the start. Even companies with a long presence in the region, or who have moved in and out of Asia during recent decades, have failed to use the information available to them effectively, so have not always performed as well as they should have done.

For this, Western firms have not been entirely to blame. In Asia, information is a highly prized asset, and its businesspeople are past masters at collecting, controlling and using it. Pre-crisis, gathering certain types of data about a company was virtually impossible. For example, an investment decision could rarely, if ever, be taken on the basis of a hard analysis of the local company's balance sheet. Any books offered for inspection would almost certainly be neither the true nor the only set. The key facts and figures would be safely locked in the head of the company owner and so, short of hypnosis, difficult to extract. Consequently, Western companies were often forced to take decisions on less than perfect financial information.

However, their failure to gather other, more easily accessible information about the country, the business environment or the background of the local partner before signing on the dotted line is less excusable. It also cost them dear. For this neglect both weakened their ability to make a deal that would safeguard their investment against some of the most common dangers of operating in the region and, even more crucially, gave the upper hand in the relationship to their Asian partner from the start. From there on, the only way for many Western companies was down.

Why this *kamikaze* approach to a region of such major importance? Why have companies adopted an almost 'what the hell, let's get in at any price' attitude and entered countries in the region in unseemly haste, only to repent at leisure as they searched for a market that never met the glowing forecasts, tried vainly to manage a huge, unskilled workforce they could not sack and, finally, realised that even if there were any profits, they couldn't necessarily repatriate them? The most basic research effort could have given them enough information to avoid such pitfalls. Fed into their strategic planning, it would have given them a much stronger hand at every stage of their entry, whether via a joint venture or, even more critically, via an acquisition. Western managers would never dream of acting like this in their home markets – at least not if they wished to stay in business. So why this flagrant neglect of basic business practice when it comes to Asia?

Ignorance is not Bliss

The speedy withdrawal of many new investors from Asia during the region's 1997–98 economic crisis and its aftermath was due largely to ignorance. Other markets in the United States and Europe might be volatile and go through periods of recession, but Western managers are well informed about these markets and their business cycles, and this knowledge gives them the faith to ride out the bad periods. Lacking the same experience or knowledge of Asia, the majority failed to balance the underlying strengths of the region against this serious but transitory period of crisis. Just as their view of Asia's potential had been exaggerated, so their view of the economic crisis and its implications was equally extreme. An economist at the Economist Intelligence Unit (EIU) in Hong Kong observed that where once, during the boom years, expatriate managers had often asked him to give a talk to visitors that would temper their unrealistically high business expectations, 'they were now trying to convince head office to stay in the region'. Both positions were based on a fundamental lack of knowledge.[1]

The Costs of Ignorance

In Asia, information can make the difference between success and failure, control and impotence. This is because information:

■ Changes the Balance of Power

In the boom years and the bad, Asian companies had the upper hand over their Western partners. In the good times, since demand vastly outnumbered supply, they were able to cherry-pick those foreign firms that they knew matched their need for technological and financial resources. Siam Cement, for example, was so deluged by companies desperate to enter Thailand that, as a senior executive remarked: 'Our financial manager is a guy who sits back and waits for them to make an offer.' Within a few years it had joint ventures with French, US, German, Italian and Mexican companies, and had diversified into auto parts, ceramics, steel, electrical machinery and building materials.

Western companies, by contrast, often failed to appreciate the reasons for their relative impotence or to draw the lesson that any failure was mainly their own fault, since, from start to finish, they had locked themselves into a vicious cycle of ignorance. Their lack of knowledge of the region and the companies in which they invested meant that when they took an equity stake, usually in a family-run business owned by an ethnic Chinese entrepreneur, they negotiated from a position of weakness. Once the partnership was up and running, their further lack of knowledge about how their partners ran their businesses, about how the systems worked, about the markets and consumers they were serving and local financial practices, handicapped them at every turn. Naturally, their Asian partners were ready to take advantage of such willing victims.

Many Western companies that retired licking their wounds after the failure of their Asian investment in effect scored a spectacular own goal. Out of ignorance, they wasted both their investment and a potential fund of goodwill: Asian companies have long memories for those who stay during the good times, but 'take away the umbrella when it rains'. For example, the US auto company, Ford, stayed in Thailand despite the currency crash and fulfilled plans for a new car plant. It also helped to establish other satellite supply companies and a dealership, enhancing its reputation in the country as a long-term 'friend'.

■ Closes Options

Those companies that had not taken advantage of their time in the region to build up a fund of business knowledge and experience were left with only one option when the downturn came: withdrawal.

By contrast, those companies that had taken a more systematic approach to investing in Asia found themselves with not just the option of staying, but of reaping a great reward. For those Western companies with faith in the long-term future of operations in Asia, based on their knowledge and experience, the currency crash was a window of opportunity to expand. Desperate to stave off bankruptcy, companies in Korea, Japan and the countries of Southeast Asia looked westwards for a foreign saviour. Many of the early deals following the crisis involved parties who had known each other for a long time, either in some form of strategic alliance or as joint venture partners. Having built up their relationship, the two sides knew and trusted each other. Consequently, the Western firms were able to increase their equity share, buy out their partner or even make acquisitions, knowing exactly what they were getting, at a good price. Thus Blue Circle, the UK-based cement company, acquired two local rivals at the modest price of $631.6 million, making itself the unassailable number one in Malaysia, where it had been present since 1953.

Other multinationals that had been waiting to break into industries previously closed to them were also able to move into the region by acquiring local companies which were in trouble. Those that had carefully prepared their positions got a bargain – a local company that was exactly the strategic fit they sought and potentially profitable. However, those that moved quickly in an opportunistic fashion, without doing the necessary research, were more likely to find themselves paying over the odds for companies which later turned out to be mired in hidden debts. The cycle would begin again.

A SWOT Analysis of Asia

Every Western manager is familiar with the concept of a SWOT analysis, an exercise in plotting the strengths and weaknesses, opportunities and threats in a company's external and internal environment, which generally prefaces important investment decisions. Out of this situational analysis arise objectives, strategies and actual plans to execute the chosen strategy.

Few multinationals would contemplate moving into a new market in the US or Europe without undertaking such an exercise. They require their business development planners to compile detailed dossiers of information about the country, the industry, its markets and consumers before reaching such crucial investment decisions. However, until recently, few companies put the same effort into Asia, despite the fact that they were stepping onto a notoriously uneven playing field where the local teams had a well-earned reputation for being sharp operators, where the culture was totally different from any they had known, where they could not communicate with local workers, managers and owners, and where operating practices were a mystery.

If Western firms are to build strength in Asia and give themselves options in the future, clearly they must approach their investment differently, and build on a solid foundation of information. What is more, having done this, companies *must act on it*. For the other unfortunate tendency has been for those companies that did put an effort into collecting information about the markets in Asia that paid for expensive reports on the political or economic risks and carefully plotted the data on a matrix of high and low desirability, to then ignore any negative indicators and go ahead with their investment anyway, on the grounds that 'We can't be left behind'.

This was frequently the case with China, where the attrition rate of Western companies has been tremendous. The reasons why joint ventures failed there have been well researched and widely publicised. One of the key reasons, it was discovered, was ignorance on the part of the foreign firm. Yet despite this, multinationals have continued to make the same mistake and enter the market without sufficient preparation. The information was there, but seemingly few bothered to look for it.

The External Environment

Many of these factors are beyond the firm's control but will affect the business environment, and so need to be fed into the final decision-making process. The data that needs to be collected on the external environment (political, economic, demographic, legal structure degree of risk, educational/skill levels) is easily accessible. For example, reports on the economic outlook and main economic indicators for each country are regularly updated by the EIU in its various country reports and research papers.

Information on government spending plans is also useful and easily obtained. Remember, most of the big conglomerates in Southeast Asia got big by investing in industries starred for growth in five-year government plans. It should not be beyond the wit of Western multinationals to look at long-term, published plans of the region's governments, especially China, to see where, for example, there are likely to be special deals or tax holidays offered to get an industry going. However, a word of caution about statistical forecasts on growth rates, market potential and so on. Be very, very wary. Government forecasts in some Asian countries reflect aspirations more than reality.

Under pressure from bodies such as the International Monetary Fund (IMF) and the World Trade Organization (WTO), countries in the region are moving towards deregulation and privatisation. But again check out the facts. Continued progress in this direction cannot be taken for granted since, in many places, strong resistance from the local population has led to a 'one step forward, two steps back' scenario. Governments that give with one hand have been known to take it away with the other. Thus, when elected in 2001, Thai Prime Minister Thaksin Shinawatra proclaimed the country open to foreign investment. He then backtracked amid fears that the foreign investors would become too influential. Privatisation was also slowed on earlier promises.

Privatisation plans for other countries such as Indonesia, China and India look good on the surface but again, beware. A little digging will reveal obstacles in the shape of entrenched vested interests in business and bureaucracy, making for a still very uneven playing field. Look at which governments are dragging their feet when it comes to selling off assets, allowing powerful but heavily indebted local businessmen to use court cases and queries about contract issues to cause delay. Check also how many parties are likely to be involved in the final decision-making process. In China, it is usually necessary to obtain approval for a contract or joint venture at many bureaucratic levels, in strict hierarchical order. This can be an unexpected hurdle that can slow down negotiations for months, if not years, as in some famous cases.

Any restructuring claims by previously indebted conglomerates also need to be verified. Which have real profitability? Is the sector you are interested in really safe to buy into, or is reform superficial? One easy way to tell is to look at what everyone else is doing. If nobody else is buying into a certain sector, however attractive, there must be a good reason. This is particularly true of the banking industry in most Asian countries; the Bank of China in China (ironically considered one of the best run), has not had any takers, while Indonesia's Bank of Central Asia, once the financial core of the mighty Salim family empire and 30% owned by the Soeharto family, was on sale for two years. Equally, the South Korean government had little success in inducing foreign firms to buy into its banking industry, while the Philippines has had a very slow time trying to sell off state assets.

Political Risks

A working knowledge of the political environment is also important, especially in assessing potential risks. This does not mean compiling a history of the region, although being aware of the reasons for friction between Japan and South Korea, or the sometimes fractious relationship between Singapore and Malaysia can help to avoid mistakes. Especially vital in China, and in countries such as Indonesia, where decentralising pressures are growing, is the need to collect and monitor information on the political scene at every level – central, regional and local. This will help to identify the ministries, people and organisations that are the most important when it comes to contacts and licences for your particular industry. Corruption is another risk to be weighed: it is a subject well documented in business journals and publications, particularly those of the corruption watch group Transparency International.

China merits a SWOT analysis by itself here when it comes to changing people at the top, rules and risks. Who will the next most powerful man be? Which 'princelings', the sons of powerful members of the Communist Party, are moving to control newly privatised companies and even existing state-owned companies? What are the foreign direct investment (FDI) rules exactly and how might they change tomorrow? Information about the latest changes to joint venture and merger rules, how strict exchange controls are (can you get your money out?), all these data are easily available and vital. Then there are China's well-charted risks to add in – labour protests are likely to get fiercer and corruption is said to be at unprecedented levels. The sell-off of state assets looks interesting, but the dynamic, modernising companies with good brands must be sorted from the moribund enterprises with outdated technology, too many workers and poor quality products with no market.

And how do you get your products to the markets you identify? Better check out the infrastructure. For non-geography graduates, a little map work on Asia is always a good idea. Where are the big markets? How far are the docks from your factory? What state are the railways/roads in? Are there toll charges? Note the bordering countries. Three of Thailand's neighbours are Myanmar, Vietnam and Laos – not known for their political or economic stability, but with a heavy involvement in the drugs trade and smuggling of contraband goods. How could that affect you?

Legislation

Information about the legal framework, that is, the rules for FDI, import tariffs and taxes and local content requirement are particularly crucial in Asia, since they vary from country to country and from sector to sector and are constantly changing. Monitor them to avoid missing out on sudden openings, or spotting new obstacles placed by governments.

Advance information about moves towards the creation of an ASEAN (Association of South East Asian Nations) free trade zone (now projected for 2010 instead of 2020) and changing AFTA (ASEAN Free Trade Association) legislation with regard to import tariffs can be vital for cost projections. For example, the implementation of the Common Effective Preferential Tariff due in 2003 and 2010 will progressively bring down agricultural products on the sensitive list, so allowing foreign producers to match the prices of their local competitors.

Another important input will be information about the country's labour laws: where can you hire and fire relatively easily, and where only after protracted negotiation? Coupled with this is knowledge about the strength and militancy of trade unions. In India, South Korea and Thailand, for example, they have strongly resisted privatisation plans, and played a powerful role in stopping foreign companies from completing proposed investments. In April 2002, ten million Indian public sector workers went on strike against legislation to make it easier to lay off workers. Make a note of these and other such developments in Asian countries. Strikes and confrontations are not what Western firms want to provoke. Their shareholders flinch from seeing company names being bandied around by workers brandishing banners characterising them as 'rapacious vultures'.

The quality of your local staff will be crucial for the success of any venture, so it is worth collecting information on the education and skill levels to be expected and where to find good employees. Competition is fierce for the best skilled workers and managers, so investigate the best way to find them. Do you use head-hunters or poach them from other companies?

The Competitive Arena

The industry/market/competitive structures and so on are another key data set. Gathering information about your competitors is always important, but in Asia this is made more complex by the number and variety of domestic competitors. Local competition in Asia can range from big conglomerates to a myriad of hole-in-the-wall operators who are ambitious to grow. Some of them will, so it is important to collect information on likely future competitors, especially those where the next US-educated, MBA-trained generation is taking over. Look out for changes in the business model as they try to implement some of the Western business methods to make them more competitive.

Multinationals tend to know a great deal about their fellow Western rivals, but be less well informed about the big Asian players and local competitors and their latest moves. Japanese investment in Southeast Asia is well known, but in fact its investment in China is even greater. Toshiba, for example, has 13 subsidiaries and six affiliated companies in China. Other Japanese firms are also pushing in, and South Korean firms are expanding rapidly in China via the purchase of stakes in companies or licensing arrangements. Even Taiwanese firms are moving in to set up factories there. Who are they and how do they operate?

In such a volatile competitive environment, changes can happen quickly, so you need to keep a strict watch on what is happening in your industry. In particular, look out for signals from industry leaders. Companies, like birds, tend to flock together, so don't be left behind by failing to spot new investment signals. For example, the move of the Asian head office operations of foreign financial services Lehman Brothers and Goldman Sachs and Philips, the Dutch electronics group to Hong Kong suggests that, post-1997, investment is shifting to Northeast Asia. Similarly, the recent trend among foreign multinationals such as Alcatel, IBM, Oracle and Microsoft to move their R&D operations to China (notwithstanding widespread intellectual property abuses in that country) appears to signal a shift in the traditional view of that country. China now seems to be making rapid progress up the value chain, changing the view of it as primarily a source of cheap labour and recipient of technology for manufacturing operations. That could change your plan. Similarly, an exodus of foreign firms from a particular country can signal that it is not the right time to invest there.

Marketing in Asia has generally been a weakness among multinationals, who have had to learn to adapt their products for different tastes, complexions, buying habits and so on. Western companies that are acutely aware of the differences between Italian and Swedish consumers have tended to regard Asia as one homogeneous market – a view that a little research could quickly correct. Some have set up excellent information systems to keep an eye on the local competitors. The shampoo, conditioners and hair colouring products of French group, L'Oréal, for example, can be seen on sale all over Asia. To maintain the company's pre-eminent place in the market, each day hundreds of packages arrive at the hair care division's headquarters in Paris. They contain every new product on the shelves, each of which is analysed to add to the information store about content, innovation, packaging and so on. Traditionally, Western firms have left the marketing side to their local partners but, for the future, they need to build up their own databases on consumer tastes and buying habits, for example the bestselling international and local products, how prices vary and how likely are price wars.

For those companies contemplating a joint venture, obviously every type of information will be needed in order to understand the different business culture they will be getting into. The potential partner's past history, how the businesses was built up, its assets (or those that are known), the background of its top managers, the skill levels of its employees, links with local/regional governments, reputation in the business community and so on. Check them out with their suppliers, distributors, competitors, in short talk to everyone you can. It will not be easy but could save you a lot of grief later on.

All this information can then be tested against your own company's internal resources: your financial, organisational and human resources, core competencies, strategic objectives and so on. Where are the weaknesses, what are your strengths? What is the chance of building a long-term, sustainable competitive advantage? Would it be better to wait – what future changes might offer opportunities/threats/potential synergies? It is all classic textbook stuff and, if thoroughly done, might help you to avoid making an expensive mistake. If you really do know your enemy and know yourself, you will be in good shape to move into Asia.

Information Sources

Information about any of the above can come from many sources. Fastest and easiest, anyone with access to the Internet can discover an enormous amount of background information about countries and companies in all parts of the region. Read the local media. The *Bangkok Post*, Singapore's *Business Times*, the *Jakarta Post*, the *Asian Wall Street Journal*, the *South China Morning Post* and Malaysia's *The Star* are among the better English-language publications in the region for local business coverage. Reading the local media is the best way to get a feel for the country and its business context – who is expanding or linking up with whom, who is borrowing money, issuing a bond or looking for an injection of equity. One expatriate had the bright idea of looking up the website of a key competitor. He was amazed at the information to be found there:

> Even information about their brands and the perceptions behind them. We had been trying to work it out for ourselves, and there it was all the time. It would have saved a lot of expensive consultants' time if we had thought to look on the web beforehand.

Many books have been written about Asia – its business context, ethnic Chinese entrepreneurs, brands and the region's politics. But one little known source is the archive of case studies written by business school faculties around the world about the experiences of companies investing in Asia, and on Asian companies themselves. Written for pedagogical purposes, the studies aim to teach managers about how business works in Asia. Companies can save themselves a lot of time if, for a standardised and modest fee, they buy relevant case studies from the clearing houses that collect and hold the cases that are written around the world.[2] Highly detailed case studies can be readily bought, for example, on the histories of Asian conglomerates or joint ventures in China. Many have a teaching note to emphasise key lessons, and perhaps a later update. Investors and companies could learn a lot for little effort, but this is perhaps too easy. Few companies avail themselves of this opportunity but many more should.

Of course, these are all secondary sources of information. The best way of all is to go directly into the field and collect it yourself. Set up an office as a listening post, make contacts with locals, fellow expatriates, embassy staff and tune into the gossip, get invited to the parties, watch what local consumers are buying, drive out of town and see where the roads run out. It will be worth your while if being Big in Asia is your aim.

Hitting the Ground Running is Preferable to Simply Hitting the Ground

The biggest challenge for many companies operating in Asia will be simply how to make money out of the region. Opinions as to its future prospects vary, some predicting another downturn while others anticipate a Chinese powerhouse. Whatever the reality, the return you get will depend on making a wise investment and this is only possible on the basis of good information.

In Strategy 7, the story of Lafarge, the French construction group, and its entry into Southeast Asia demonstrates perfectly the importance of preparation in determining a successful outcome. It shows how collecting the right information and preparing the ground thoroughly can ensure that you really do hit the ground running, ready to beat the competition and make the right acquisitions at the right price. As a result, Lafarge is well on the way to becoming Big in Asia.

Remember

■ Ignorance is not bliss. Ignorance means:
- A weak negotiating position
- Weakness in understanding the terms of a contract you sign
- A weak position in the ongoing relationships with your partner
- Weakness in anticipating future threats or opportunities
- Few options.

■ Information gives:

- Choices
- Power
- Leverage in negotiations
- A long-term future
- The potential to become Big in Asia.

Finally, also remember that:

■ To remain competitive and plan future moves with confidence, information collection never stops.

Notes

1   *Asian Wall Street Journal*, 'Asian CEOs Talk Recovery', 2 February, 1999.
2   Websites: http//www.ecch.cranfield.ac.uk and http//www.ecchatbabson.org.

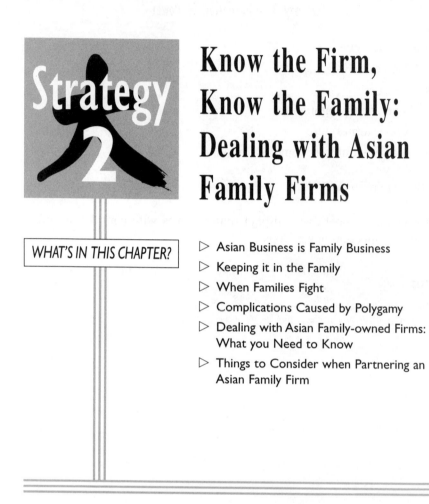

Know the Firm, Know the Family: Dealing with Asian Family Firms

Asian Business is Family Business

Asian business is family business, so if you want to be Big in Asia, you must be ready to do business with Asia's families. Yet much of the literature on modern firms is based on the assumption of wide ownership, but in Asia, ownership is anything but wide.

Most firms in Asia outside China and Japan are founded, owned and managed by single families. This means that existing management theory that relates to corporations and firms is largely misleading when applied to Asia.

Analysts' reports and even due diligence studies also often ignore the role of Asia's families. Analysts' reports, even those produced locally, might go into detail on P/E (price/earnings) ratios and other multiples, but then neglect to mention anything about companies' shareholders – the fact that there might be a single controlling shareholder and it is a family. Yet Asian families have an enormous influence on the structure and behaviour of Asian firms. Sometimes, who owns a firm is more important than what it actually does.

Partly, the problem is that US researchers and MBA programmes make the mistake of assuming that the US model applies to the rest of the world. It could not be more different in Asia. Most large American corporations do not have a single controlling shareholder, while most large Asian companies do. And it is not a large pension fund or some other hands-off investor but a family, with a whole range of motives, only one of which might be maximising their rate of return. Indeed, internal accounting standards might be so poor and the companies so complex and lacking in transparency that even the controlling family might have little idea as to the actual rate of return. Many are happy so long as they have cash at their disposal whenever they want it, cash flow often being mistaken for profits in Asia.

A World Bank study published in 1999 analysed 2,980 publicly traded companies in Hong Kong, Indonesia, Japan, Korea, Malaysia, the Philippines, Singapore, Taiwan and Thailand. It focused on the largest public companies in these countries.[1] The study found that more than half were controlled by a single shareholder, usually a family. Ownership was widest in Japan, where less than 10% of listed companies are now controlled by families. Elsewhere families controlled on average at least 60% of the large listed companies. There was also significant state control in Indonesia, Korea, Malaysia, Singapore and Thailand. The World Bank study also found that the smaller and older the firm, the more likely that it was controlled by a family. Separation of ownership from family control was also found to be rare. Asia's families want to manage the companies they own, which presents its own problems. Many may be entrepreneurs, but many are not managers. So, it's not only the food and the climate that foreign executives will find different in Asia.

Keeping it in the Family

The companies of Asian business families serve many purposes. Experience shows that they mean more than wealth alone. Witness the number of Asian families that fight to keep their companies long after they should have sold out had they wanted to keep their wealth intact. For many, the company is synonymous with the family.

Maintaining family control is paramount. That is not good news for minority shareholders or joint venture partners. It also means that something other than commercial factors are at play. And what that means is that the motives of outside investors (who generally rate return maximisation as a priority) who wish to link up with Asian firms typically will differ from the motives of the business families.

In Asia, control of large groups of companies is enhanced by arranging the companies into pyramid structures, with a family-owned, private holding company at the top and subsidiaries beneath it, some of which are publicly traded. Those companies in turn control other subsidiaries. The further down the pyramid, the more the family's equity is diluted but due to clever use of voting rights control is not. Consider a family that owns 51% of the equity and thus 51% of the voting rights in Company X. This company in turn is the largest single shareholder in Company Y with 20% equity. The rest of Y's equity is widely held and no other shareholder owns more than 2% of the remaining equity. Thus the family can control Company Y even though it has only 10% of its cash flow rights.

Typically, the better quality, higher yielding assets are nearer the top of the pyramid and those assets the family values less are nearer the bottom. Changes in how the family views an asset can be seen by how it is passed up and down the pyramid. Assets viewed as deteriorating in value get sold on down the pyramid so that the family's direct and indirect equity in them falls. But all the while, the family's control over them is likely to remain unchanged. Control over the group is further enhanced by deviations from the one-share-one-vote rule that allows voting rights to exceed cash flow rights.

The other important means of control of a group is to bind companies together through complex cross-shareholdings and related-party transactions. These make it difficult for individual companies to be sheared off from the rest of the group. It also makes it difficult for the group to be broken up in the event of a family dispute – many Asian business patriarchs deliberately leave behind intricately enmeshed groups to force the family to stay together. The strategy often works if for no other reason than because no one is able to unravel the family's corporate holdings. Elaborate cross-shareholdings also make the ultimate ownership of each unit difficult to ascertain, which has the effect of reducing group transparency and making it less vulnerable to takeover by outsiders.

The desire to keep companies under family control can mean that many families do not raise capital and bring in outside investors when their companies need it. Sometimes companies are pushed to the point of insolvency before their controlling families are ready to accept other shareholders. The result is that many Asian business families prefer to borrow rather than issue new shares which might see a dilution of their control. This pushes their gearing ratios beyond what is optimal, making them vulnerable at times of crisis. The desire to preserve family control is an indulgence that can mean that bondholders, creditors, minority shareholders and joint venture partners are forced to bear greater risk than they would otherwise.

Family-owned and managed companies pose problems everywhere. Look at the collapse of the Robert Maxwell-owned Mirror Group Newspapers in the UK. The UK government report in 2001 into the collapse highlighted a range of problems in the group that had as its source the group's family control.

Maxwell's son Kevin was quoted in the British media at the time as saying that no one should work for a family business. The temptation to flout the law to save the family empire is substantial:

In family-run businesses, the conflicts of interest with outside shareholders are so deep and so impossible to deal with that I don't think it is either safe or fair for

---

Asian family-controlled firms exist for things beyond making profit

They also exist:

- To give family members a job

- To hold the family together

- To honour the ancestral founders of the firm

- For the family's prestige and honour.

These are things that most Asian business families care deeply about. They are motivations not cared for by most outside partners and investors or regulators.

family relations to be exposed to those types of pressures, if you are brought up in a family business, you view the continuity of that business as almost sacred, as a duty. You do everything you can to save it and you lose sight that you are just a manager, no different from the hired gun who you pay a large sum to … one's sense of duty to the family overrides everything.[2]

So problems with family-owned business are not unique to Asia; but what is unique, at least compared with the more mature economies of the West, is the degree of control that families have over Asia's corporate sector.

Some Asian family-run business groups are not profitable at all. They are not required to be. Some groups have become large and complex because the families behind them have become large and complex. Agility and flexibility have been sacrificed to keep the family working together. Working in the family business has become the only way to profit from it for some Asian families. This was the case for Li & Fung, one of Hong Kong's most prominent trading companies today. Two brothers, William and Victor Fung, decided to modernise and streamline the company but first they had to buy out the interests of some 30 cousins so that they would have a clear run at achieving their aims. The company was not profitable in the latter years of its broad family control. It was also sluggish and old fashioned. Today, it is profitable, agile and admired.

Some Asian business families do anything to avoid bankruptcy or shedding companies when they should. They do this to avoid the loss of prestige and 'face' in the local business community, but also to uphold the honour of the family's ancestors. Many Asian business families would see it as unfilial to sell or liquidate a company that a grandfather or great-grandfather had founded. It is another important motivator in corporate Asia that is at odds with the interests of outsiders.

Unravelling Multi-Purpose Holdings

The unravelling of Malaysia's Multi-Purpose Holdings Bhd (MPHB) a group of companies controlled by Lim Thian Kiat (or T.K. Lim, as he is better known) around 1999 demonstrated what can happen to a group when a single shareholder arranges it not for transparency or profits but simply to exert control. Lim had structured MPHB in the pyramid manner described above. And the cement that he used to hold the pyramid together was a highly complex array of cross-shareholdings.

Lim acquired MPHB in 1989 through his family company, Kamunting Corp. He developed it into a sprawling conglomerate, building it up in such a way that he personally owned very little of most of its subsidiaries. MPHB grew to encompass a bank, several property companies, gaming and shipping. At least seven group members were listed on stock exchanges in the region. Using the classic pyramid structure of holding companies and cascading subsidiaries, Lim was able to control a great deal with very little equity, and a high proportion of the equity that he did have was borrowed. Lim had no direct and little indirect equity in companies at the base of the pyramid, but they were still part of the MPHB group and he was able to control them through cascading voting rights as if he did own them. Less than 10% of the equity in some of these companies was attributable to him.

Ultimately, the group suffered from poor management and high indebtedness. By the time of the Asian economic crisis, MPHB and Lim were in deep financial trouble. The size of the group and the size of its debts saw the Malaysian Government step in. The then Finance Minister Daim Zainuddin gave Lim the option of facing bankruptcy proceedings, probable prosecution and probably being left with nothing, or going quietly, handing over control of the group to new managers and being left with his personal assets. He opted for the latter and departed Malaysia for London. The government did not buy into the group. Instead, Daim 'invited' in several businessmen who he felt could sort out the troubles at MPHB.

They set about unravelling the group's highly complex ownership structure. The process of picking their way through the intricate mixture of cross-shareholdings and loan guarantees took around a year. The aim was to divide the group into its key components – stand-alone companies that could then be separately listed on the stock exchange as independent companies. As Lim's structure was unscrambled, the true extent of the group's borrowings became clear. What also became clear was how little equity Lim actually had in the group. He was able to control billions of dollars in assets with a personal stake measured only in the tens of millions.

When Families Fight

Family ownership and management means that much of corporate Asia is exposed to the risks of family infighting. When business families fight they tend to take their eye off the ball when it comes to their business affairs. Carve-ups become inevitable and much time is spent trying to determine who owns what and who can have what. Rarely are break-ups clean and quick. The elaborate structures of many family-owned groups are designed precisely to ensure that they will not be.

Corporate interests potentially face harm by such break-ups. Splitting up the pie becomes the focus of the family's attention rather than expanding it. Having a local family that is embroiled in infighting as a business partner is a real risk in Asia and one that needs to be quantified. It is a problem not restricted to obscure, small firms in Asia's more immature markets. Blue-chip firms and families with excellent reputations are all as much at risk.

Among the more prominent Asian business groups whose controlling families have engaged in public brawling that has often led to negative media coverage and ended up in the courts are: Malaysia's Tan Chong Group (the Tan family – the company is a prominent distributor of passenger motor vehicles in Asia); Singapore's Scotts Holdings (the Jumambhoy family – the company, which the family lost, owned property and serviced apartments); Wah Kwong Shipping (the Chao family – the company is one of Hong Kong's main shipping companies); and Singapore's Yeo Hip Seng Holdings (the Yeo family – the company is a beverages and condiments manufacturer). In the cases of the Jumambhoy and Yeo families, the infighting led to them losing control of the companies they had founded.

Each of these examples involves listed companies that have enjoyed some of the best reputations in their respective markets for shareholder responsibility. The assets of each have been first rate. But what let the side down was factionalism in the controlling families.

There is growing recognition of the problems of family control among Asian business families themselves. The problem is what to do about it. Restructuring Asian family firms is a growing business for management consultants.

Several of the bigger business families in the Philippines noticed that at their third-generation level there was much intra-family rivalry and squabbling. 'They're all cousins now' was the observation – and cousins are not nearly as naturally cohesive as siblings. So around the mid-1990s, a Harvard Business School academic was hired to advise them in a five-day seminar in Manila on how to manage change in their family-run businesses. Word was sent to other big local business families and they too were invited to send along representatives and help share the cost of the seminar. Around ten of the biggest business families in the Philippines including the Tuason, Elizalde, Zoebel/Ayala, Cojuangco and Soriano families all participated, each sending along several representatives.

One of the attendees interviewed by the authors said that the academic presented two basic options. One was that the families could stay together. Strategies on how to manage this without fighting were then presented. The other option was to split up. Ways in which this could be achieved fairly and without acrimony were then looked at. The biggest issue is not necessarily how to divide assets but how to value them so that they can then be divided. Methods for this also were examined. Some of the families made some changes. Most opted to defer their decision making. Perhaps it was felt that changes made now would simply bring future squabbles forward.

Complications Caused by Polygamy

An added complication to family ownership and management in Asia is that many of Asia's earlier business generations were polygamous – the business founders had more than one wife concurrently. Polygamy is still practised by some of Asia's biggest entrepreneurs today. It is not the fact of polygamy that is problematic but its results. Sets of rival children each grouped under their respective mothers attempting to assert their claims over one set of corporate assets are not helpful to the health of those assets.

Asia's royal families have long been polygamous. The current Sultan of Brunei has two official Queens. Thailand's King Mongkut – the king in *The King and I* – was astonishingly polygamous. He had 23 official wives and another 42 concubines. He had dozens of children as did many of his relatives and predecessors. There are thousands of Thais today who can lay claim to royal blood if not a royal title.

Other examples, in Asian business today, include:

■ Eka Tjipta Widjaja, the founder of Indonesia's Sinar Mas group of companies (8 or possibly 12 wives and more than 40 children)

■ Tiang Chirathivat, the founder of Thailand's Central Group (several wives, 26 children – 14 sons and 12 daughters – and more than 40 grandchildren)

■ Srisakdi Charmonman, the head of Thailand's KSC (31 brothers and sisters and their children now account for an extended family of more than 300)

■ Chew Choo Keng, the founder of Singapore's Khong Guan biscuits (5 wives, 23 children)

- Thaworn Phornpapha, the founder of Thailand's Siam Motors (3 wives and 13 children)

- Stanley Ho, the Hong Kong founder of the casino industry in Macau (at least 3 wives and 17 children).

Polygamy has its costs though. Large nuclear families are prone to faction-alism if only because of their size. But this is more so when a family comprises an explosive mix of brothers, half-brothers, endless cousins and so on coupled with sometimes enormous corporate wealth.

Dealing with Asian Family-owned Firms: What you Need to Know

When outside companies seek to link up with Asian companies, it pays to determine if the local firms are controlled by a family. It pays not only to assess the health of the company but also the health of the family:

- Does the family have a history of infighting?
- What are the risks that infighting might break out?
- How complex is the family? Are there potentially rivalrous sets of half-siblings?
- Are ownership issues settled among the various branches of the family or is that yet to be determined?
- Is the family's equity in the company ascribable on an individual basis or a joint stock basis?
- Is there a clear succession for the current family head/CEO?
- If a successor has been chosen, will this choice hold after the death of the current patriarch or will it be challenged?
- If fighting does break out, is there a professional management team in place to pick up the slack as family members get on with attacking one another?
- If the family splits apart, how amenable are its corporate assets to being split apart? Will the breaks be easy or destructive to the businesses concerned?
- If you have joint ventures or MoUs (memorandums of understanding) with a family-controlled concern, are your agreements with the family holding company or with individual subsidiaries? If the former, what will happen if the family holding company is wound up?

These are legitimate questions if you intend to go into business with an Asian business family in any significant way.

Things to Consider when Partnering an Asian Family Firm

- Ensure that due diligence covers not just the state of the firm but the state of the family.
- Ask to meet various family members, get to know them and stay on good terms with them all.
- Don't just deal with family members. Also get to know the family's professional managers.
- Preferably sign agreements with companies other than family holding companies. If families fight, it is their family holding companies that are liquidated first.
- If the family is already factionalised, partner an entity that has clear individual owners if possible rather than one that is owned by the 'family' as a whole.
- Attempt to get as clear as possible an explanation of the family's corporate holdings, including which companies are subsidiaries of what and where the cross-shareholdings are, so that you'll have an understanding of where your venture sits relative to the family's other assets should a family dispute arise and the assets are to be divided up.

Notes

1 Claessens, S., Djankov, S. and Lang, L. *Who Controls East Asian Corporations?*, World Bank, Washington, February 1999.
2 *Sunday Times*, 'Kevin Maxwell: don't ever work for a family business', 1 April, 2001.

Understanding Asia's Overseas Chinese

Asia's Movers and Shakers

The influence of ethnic Chinese businesspeople in Asia is now well known. Approximately 30 million ethnic Chinese live in Hong Kong and Southeast Asia today. They control companies and capital way in excess of that suggested by their numbers, to the point where doing business in Asia outside Korea and Japan usually means doing it with an overseas Chinese business partner. The name might be Thai, Indonesian or another local variant, but more often than not, the local will still be ethnically Chinese. Everyone knew the founder of Bangkok Bank as Chin Sophonpanich, for example, but Chin Pik Chin was his original, Chinese name.

Table 3.1 Southeast Asia's Chinese

Country	Total Population	Ethnic Chinese % (estimated)
Indonesia	235 million	2.2
Malaysia	23.1 million	26.0
The Philippines	84.6 million	2.0
Singapore	4.6 million	76.0
Brunei	360,000	13.0
Cambodia	13.1 million	2.0
Myanmar (Burma)	42.5 million	3.0
Vietnam	81.6 million	3.0
Laos	5.9 million	0.5
Thailand	64.3 million	10.0

No one ever got Big in Asia by being ignorant of the detail. Certainly not the overseas Chinese. As we shall see, being better than almost anyone else at getting information is how they have made their fortunes. And an important step to success in Asia is to understand the overseas Chinese – their business, their culture and the many differences among them.

The wealth of Asia's overseas Chinese received a battering during the region's economic crisis of 1997–98. Many went into the economic crisis highly leveraged and with their debts unhedged. Debts ballooned in local currency terms in the crisis, asset prices collapsed and banks and finance companies were shut down, nationalised or merged. The Indonesian corporate scene had been almost entirely owned by local Chinese if not foreign or state-owned. But many Chinese had to pledge their assets in return for state-sponsored bailouts of their banks. Chinese elsewhere suffered too, although in lesser degrees. They have been weakened in absolute terms, but in relative terms, their dominance remains intact.

Many of Indonesia's big Chinese families all but relocated to Singapore after the economic crisis and with political uncertainty, legal problems and harassment at home. The Salims (Salim Group), the Gondokusumos (Dharmala Group), the Widjajas (Sinar Mas Group) and the Nursalims (Gadjah Tunggal Group) were among those to shift family members to Singapore from where they continued to manage their Indonesian interests.

Chinese are not just Chinese

The forebears of the majority of Asia's overseas Chinese emigrated from China comparatively recently – mostly in the nineteenth and early twentieth centuries. They were economic migrants and their departure from

China often coincided with famines or civil strife. Today China has 29 provinces, but the great majority of Asia's overseas Chinese ancestrally come from just three of them: Guangdong and Fujian Provinces on the South China Sea in the bottom southeast corner of China and Hainan Province, an island off the southern tip of Guangdong. China might have over a billion people but the overseas Chinese have cultural, family and language ties with relatively few of them. So it is true that many of Asia's overseas Chinese have ancestral and family connections that can be useful in opening doors but those particular connections are not at all broad.

Asia's overseas Chinese are not a monolithic group. Many are now second, third or more generation residents of the countries in which they live and so have taken on many of the local ways and culture as their own. Also, there are important differences among the Chinese in any given location and between the Chinese outside China and those in mainland China. Understanding these differences is essential to understanding the overseas Chinese as businesspeople.

The native tongue of almost three-quarters of all Chinese who live in China is Mandarin (or *Putonghua*, as it is called in Hong Kong), but it is the ancestral tongue of perhaps less than 5% of Hong Kong and Southeast Asia's Chinese. Mandarin is the language of northern China, not southeastern China where most Southeast Asian and Hong Kong Chinese have their origins.

All speakers of Mandarin or one of the many Chinese dialects share the same written language but pronunciations can differ so much that most of the dialects of southeastern China – and hence the dialects of most Southeast Asian and Hong Kong Chinese – are not intelligible to Mandarin speakers.

The main ancestral languages of Asia's overseas Chinese are Hokkien, Cantonese, Hakka, Teochiu, Fuzhou/Hokchia, Hainanese and Henghua, probably in that order:[1]

- *Hokkien* is the dialect for those with origins in southern Fujian Province. Hokkien is the dominant ancestral dialect of Singapore's Chinese and the Chinese in the Philippines. The Quek family of Malaysia and their cousins, the Kewks of Singapore, both of which own business groups called Hong Leong in both countries, are among Asia's richest overseas Hokkiens. The Tan family of the Philippines, who founded Jolibee Foods, are also Hokkien.

- *Cantonese* is the ancestral dialect of those with origins in much of Guangdong and Hong Kong. Cantonese speakers dominate Hong Kong and the Chinese communities of Kuala Lumpur (but almost nowhere else in Malaysia) and Saigon. Ronnie Chan of Hong Kong's Hang Lung property group is a prominent Cantonese businessman.

- Hakka (or Keh) is the language of a group of Chinese who in recent centuries have been sprinkled throughout northern Guangdong, southern Fujian and further inland. This dialect group further divides into sub-dialect groups such as Huizhou, Taipu, Fengshun, Meixian, Popo and Yongding. They have no single ancestral homeland in China due to their past continual migrations. Hakka are found everywhere but do not form a majority of the Chinese in any particular country. They do dominate in some regions though, for example in the Malaysian state of Sabah where almost 60% of the local Chinese are Hakka. The Lamsam family of Bangkok who founded the Thai Farmers Bank is a prominent Hakka family.

- *Teochiu* (or Chiu Chow [Chaozhou] as it is spelled in Hong Kong) is the dialect of those from the Shantou area of northern Guangdong. Most Thai Chinese (perhaps 80%) are Teochiu and it is the second most prominent ancestral dialect among Singapore's Chinese. The five big entrepreneurial families of Bangkok are the Wang-Lee, Sophonpanich, Tejaphaibul, Srifeungfung and Chearavanont families. Not only are they all ethnic Chinese but they are all Teochiu. Hong Kong's Li Ka Shing is Asia's best-known Teochiu/Chiu Chow businessman. Eka Tjandranegara, founder of Indonesia's Mulia Group, is another prominent Teochiu.

- *Fuzhou* is the ancestral dialect of those from around Fuzhou city in the northern tip of Fujian, and *Hokchia* is the closely related dialect of those from the area around nearby Fuqing. Members of these groups can be found everywhere but most of Southeast Asia's Fuzhou Chinese are to be found in Malaysia, particularly in Sarawak, and most of the Hokchia are to be found in Indonesia. The Fuzhou and Hokchia are numerically a very small group, but are disproportionately represented among the ranks of the highly successful overseas Chinese businessmen. Hong Kong-based Malaysian Robert Kuok is perhaps the most prominent overseas Fuzhou businessman. Indonesia's Liem Sioe Liong who founded the Salim Group is an important Hokchia.

- *Hainanese* (or Kheng Chew) is the language of those from Hainan Province. There are Hainanese Chinese across Southeast Asia but they are always in a minority. The Thai-Chinese businessman Sondhi Limthongal, who founded Thailand's M Group, is Hainanese.

- *Henghua* is the language of the smallest group who ancestrally come from the Putian area, close to Fuzhou in China. They are found in small numbers across Southeast Asia. Indonesia's Sjamsul Nursalim (founder of the giant Gadjah Tunggal Group) and Mochtar Riady (founder of the equally large Lippo Group) are prominent Henghua.

However, it should not be assumed that all Chinese in Southeast Asia can actually speak or read their ancestral dialect or in fact any Chinese. Many cannot – many have no Chinese language abilities whatsoever. A high proportion of Indonesian Chinese are in this category. Some Indonesian Chinese are not even aware of what their ancestral dialect is. William Soeryadjaya, the founder of Astra Group, Indonesia's largest listed company, is one prominent Indonesian Chinese who cannot speak Chinese – Dutch is his preferred language and that of several of his key senior executives.

Chinese who have been in their countries of residence for many generations and have become highly acculturated with local ways, such as William Soeryadjaya, are called the *Peranakan* in Indonesia and the *Babas* in Malaysia and Singapore. But acculturation need not mean assimilation. There is much resentment in Indonesia against all Chinese. The Chinese are most assimilated in Thailand, where many have intermarried with ethnic Thais. Many and maybe most Bangkok people can claim some Chinese ancestry, including King Bhumipol Adulyadej himself whose mother was half-Chinese. Elsewhere, intermarriage has been less common. In Malaysia, it is rare but that is changing. Marriages between Malay men and Chinese women who convert to Islam and take Muslim names are becoming more common. Wan Azizah Wan Ismail is ethnically Chinese. She married former Deputy Prime Minister Anwar Ibrahim and is now an opposition politician in her own right.

There is one other important migrant Chinese group in Asia and that is the Shanghainese of Taiwan and Hong Kong. They fled mainland China in 1949 in the wake of Mao's Communist takeover. Many were successful industrialists in Shanghai but left with little of their wealth intact. They started anew and today some of the wealthiest families in Hong Kong and Taiwan are actually old Shanghainese families, whose ancestral dialect is Shanghainese.

They have become important investors again in Shanghai and Ningbo. Typically they rebuilt their fortunes in textiles and clothing – Hong Kong owed its initial prosperity to the textiles industry built up by the Shanghainese refugees. Almost all cotton spinning mills in Hong Kong or those owned by Hong Kong investors in nearby Guangdong are actually owned by migrant Shanghainese. Peter Woo of the Wharf/Wheelock Group, David Wong of Dah Sing Financial Holdings, the Kwok family of Wing On Group and Henry Tang of the Winsor Textile Group are among the prominent Shanghai-descended businesspeople in Hong Kong today. Shipping in Hong Kong is controlled by three big Hong Kong Shanghainese families – the family of the late Y.K. Pao (World-Wide Shipping), the family of C.Y. Tung (Orient Overseas) and Frank Chao and his family (Wah Kwong Shipping). Tung Chee Hwa, Hong Kong's first chief executive and son of C.Y. Tung, is of Shanghainese descent. In Taiwan, one of the richest families, the Hsu family, is originally from Shanghai. They own the massive Far Eastern Group which includes Far Eastern International Bank, Far Eastern Textiles, Asia Cement, U-Marine Shipping and Far Eastern Department Stores. It is important to remember that most Chinese in Hong Kong and Taiwan are the children or grandchildren of refugees. Hong Kong and Taiwan are not their places of ancestry.

What's in a Name?

Quite a lot, if you are Chinese. Overseas Chinese tend to have traditional surnames which, when rendered in English, reflect their ancestral dialect and thus their place of Chinese ancestry. There are more than 6,000 possible Chinese surnames, although many have died out. There are far fewer surnames among Asia's overseas Chinese because their ancestral homes are mostly in the southeast corner of China. There are around 500 surnames in use among Singapore's Chinese but there are several that are particularly common. The three most common are Tan (9.9% of all Singapore's Chinese), Lim (6.9%) and Lee (4.6%). Each of these is the Hokkien pronunciation, reflecting the dominance of the Hokkien among Singapore's Chinese. The same Chinese characters used to denote Tan are pronounced as Chen in Mandarin, Chan in Cantonese and Ting in Fuzhou. Thus someone who has the surname that's spoken as Tan will have the same Chinese characters as someone who is Fuzhou and who calls themselves Ting. Both the surnames read the same but are spoken differently. Wong, one of the most popular surnames in Hong Kong, is the Cantonese rendering of 'Ong' in Hokkien or 'Heng' in Teochiu.

When Chinese meet each other for the first time they are often eager to know each other's surname. Pronunciations differ so widely that they often need to write their names to show each other the actual Chinese characters. If they share the same surname, they are 'kinsmen' and right away they share a bond. Traditionally, Chinese with the same surnames were forbidden to marry as it was believed that they had the same ancestor.

Chinese surnames can reveal a lot. Any recognition of this and interest shown in the ancestral origins of many Chinese is often met with surprise and delight. After all, it is something that interests many Chinese.

Why the Success in Business?

Asia's overseas Chinese have been so successful in business largely for two reasons. Many of Asia's ethnic Chinese businesspeople have a dual role. They are well-entrenched citizens in their home countries, but they also operate at a regional level, using their family, clan, dialect and other ties with Chinese in other countries to invest and trade. These international networks of family relations and friends allow them to operate across markets. Shortages in one market can be matched with excesses in another. Trade is nothing if it's not about leveraging information ahead of competitors. The networks allow for that information to be gathered in and used.

This tendency to do business on the basis of connections means that Chinese businesses often become eclectic and unwieldy. Consider a typical Chinese shop in any Chinatown. It might be filled with a bizarre array of items – packets of seeds along with pairs of rubber gloves, children's toys and woks. Decisions on stock purchasing are driven not so much by customers' needs but with which suppliers the owner has personal connections. Thus the range of stock is driven by supply rather than demand. Now upscale that shop a few thousand times and you have a typical Chinese-owned conglomerate, its scope of opportunities determined not by strategy and complementarity but by opportunity. Such a structure is optimal only in certain economies at particular stages of immaturity.

The second factor in the commercial success of Asia's overseas Chinese is that they have institutions that allow them to operate in environments where legal protection is poor. By doing business within their communities and having additional legal contract enforcement mechanisms, such as a highly developed sense of 'face' whereby being a bad debtor is simply too humiliating for oneself and one's family, and having chambers of commerce within which disputes can be settled without recourse to the law, the overseas Chinese are at a significant competitive advantage to other ethnic groups which do not have these mechanisms.

The overseas Chinese tend to be among the first investors in 'new' or opening markets (such as Myanmar, Vietnam and Cambodia) or dominate old markets (Indonesia, the Philippines and Thailand) where legal systems are marred by corruption and poor drafting of laws.

East Timorese Chinese were among the first investors back into East Timor after the country seceded from Indonesia and the United Nations set up a provisional government. Many families had fled with the Indonesian invasion of 1975 and had not been back for 25 years. One family, the Japes, had settled in the northern Australian city of Darwin where they had set up local hardware and bedding franchises. They set up a store selling furnishings, hardware and home appliances in Dili shortly after the UN's arrival, and relied on extended family members to run it.

Once legal systems develop so that all groups can do business on the same basis then the overseas Chinese lose much of their comparative advantage. That is why Western multinationals do well in Singapore (with its first-rate legal system) and why Australia's 3% ethnic Chinese community does not control 70% of that country's private, corporate capital.

The overseas Chinese have also been adept at filling market niches – gaps in economies where there is a demand for some product or service to be supplied but where local social and cultural constraints inhibit that demand being fulfilled. For example, Islamic laws prohibit usury but the Chinese have no such religious constraints, and so early on became the money lenders across Malaysia and Indonesia. Hindu restrictions on 'unclean' occupations dealing with dead cattle have seen Hakka Chinese in Calcutta dominate the city's leather industries, with most of its several hundred tanneries being run by the small local Chinese community.

Local investment flows around Asia often can be explained by looking at the ancestral and historical links of Asia's overseas Chinese. For example, trade and investment flow across the Straits of Malacca between Medan in Indonesia and Penang in Malaysia largely because both places are dominated overwhelmingly by Hokkien Chinese. Taiwan invested billions of dollars in Penang's massive electronic components industry because the local infrastructure is good and the government offers lucrative incentives but also because the Chinese in Taiwan and Penang overwhelmingly share a common Hokkien ancestry. Singapore and Hong Kong have been the biggest investors in Myanmar in recent years because it was to Singapore and Hong Kong that many Burmese Chinese fled in the 1960s and they are now taking advantage of the Myanmar government's new pro-market policies to invest in their old homeland. And then of course many of Asia's overseas Chinese have used local knowledge and connections to invest in their ancestral homes in China itself.

Occupations and Dialects

Historically, overseas Chinese of certain dialects dominated particular occupations. For example, opticians, Chinese herbalists, tailors, pawn-brokers and tin miners in Malaysia and Singapore usually were Hakka Chinese. Electrical shops were run by the Hokkien and rice export-import agencies, antique and curio shops and fishmongers by the Teochiu. These linkages have tended to break down but are still important to explain some patterns observed in overseas Chinese business today. The Henghua Chinese were traditionally found in occupations associated with transport. They owned bicycle shops and were even bus drivers. Gadjah Tunggal group is Indonesia's largest manufacturer of rubber tyres. (Its tyres are the number one imported tyre to the United Kingdom today incidentally.) The company had its start in this sector by making tyres for rickshaws. The owner and founder of Gadjah Tunggal is Sjamsul Nursalim, a Henghua Chinese. The family started in the business because of its traditional assoc-iation with the Henghuas – other Henghuas were already in it so the Nursalims followed.

One traditional occupation–dialect linkage that still holds is the promi-nence of Teochiu traders in the cross-border trade for rice, fresh fruit, vegetables, poultry and seafood across Southeast Asia and Hong Kong. Much of it is sourced from Thailand, where Teochiu Chinese are domi-nant, and then distributed around Asia by local Teochiu traders. Also, cold storage facilities are often owned by Teochiu businesspeople. Teochiu families also control much of the integrated poultry raising and processing in Thailand, Malaysia and Indonesia. If your business is in these sectors, you can expect to find yourself dealing with the Teochiu.

Chinese Associations

Traditionally, Asia's overseas Chinese have been great joiners of clubs, chambers and societies. Partly it is a function of their having been a migrant minority culture. Migrant minorities tend to form themselves into self-help organisations to deal with an uncertain or even hostile new envir-onment. But also the number and variety of organisations suggests how fractured and non-monolithic overseas Chinese communities are. This is because many traditional overseas Chinese organisations are based around Chinese ancestral origins, their dialect group or their surname or clans.

Guilds were also popular for both controlling entry into a sector and the worship of the craft's patron deities.

Some of these groups have formed international bodies that meet annually or biennially at massive conventions. For example, World Fujian Conventions have been held which have drawn together thousands of Chinese, who have their ancestral origins in China's Fujian Province, for several days of feasting, seminars and networking. Overseas Hakkas, Hainanese and Fuzhous have held similar events. And every two years a World Chinese Entrepreneurs' Convention takes place. (The 2003 Convention was held in Kuala Lumpur, for example.) These have met with mixed success depending on the quality of the organising skills of the host Chinese chamber but they always attract thousands of participants. Non-Chinese attend as well – eager to make new business contacts in the overseas Chinese business community.

And then there are the Chinese chambers of commerce. Historically, these regulated the business affairs of the community and adjudicated in disputes. The chambers provided venues where legal disputes could be solved 'in-house'. Today they are important around Asia to act as a single voice to lobby government, promote business within the community and assist with international trade promotion. There are many local Chinese chambers of commerce across Asia but there is usually a main chamber in each country (see below).

Many have websites, their own newsletters that often accept advertisements from outsiders and some offer associate membership to non-Chinese. It is always worth making contact with the local Chinese chamber but it is surprising how few Western businesspeople do on coming to Asia. Some chambers are better resourced and organised and are more welcoming than others, but they do provide a route into the wealthiest sector of the business community in every East Asian country bar Korea and Japan.

The younger generation of overseas Chinese businesspeople tend not to join or at least not be active in the more traditional Chinese associations. Instead they join other groupings. Rotary and other service clubs have taken off in some parts of Asia. Various local industry and trade associations that need not be exclusively Chinese are also important. Classmate and alumni associations are very important among the younger generation of foreign-educated overseas Chinese. Such associations allow networks started at overseas tertiary education institutions to be maintained. This is important, for many parents send their children to US, British and

Australian institutions for both education and networking opportunities with other well-to-do Asian classmates. Associations such as these are also more accepting of non-Chinese. In fact, many of the new generation of overseas Chinese find traditional Chinese organisations too limiting. They want to grow their contacts and businesses in the Chinese community but also beyond it.

Contacting Asia's Chinese Chambers of Commerce

Covering all bases in Asia means also covering the local Chinese chambers of commerce. As has been mentioned, they are not strictly for Chinese – indeed some are welcoming to non-Chinese. The chambers exist for the benefit of the local Chinese business community rather than as clubs designed to exclude outsiders. The following list gives names and addresses of the main chambers in Asia:

Brunei
Chinese Chamber of Commerce
72 Jalan Roberts
2–4 Floor
Bandar Seri Begawan 1902
Brunei

Myanmar (Burma)
Myanmar Chinese Chamber of Commerce & Industry
No. 84, 8th Street, Lanmadaw Tsp
Yangon, Myanmar

Hong Kong
Chinese General Chamber in Hong Kong
7/Fl, 24 Connaught Road, Central
Hong Kong

Malaysia
Associated Chinese Chambers of Commerce and Industry of Malaysia
8/F Office Tower, Plaza Berjaya
12 Jalan Imbi
55100 Kuala Lumpur
Malaysia

The Philippines
Federation of Filipino Chinese Chambers of Commerce & Industry
6/Fl Federation Centre
Muelle de Binondo Street
Metro Manila
The Philippines

Singapore
> Singapore Chinese Chamber of Commerce and Industry
> 47 Hill Street # 09-00
> Singapore 179365

Thailand
> Thai Chinese Chamber of Commerce
> 233 South Sathorn Road
> Bangkok 10120
> Thailand

Note

I This list is amended and extended from Backman, M., *Asian Eclipse: Exposing the Dark Side of Business in Asia*, John Wiley & Sons, 1999, 2001.

Understanding Asia's Overseas Indians

The Overseas Indian Century has Arrived

Globalisation, the proliferation of English as the world language of business, the rise of the service sector and the importance of technology – all things that favour Indians and overseas Indians – mean that the importance of the overseas Indians is changing relative to that of the overseas Chinese. In short, the overseas Chinese are losing ground. As a commercial diaspora, overseas Indians – as many as 25 million Indians live outside India – have never been as important as they are now, and their influence is increasing.

India is also becoming more important to the world economy as its high-tech sectors compete on cost and quality better than almost anyone else. Business processing (BP) functions increasingly are being outsourced to firms in India. India is now a mainstream option when it comes to North American corporates outsourcing their back-office functions. General Electric now has more than 10,000 staff at its BP operations in India. British Airways, P&O Nedland, ABN Amro, ING, American Express, Agilent Technologies and Cap Gemini have all shifted some of their BP operations to India. Even the Washington-based World Bank has moved most of its global accounting operations including payroll processing to Madras in India. Now more than ever it is time to learn about the emergent power of the Indian diaspora in business.

Overseas Indians are adding management and high-tech capabilities to their traditional capabilities in trading. Very few multinational corporations have expatriate CEOs in India. The skills base and English-language proficiency in India is such that it is not necessary. The CEOs sourced locally are usually highly educated professionals rather than members of the old Indian business families. There are also plenty of examples of Indians who are the CEOs of multinational corporations worldwide, as we shall see.

But Indians are not just Indians. Like the overseas Chinese, there are many cultural, language and religious differences among them. Indeed, Indians tended to migrate not as Indians but as Jains, Gujaratis, Sikhs, Muslims, Tamils and so on, and they settled on that basis. These are differences that Indians themselves recognise.

Indians, again like the overseas Chinese, have traditional surnames that convey a considerable amount about their ancestral origins. Most Indians can identify which Indian state another is from, whether they are a Jain, a Parsi, a Tamil, which Hindu caste and so on, simply by that person's surname. With that comes a whole host of other assumptions and information.

The differences among Indians help to explain a lot about where and with whom they do business. Hiring practices can also be explained by looking at Indian subgroups, for it is often when Indians and overseas Indian firms choose their staff that group loyalty is at its most apparent.

The clan networks among overseas Indians are weaker than those of the overseas Chinese. Overseas Indians also have a less sentimental attachment to their places of ancestry. They are more likely to invest in India if they think that they will make a profit rather than out of some sense of duty. Of course, networks are always useful for reducing information costs and alerting businesspeople to unexploited opportunities here and risks there, so, as with the overseas Chinese, ethnicity and ancestry drives a certain amount of Indian trade and investment.

Relationships among Indians tend to lack the emotional aspects of the *guanxi* (personal connections) of the Chinese. Their relationship building is grounded in more practical considerations and focused on recognisable pay-offs. Friends may not see each other for years but when they do it is as if they have never been apart. Relationships are more easily built, because they tend to be built less with a shared history in mind but with a view to future rewards. The more clearly defined those rewards are, the more intense the relationship building will be. However, treacherous behaviour is met with permanent estrangement. Pragmatism only goes so far and grudges can run deep.

The explicit 'what's in it for me' attitude has deep cultural underpinnings built up by a long history in India of a broad system of patronage that also cuts deeply into all levels of society. But it is one that other cultures find grating. Local resentment towards Indians across Asia can be high, particularly in their role as employers. (Ethnic Indian businesspeople have a reputation for sharp business practices in Bangkok as in other Asian cities. 'If you see a snake and an Indian, hit the Indian first' goes a common Thai saying.) This is a problem that many Indian expatriate managers must come to terms with when they are posted to East Asia.

In the words of one Western businessman who sells high-end food products across Asia:

> doing business with Indians and in India is different to doing it with the overseas Chinese or in China. In China and Southeast Asia one must first establish the trust and the relationship, then matters relating to making business comes next. And only then, once the relationship has been developed, and the scope of the business to be done has been determined is the matter of contracts raised. In India it's about making money first. Developing the relationship follows and then comes discussion about contracts.

The need for very clear rewards means that India and many overseas Indian communities are beset with an all-embracing patronage system, in which little is done on principle alone. Samy Vellu, the head of the Malaysian Indian Congress, Malaysia's main Indian political party and a member of the ruling coalition, is both public works minister and sits atop a very extensive and deep network of patronage. The network reaches all layers of local Indian society to deliver the majority of Malaysian Indian voters to the ruling coalition. Vellu is often blamed for the nepotism and patronage that is part of Indian politics in Malaysia but he is a product of the culture in which he must work, so change, if it is desired, will be slow.

Traditionally, Indian family businesses are joint stock companies with each son or family member jointly owning all the assets. This can lead to some spectacular bust-ups when Indian families fight. Assets not being assigned to individual family members as a matter of course means that if they want to take their inheritance and strike out on their own, it must first be determined how the family's assets are to be divided. A recent spectacular case of an overseas Indian family breaking apart with the family losing control of the family firm was the Jumabhoy family of Singapore, which had built up the retail and property group Scotts Holdings. The family fought and Scotts is now owned by a Singapore government-linked company.

While corporate structures of many overseas Indian family-run firms lag behind when it comes to modernisation, overseas Indians are at the forefront of adopting new technology. The Internet has become an important way for overseas Indians to stay in touch with their own subgroups and developments in their ancestral regions in India in a way that far exceeds the use of the Internet by the overseas Chinese. Overseas Indian sites have proliferated. They are well maintained, well resourced and up to date. They are an excellent means for Indians to stay informed about each other and for outsiders to have a window on the astonishing vibrancy of overseas Indian business.

Asia's Overseas Indians

Indians are spread across Asia, but in far smaller numbers than the overseas Chinese. The main communities in East Asia today are:

Hong Kong	where there are about 80,000 Indians.
Malaysia	where there are about 1.8 million ethnic Indians.
Singapore	where there are about 250,000 ethnic Indians.
Thailand	where there are possibly as many as 100,000 ethnic Indians.
Myanmar	although it is not clear how many ethnic Indians live in Myanmar. Possibly several million. Today Indians are more plentiful than Chinese on the streets in Yangon (Rangoon).

There are other small Indian communities in the Philippines and Indonesia, and even in Korea and Japan. Overseas Indians can be divided again according to several very different commercial minorities.

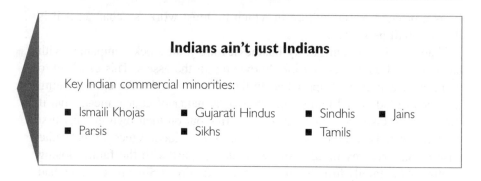

Indians ain't just Indians

Key Indian commercial minorities:

- Ismaili Khojas   ■ Gujarati Hindus   ■ Sindhis   ■ Jains
- Parsis   ■ Sikhs   ■ Tamils

The Ismaili Khojas and the Gujarati Hindus Overseas

A large proportion of ethnic Indians outside India have their ancestral
origins in India's Gujarat State. For example, around 40% of the Indians
in the New York area are from here. But, more particularly, many are from
the Kutch region, a dry, barren area with few economic activities. Kutch,
a small princely state in the northwest of Gujarat adjacent to what was
Sind, has given rise to a surprising number of global commercial Indian
networks. Many of the Kutchi merchants who emigrated to trade
anywhere from Asia to East Africa often came from only a handful of
villages. Among them were Lohana Hindus, Bhatia Hindus, Muslim
Ismaili Khojas, Bohras Muslims and Sunni Memons. Indians are not just
Indians, but nor are Indian Gujaratis simply Gujaratis. The story is far
more complex.

The Indians who settled in East Africa tended to be Ismaili Khojas and
Gujarati Hindus. The Ismaili Khojas, who today number 15–20 million,
were economic migrants. Many went to Zanzibar and Uganda. Ismaili
merchants formed trading networks that linked Bombay with Zanzibar,
Kampala, London and the Middle East, particularly Oman. Spices, textiles
and ivory were traded.

The 'Africanisation' campaigns of the 1970s saw tens of thousands of
Indians expelled but rarely did they go to India. The dictator Idi Amin
forced out thousands from Uganda in 1972. He made the point that only a
third of Uganda's Indians had taken out Ugandan citizenship. Many in fact
held British passports and so 27,200 Ugandan Indians resettled in Britain.
Others fanned out across the world, so that today there are Ismaili Khoja
and Gujarati Hindu communities in many countries. There are 45,000
Ismailis in Canada, many from Uganda. Those who sought refuge in the

United Kingdom took up the businesses they left behind in Africa – shop-keeping and small-scale trading. Today ethnic Indians run as many as 60% of all independent retail stores in the UK.

The Khojas are a subset of the Nizaris who are a subset of the Ismailis. The Ismailis in turn are a subset of the Shiite Islamic sect and the Shiites are a breakaway group from the dominant Sunni Islamic sect. Today, the Nizaris are the dominant group within the Ismaili community, and the two terms now tend to be used interchangeably.

The Aga Khan is the spiritual leader of the Nizaris and thus the Indian Ismaili Khojas. There is even an Ismaili flag and this is used when the Aga Khan visits friendly countries. The Aga Khan used what influence he had with prime ministers and presidents around the world to have third countries accept Khoja refugees from Africa after their expulsion in the 1970s.

Earlier Aga Khans were based in Iran, then India and now France. Nizari-Ismailis are exhorted to save and to pay a monthly tithe from their savings. The tithes are paid to the Aga Khan, and although the tithes historically have been used for charitable works in the Nizari-Ismaili community, the sums collected were regarded as the personal property of the Aga Khan.

Today, the Aga Khan, who lives outside Paris, is supposedly one of the wealthiest men in the world. The various Aga Khans' private fortunes have made them independent of the tithes of their followers so that the tithes can be distributed as charity. The Aga Khan and his charitable foundations claim to give around US$100 million away each year to Third World development projects.

The most prominent business family in East Asia today with Ismaili Khoja roots is Singapore's Jumabhoy family, the founders of Scotts Holdings and the Ascott serviced apartment group. The family's patriarch Rajabali Jumabhoy (who died in 1998) arrived in Singapore from Kutch in 1918. He imported dates from Persia and exported timber from Java. He amassed a small fortune that he used to branch into other businesses. In 1952, the elder Jumabhoy passed control of what was, by then, the family's property business to his son Ameer Rajabali Jumabhoy, and in turn Ameer's two sons, Rafiq and Iqbal, became involved. Outside Scotts, the Jumabhoys held the A&W Restaurants fast-food franchise in Singapore, substantial duty-free shopping concessions at Singapore's Changi Airport and commenced real estate development outside New Delhi. Today, the family's wealth is much diminished after it lost control of Scotts Holdings in 1998 due to family infighting. The various Jumabhoys now pursue business activities independently of one another.

The Sindhis

Another important Indian diaspora are the Sindhis – Hindu Indians from what is now Pakistan. Most left the province of Sind when it became the new Islamic nation of Pakistan. But others left well before then to become merchants and traders as far afield as China and Africa. There are Sindhis everywhere, from Asia to North America to Europe. Many overseas Sindhis have 'ani' as the suffix to their surnames, as in 'Mirchandani' or 'Tolani'.

The most prominent Sindhi-owned business group in India is the Escort Group owned by Rajan Nanda. Escort has three main divisions: telecommunications, construction equipment manufacturing and motorcycle manufacturing. While Sindhis in India are by definition a migrant group, they are comfortable and fit in well with the majority Hindu culture. They do not face the acculturation pressures faced by migrants elsewhere.

The most prominent overseas Sindhi business family in the world is the billionaire London-based Hinduja family, with interests in finance, oil and telecoms. Initially, the family made its fortune not in India but in Tehran, before settling in London. The Hindujas first became well known to average Britons when they were linked to a political controversy over 'cash for passports', as the tabloid press put it.

In East Asia, Hong Kong's Harilela family is the most prominent Sindhi business family. They originated from Hyderabad. Lilaram Harilela was the family patriarch. He had six sons and today they run the family's business, headed by second son Hari. The family started in trading and then in the 1970s made its wealth in tailoring. They then diversified into property, electronics and software.

The family ventured into hotels with the construction of Hong Kong's Imperial Hotel and then the 650-room Holiday Inn Golden Mile. They now own Holiday Inns in Hong Kong, Singapore and Penang, the Sheraton Belgravia in London, a Quality Hotel in Montreal, Canada, a Westin Resort in Macau, the W Hotel in Sydney, the Grand Stanford Intercontinental Hotel in Hong Kong, the transit hotels at Singapore's Changi Airport and the Crown Plaza Hotel in Bangkok. The hotel interests are all privately owned by the Harilela family. Even the left-luggage service at Changi Airport is operated by a Harilela-owned company.

The Harilelas jointly own their business interests in the joint stock arrangement that is common among Hindu Indian families. And this communal arrangement follows through to their living arrangements. More than 40 members of the family – the six brothers, their sisters and all the wives and children – live in one large compound in Kowloon, Hong Kong.

It has almost 90 bedrooms and garage space for more than 30 cars. Members of the younger generation are not encouraged to move out on their own, instead, more wings have been added to allow them more privacy.

The controversial brothers Raj and Asok Kumar of Singapore are from another prominent East Asian Sindhi family. They own the Royal Brothers property group in Singapore. Their father founded a chain of silk stores in Singapore in 1947. The brothers' speculation in property at one stage included a chain of hotels in Australia and New Zealand, around 400 shop units in Singapore and Mumbai's Searock Hotel. However, their fortune waned when they were charged in 1997 with attempting to bribe a senior banker.

Another prominent Sindhi family in Singapore are the Melwanis, who own the popular Modestos restaurant in Singapore, among a wide portfolio of investments. They are also major shareholders in Malaysia's Melium group, a fashion and lifestyle-based group of companies.

The Jains Overseas

Another Indian subgroup is the Jains. The Jain religion is a subsect of Hinduism but is more like Buddhism with its emphasis on not harming living creatures. Jains are strict vegetarians. They are also remarkably clannish. There are worldwide Jain conventions, such as the Eleventh Biennial Jain Convention that was held in Chicago in July 2001. Religious observances and celebrations are another force that binds the Jain diaspora.

There are about 3.5 million Jains in India (concentrated in Rajasthan, Gujarat and Mumbai) and a small number overseas. Jains are viewed in India as disproportionately commercially successful and are often compared with Europe's Jews.

But the overseas Jains also exert an influence that is way out of proportion to their numbers. They have done this by capturing a large part of the world diamond trade. Many of the overseas Jains involved in the diamond trade are from Palanpur, a town on the Gujarat-Rajasthan border. With such a specific ancestry, many sharing the similar surname of 'Mehta', it is common today to find diamond traders from London to Israel with the surname of Mehta.

The international diamond trade works on secrecy, trust and strong cross-border connections. It had been the preserve of a small, powerful group of Hassidic Jews until the 1980s when the Jains moved in. Almost all the Jain firms involved in the business are owned and run by families and the diamonds are handled internationally via networks of brothers and cousins which span Europe, the United States and Asia.

Jain diamond merchants and cutters now dominate the diamond trade in Tel Aviv and Antwerp and they control about half the world's gem-quality cut diamond market. Rough gems are imported by Jain-owned firms in Mumbai from dealers in Antwerp, London, New York and Tel Aviv from where they are taken to Jain-owned cutting and polishing factories in Gujarat and then back to Mumbai and re-exported to gem centres around the world. Bangkok too is becoming more prominent in the diamond cutting and polishing trade with the small Jain community there handling much of the business.

The Gembel Group is one of Belgium's more prominent diamond cutters and exporters. Based in Antwerp, it was founded in 1956 by Kirtilal Manilal Mehta, an Indian-born Jain. He claimed to have helped 1,800 other Jains set up their own diamond businesses in Antwerp. Gembel now has a network of offices in Belgium, New York, Israel and Mumbai and each is managed by a Mehta family member.

B. Vijaykumar & Co is another Jain-owned diamond firm. It is India's largest importer of rough diamonds and was founded by the Jain businessman Vijay Shah. The company has cutting and polishing factories in Bangkok, Antwerp, Tel Aviv, Mumbai, Surat and Palanpur, collectively employing 22,000 people.

The way in which the Jains have moved in on the multi-billion-dollar diamond trade and turned it on its head in less than three decades is remarkable. Jain entrepreneurs have gone right to the heart of the old Hassidic diamond networks – even placing family members in Tel Aviv itself – to capture the industry. The Jains have given the established diamond firms such as De Beers and Argyle Diamonds a whole new cultural setting to get used to.

The Parsis

The Parsis are another subgroup. They are from India but ethnically are not Indian. They are descended from Parsi families who migrated to Bombay from Persia in the eighth century, to escape Muslim persecution. Their religion is known as Zoroastrianism, one of the world's oldest religions but one that is now close to dying out.

There are probably no more than 140,000 Parsis worldwide (about 80,000 live in Mumbai). They are a tiny, close-knit community and their commercial influence has been out of all proportion to their numbers.

Initially, the Bombay Parsis were involved in spinning and dyeing. The giant Bombay Dyeing and Manufacturing Company is still owned by the Mumbai Parsi Wadia family. Financing is another Parsi activity. Wealth from spinning and financing was put into property so that, by 1855, Parsi families were believed to own approximately half the island of Bombay. Property developers today wanting to move into Mumbai find that more often than not they must deal with Parsi landlords.

Several of India's most famous business families are Parsis, including the Tata, Modi and Wadia families. The Tata Group, controlled by the Tata family, is India's largest industrial group with sales of around US$10 billion annually and encompassing around 30 listed companies and many more private ones. It is not a bad result for a family that is not strictly ethnically Indian. The massive Mumbai-based Godrej Group is another prominent Parsi-owned enterprise, owned by the Godrej family. It is an important producer in India of non-perishable consumer goods.

Prime Minister Indira Gandhi's husband, Feroze Gandhi, was a Parsi. Prior to the marriage he had spelt his surname 'Ghandy'. The later rendering appears to have been an opportunistic and erroneous attempt to suggest a link to Mahatma Gandhi. The late Freddie Mercury, lead singer of the rock group Queen, was a Parsi. His real name was Farookh Bulsara and he was born in Zanzibar to a local Parsi family. World-renowned conductor Zubin Mehta is another Parsi.

Traditionally Parsis have been involved in money lending outside India. The Parsi linkage with money handling is why the finance column in the Hong Kong-based weekly magazine, the *Far Eastern Economic Review* is called 'Shroff'; Shroff being a common Parsi surname. It is also why offices in Hong Kong that handle small payments such as parking fees in high-rise car parks are called Shroff offices. Parsi Road in Singapore runs between Singapore's Monetary Authority building and its car park, a further allusion to the historic money handling role of the Parsis.

The Parsis were especially prominent in business in Hong Kong. Twelve of the 62 founding members of the Hong Kong General Chamber of Commerce were Parsis. Most of the rest were British. (There were no founding Chinese members, local or otherwise.) Many Parsi surnames particularly in Hong Kong have 'jee' as a suffix. Ruttonjee Estates is a big commercial property company in Hong Kong, owned by the Parsi Shroff and Ruttonjee families. These families still maintain close links with the Parsi community in Mumbai. Today, however, there are thought to be just 200 Parsis left in Hong Kong.

The Sikhs

There are about 14 million Sikhs in India, mostly in the Punjab region, but they are found all over India. The Sikh religion is comparatively modern (about 350 years old) and was established to combine elements of Islam with Hinduism – Sikhs cremate their dead, for example, but are opposed to idol worship. Observant Sikh men do not cut their hair, keeping it twisted over their heads and hidden in a turban. Not all Sikh men do this and so today there are many Sikhs who have the appearance of other Indians. However, all Sikh males have the surname 'Singh', although it may not always be used. All Sikh women have the surname 'Kaur'.

Sikhs in India are yet another small group that is disproportionately wealthy. They tend to be involved in commercial activities with a mechanical emphasis. Many are sports fanatics in and outside India and choose businesses that have a linkage to sport. Local Sikh families run most sports goods stores in Kuala Lumpur. Similarly, East Asia's biggest regional chain of sports goods stores is Royal Sporting House, founded in Singapore by local Sikh J.S. Gill. Today there are more than 200 Royal Sporting House stores across Asia and the group manages Lacoste, Golf House, Greg Norman, Reebok and Nautica stores in Singapore, all of which have a sports focus.

Thailand's Sikh community is prominent in that country, although numerically small – about 25,000 – and most are in Bangkok. Tailoring in Thailand is an occupation dominated by Sikhs, especially in Bangkok, Phuket and Pattaya. They run the tailoring stores, import the necessary fabrics and contract out the actual tailoring mostly to ethnic Thais.

Sura Chansrichawla is Thailand's most prominent Sikh businessman. He controlled Thailand's Laem Thong Bank before losing it in the wake of Asia's financial crisis of 1997–98. The bank had been brought to the point of collapse by Sura after he had it extend huge loans to his other business interests. He also founded Thai Prasit Insurance Co. which he sold in April 2000. He has claimed to have owned seven hotels in India. Today, Sura concentrates on real estate holdings and, true to the typical Sikh interest in sports, is well known as a big donor to sports development in Thailand.

Kartar Singh Thakral is another prominent Southeast Asian Sikh. He was born in Bangkok and went to Singapore with his father in 1952 to set up a textile trading business. He made Singapore his home and he now holds Singapore citizenship. His business interests are in property and electronics, spanning Singapore, India, China and Australia. Among Thakral's Australian assets are the All Seasons Premier Menzies Hotel and Wynyard Retail Centre in Sydney, All Seasons Premier Pacific Bay Resort in Coffs Harbour, the Novotel on Collins Hotel, Hilton on the Park Hotel, and Australia on Collins Shopping Centre in Melbourne. Thakral is the patron of the Singapore Sikh Welfare Council.

The Tamils

Southern Indians, particularly Tamils, dominate Malaysia's Indian community today. In fact more than half Malaysia's Indians, or about one million, are Tamil. The forebears of the vast majority came from what is now Sri Lanka. They came during the colonial period to work as indentured labourers in the rubber plantations. A small group came from mainland India. They were better off and better educated and tended to take jobs in the colonial civil service.

Today, Malaysia's Tamil community tends to be among the poorest Malaysians and many still live on rubber plantations where salaries and government services are poor. They do not have a strong voice in government and their relative poverty is a perpetual social and political issue in Malaysia. There are around 111,000 Tamils living in Singapore, where they tend to work as labourers, security guards and shop assistants.

The best-known Tamil businessman in East Asia today is Malaysia's T. Ananda Krishnan. He built his billion-dollar fortune from oil trading in Malaysia, telecommunications and property. He built Kuala Lumpur's twin Petronas Towers, the tallest buildings in the world. He keeps a very low profile, is rarely photographed and almost never appears in the media. He was on good terms with Malaysia's former Prime Minister Mahathir Mohamad, which fact helped to smooth his way to the upper echelons of Malaysian business.

The most prominent ethnic Indian conglomerate in Indonesia is the synthetic textiles-based Texmaco Group, founded by the Marimutu family and headed by Marimutu Sinivasan. The Marimutus are also of Tamil descent. Texmaco owns several massive factories in Indonesia and invested heavily in India prior to Asia's and its own financial crises. The Marimutu family intended to build a US$700 million power plant in India, for example. They paid US$48 million in 1997 for UK-based clothes manufacturer SR Gent which supplies clothes to the UK retailer Marks & Spencer. The Group's management is dominated by Marimutu family members and other ethnic Tamils, notwithstanding its massive operations in Indonesia. By 2004, Texmaco Group remained under the Marimutu family's management but the bulk of its shares had been ceded to the Indonesian Bank Restructuring Agency (IBRA). The family's financial difficulties had become accute. Marimutu Manimaren, the younger brother of Marimutu Sinivasan, chairman of the Group, threw himself to his death from the window of a central Jakata hotel tower in August 2003. A consortium that included the son of former Malaysian Prime Minister Mahathir was named as a possible bidder for IBRA's stake in the Group.

Overseas Indians in the West

London is an important focus of the old Indian diaspora and from there the Indian linkages and networks spiral back to India, Africa, the Caribbean, Hong Kong and the rest of Asia. Indians are prominent in the Americas as well. Ethnic Indians run almost half of all small motels across the United States. One of the oldest Indian names in business in the United States is Amar Bose who founded the Bose Corporation in the 1950s. Today the Massachusetts-based company is the world's largest manufacturer of high-

Table 4.1 Recent Indian heads of worldwide multinational corporations

Name	Company	Period	Place of Birth
Rajat Gupta	CEO, McKinsey	Appointed 1994	Calcutta, India
Jamshed 'Jim' Wadia	Worldwide Managing Partner, Arthur Andersen; Chief Operating Officer, Linklaters	1997–2000 Appointed 2001	India
Arun Netravali	President, Bell Labs	1999–2001	Karnataka, India
Sanjay Kumar	President and CEO, Computer Associates	Appointed 2000	Colombo, Sri Lanka
Rana Talwar	CEO, Standard Chartered Bank	1997–2001	India
Aman Mehta	CEO, HSBC	1998–2003	India
Rono Dutta	President, United Airlines	Appointed 1999	India
Rakesh Gangwal	President and CEO, US Airways	1998–2001	Calcutta, India
Victor Menezes	Chairman and CEO, Citibank	Appointed 2000	Pune, India
Shailesh Mehta	CEO, Providian Financial Corporation	1994–2001	India
Pradman Kaul	Chairman and CEO, Hughes Network Systems	Appointed 1990	India
Rajiv Gupta	Chairman and CEO, Rohm & Haas	Appointed 1999	Mumbai, India
Ramani Ayer	CEO, Hartford Financial Services	Appointed 1997	India
Arun Sarin	CEO, Vodafone	Appointed late 2002	India

quality loudspeakers, and state-of-the-art Bose sound systems are sold around the world.

The United States is also the focus of recent migrations from India, particularly California's Silicon Valley. The overseas Indians of old were traders and shopkeepers. The new generation of overseas Indians are professionals, who do not need to have their own companies and are comfortable working for others. So, today, ethnic Indian professionals can be found heading up some of the world's most important corporations, as shown in Table 4.1.

Their surnames suggest more than that they are simply of Indian descent. Jim Wadia is a Parsi, and Pradman Kaul's surname suggests that he is ancestrally from the Kashmir region, for example.

Research by University of California, Berkeley, associate professor AnnaLee Saxenian indicates that about one-third of the engineers in Silicon Valley are of Indian descent, while 7% of the high-tech firms are led by Indian CEOs. Two of the most prominent are Vinod Khosla, co-founder of Sun Microsystems, and Sabeer Bhatia who founded Hotmail and sold it to Microsoft for US$400 million.

Many Indians also work in the financial sector as fund managers, analysts and stockbrokers. Accordingly, Indians were prominent among the victims of the 2001 terrorist attacks on New York's World Trade Center.

Networked Investment

Examples of cross-border joint ventures between overseas Indians are not as common as among overseas Chinese, but they do happen. Singapore's Jhunjhnuwala family owns Singapore's Hind Development Group. The company had its start in 1997 when it acquired the Oberoi Imperial Hotel in Singapore from India's Oberoi family. Today the Jhunjhnuwala family is involved in property development in Singapore, Hong Kong and Australia and running northern Indian food restaurants in Singapore. The family has around 50 members today in Singapore. Originally from India, they were based in Burma until the 1960s exodus when the Burmese government nationalised industry. The family acquired listed industrial paint-maker Shalimar Paints in India in 1988, but it was the early acqui-sition of the Imperial Hotel from fellow Indians that provided their real start in business.

Two Indian families founded the G. Premjee Group in 1868 in Burma, principally to trade in rice. They moved to Bangkok in 1918 and today the group employs more than 2,000 people in 200 subsidiaries involved in trading, shipping, tourism and real estate. Singapore's Jumabhoy family chose Shah's G. Premjee Group as its local partner for its Bangkok Palm Court serviced apartment development – another example of cross-border overseas Indians linking up. The Group still sources rice from Thailand, Myanmar, India, China and Pakistan and sells it to East Africa via local Indian importers there. Its listed Precious Shipping is Thailand's largest shipowner. Nearly all the Group's top executives are Indian. In 1999, the group's Thai-Indian head Kirit united with India's Ballarpur Industries and its president Lalit Mohan Thapar to oust the expatriate American management of Thailand's Phoenix Pulp & Paper.

Thailand's Sikh businessman Sura Chansrichawla (mentioned above) co-owns Bangkok's Holiday Inn Crown Plaza Hotel with the Hong Kong-based Indian Harilela family – another example of cross-border overseas Indian cooperation. The Harilelas were part of an initial rescue bid to pump funds into Sura's Laem Thong Bank as it faltered with the Asian crisis in 1998. (The bank was ultimately absorbed into a state-owned bank which itself was then sold to a Singapore bank.)

The Silicon Valley Technology Group, founded in San Jose by Anil and Sucheta Kapuria, also benefited from finance from the Harilelas in its early days.

Indorama Group (also known as the Irama Unggal Group) is another Indonesian Indian-controlled conglomerate and, like Texmaco, it concentrates on textiles. It is owned by the low-profile Lohia family and has expanded across Asia using Indian family members and Indian expatriates in its offices in Indonesia, Thailand, Turkey, India and Sri Lanka. Polyester and worsted yarn is produced in Thailand, Indonesia, India and Sri Lanka. It is a case of an overseas Indian family expanding to wherever it has family and personal connections. It has around US$600 million in assets. The Lohia's bought Thailand's ailing Siam Polyester in 1998 for approximately US$5 million and installed a family member to oversee it.

Indian Chambers of Commerce in Asia

There are Indian chambers of commerce across Asia as there are Chinese chambers. They provide good starting points for outsiders wanting to access the local Indian business community, and also good entry points for newly arrived Indian businesspeople.

The main body in Hong Kong is the Indian Chamber of Commerce Hong Kong. It was established in 1952 and today has hundreds of members. It is a member of the Council of Hong Kong Indian Associations.

The main body in Malaysia is the Malaysian Associated Indian Chamber of Commerce and Industry. In Singapore, it is the Singapore Indian Chamber of Commerce and Industry. In Myanmar, it is the Myanmar India Business Club; in Korea, the Indian Merchants Association; in Japan, the Indian Chamber of Commerce; and in the Philippines, the Filipino-India Chamber of Commerce.

Indonesia has an organisation called the Gandhi Seva Loka. It is a well-funded foundation for Indonesian Sindhis. It recently built modern, three-storey premises in central Jakarta, called the Graha Sindhu (Sindhi House). The foundation acts as a Sindhi chamber of commerce and cultural centre.

In 1999, a move was made to unite these bodies at a regional level and so the Asia Pacific Indian Chambers of Commerce (APICCI) was formed in Singapore. The founding members of this new body comprise all the Indian chambers above plus chambers in India itself, Japan and Korea.

There are also Indian chambers of commerce in many other parts of the world. But perhaps the most renowned of the American chambers is IndUS Entrepreneurs. It comprises a large group of mostly Silicon Valley-based ethnic Indian entrepreneurs. Its main function is to hold monthly meetings for networking. There are chapters in Atlanta, Austin, Bangalore, Boston, Chicago, Chennai, Dallas, Delhi, Hyderabad, Los Angeles, Mumbai, New York, Seattle, and Vancouver BC, thus providing a formal basis for networking across North America and India.

The overseas Chinese were Asia's most important commercial diaspora in the twentieth century. Southeast Asia's share of the Asian economic miracle was their doing with the help of largely benign government policy.

But it will be the overseas Indians who will be this century's important diaspora in Asia. And probably the most important economic diaspora in the world.

Ignore them at your peril!

Dealing with Information Ambiguity, Local Consultants and Accounting Firms

Information – Asia's Scarcest Commodity

Getting good information in most of Asia is not easy. Due diligence reports with gaping holes, local partners with fingers in many pies (most of which are kept hidden), vaguely specified contracts, companies with three or more sets of books, rumours that are never confirmed or dismissed – such are the joys of operating in Asia. Information is like gold in Asia – it's valuable, scarce and no one ever has enough. And when legal structures are poor in Asia, remedying mistakes can be difficult. So it pays to do your research first. But how do you get good, timely and reliable information?

The media in Asia is often poorly resourced and compromised by its owners' other businesses. Journalists from Thailand and China to

Indonesia and the Philippines are paid so poorly that many accept payments either not to write bad news stories or provide companies with only favourable coverage.

Asian entrepreneurs generally prefer low or no profiles and nor are their businesses transparent. Statutory filings are rarely required and, even if they are, the requirements may not be complied with.

Government statistics are poor in much of Asia and in Vietnam, Indonesia and China are more for propaganda purposes than recording reality. It all adds up to an information-poor environment. When information is available, it is often tainted or simply fabricated.

Due diligence reports out of China, for example, might come with documents, some of which are not even photocopies, but hand-written copies of documents that have been sighted. Managers will need to make their own judgments about the reliability and reputation of the due diligence firm they are dealing with to decide if they should accept this sort of 'evidence'. Sometimes there's no choice.

Managers in Asia must learn to operate with not as much information as they typically have at home and learn to interpret what they do have. 'Bad news never travels up' is an adage nowhere more true than in Asia. The reticence of employees in Asia to report bad news to superiors can mean that managers – and joint venture partners – can be left in the dark until it's too late. Information *about* companies is often hard to get but also information *within* companies may not flow as it should.

Head offices must also understand that their Asian offices may not be able to supply all the information which they would normally receive from more mature markets. If they don't, opportunities may be lost. In this regard, regional managers in Asia will need to learn as much about managing head office expectations on this as operating in an information-scarce environment.

Business intelligence gathering has become big business in Asia. New York-based Kroll Worldwide is one of the market leaders. It was one of the first to tackle business information constraints in Asia in a serious and professional manner. Former CIA (Central Intelligence Agency), FBI (Federal Bureau of Investigation) and ASIO (Australian Security Intelligence Organisation) officers were initially among its staff. The company's Asian operations specialise in providing corporate due diligence assessments, particularly in China, investigating fraud by joint venture partners and helping to enforce copyright protection.

Another company is the Hong Kong-based Hill & Associates. Most of the principals of the company are former senior officers of the Hong Kong police force. There are one or two former FBI officers too. The company specialises in intellectual property protection, advising on the physical security of Asia-based personnel and general investigation. It also provides bodyguard protection for Hong Kong's billionaire businessmen and their families. Like Kroll, Hill & Associates has offices around Asia.

Apart from these two companies, there are many local companies willing to offer local 'intelligence' gathering services, devise market entry strategies and so on.

Local Business Consultants

One way to solve the information gap in Asia is to hire local business consultants. But many are not all that they're cracked up to be and some, with their vested interests, are simply downright dangerous. Many are Western expatriates who like Asia, didn't want to go home, decided to stay and set up in business, running business partner matching services and providing market entry advice.

Local consulting firms face problems like any other firms in Asia. They face difficulties in hiring local employees who are able to think creatively and analytically and who have the ability to be sceptical of whatever information they come across as part of their corporate and industrial research. And many of the local firms that do not have the backing of an international brand name accordingly attract lower fees and thus cannot usually afford local staff of sufficient calibre.

So instead of hard-edged research, they often congregate at the lower end of the spectrum, offering the types of service that the bigger names don't want to soil themselves with. They can 'buy' data from government officials on your behalf, find you the 'right' local business partner and help you get around the US Foreign Corrupt Practices Act.

One of the biggest problems when it comes to engaging local consultants is that of faked data. Research staff unable to find the information needed or who simply want to cut corners might be tempted to make it up. This is especially so in an information-scarce environment that makes obtaining supplementary data for cross-verification purposes expensive, if not impossible, to obtain. Japanese firms tend to go through the research results they pay for and strip them apart, wanting to know how the information was collected, by whom and from where. Western clients tend not to do this and routinely accept research reports from local consultants at face value. They shouldn't.

How to avoid such problems? Of course there are smaller companies that are genuinely reputable and try the best they can with limited resources. Another possibility is to approach big name firms. These tend to hire good local talent, pay them accordingly and, most importantly, train them. One risk, however, is that these larger firms use their big names to pull in clients but then subcontract work to small local consulting firms whose calibre and staff they have little control over.

A US$100,000 research project, for example, might be awarded to the consulting arm of one of the big international accounting firms. One of the reasons why the firm is given the project is because of its big name and reputation ('no one has ever been fired for choosing McKinseys' as some say). The client is prepared to pay to have the brightest and the best working on its brief. But the accounting firm then seeks to subcontract out the entire project to a smaller local research firm – the sort of firm the principal client had hoped to avoid. In turn, the smaller firm seeks to break up the brief and further allocate it to several more small firms – all without the principal client's knowledge. Each step in the chain requires its cut and before long perhaps almost two-thirds of the total fee is chewed up by cascading margins. This tale is not so far-fetched. In fact, it is based on what actually happened.

The vested interests of local consultants can pose more problems. What are all the family and equity connections of the owner and all the staff that can affect the advice that they give to clients? Another more potent problem is confidentiality. Information is bought and sold in Asia like nowhere else. But information need not be sold for confidences to be broken. Idle secretarial chatter between firms in Asia can be a big problem. One expatriate employee in Jakarta was approached by a head-hunting firm for a position elsewhere. The potential candidate was not particularly interested but handed over his CV anyway. A secretary in the client firm was friendly with the expatriate's existing employer's wife and wasted no time in telling her that the expatriate was looking for work elsewhere. He wasn't, but suffered accordingly. Similarly, no consulting assignment in Asia, or anywhere for that matter, should be awarded without the consultants agreeing to strict confidentiality provisions. And yet, it's amazing how often Western firms are willing to accept standards in Asia that are far lower than what they would expect elsewhere when it comes to these sorts of provisions.

Caveat Emptor: Auditing in Asia

Hire an external auditor, pay him hundreds of thousands of dollars and then call him 'independent' – the practice is bizarre anywhere and nowhere more so than in Asia. Audits are not just audits. Managers intent on investing in companies in Asia need to assess the professionalism of the auditor as well as the audited accounts.

The first problem is that accounting standards differ from country to country. A profitable company in one jurisdiction might well be unprofitable in another, depending on what is permitted as income, costs, assets and so on. Hong Kong's Pacific Century Cyberworks, for example, reported a loss of US$884.6 million in Hong Kong for the year 2000 under Hong Kong's accounting rules. One unit's American depository receipts were listed on the New York Stock Exchange, so it was required to report its results under US standards as well. And its loss under US rules was more than double the Hong Kong figure, at US$1,867.9 million – two very different results for the one company. Worldwide harmonisation of accounting standards is in sight, but in the meantime, managers need to be aware of the potential for these sorts of discrepancies.

Western accounting firms have been instrumental in moving Asia's corporate governance standards further along the track to modernity. But, given Asia's economic crisis, have they been doing a good enough job? And if the Enron–Arthur Andersen debacle of 2002 can happen in the relatively well-regulated US market, then what does an auditing report mean in China, Indonesia, Thailand or India, even if it is conducted by a worldwide accounting firm?

Local auditing firms without worldwide reputations to protect should be immediately suspect, particularly in economies where regulatory and supervisory systems are weak. China is the classic case. There are many cases of local accounting firms helping to cook the books in China. Sometimes it is the accountants that initiate the 'service'. China's official news agency Xinhua reported in 2001 that accountants working at the Hubei Lihua accounting firm had helped eight listed A grade share companies to falsify their accounts since 1998. The fraud, as reported, was not terribly sophisticated. It simply involved the accounting staff signing off on accounts 'regardless of their truth'. They did so for money.[1]

But then how much better are audits conducted by international accounting firms? The name might be global but the staff and the practice generally are local. The fiasco over the adequacy of the audits conducted by Deloitte Touche Tohmatsu in Hong Kong of locally listed 'red chip' Guangnan (Holdings) Ltd is a case in point. Audits commissioned from KPMG suggested discrepancies in Guangnan's audited accounts of some US$1.07 billion. These were followed in 1999 by the unprecedented withdrawal by Deloittes of its 1997 audit report of Guangnan.

The debacle over Asia Pulp & Paper (APP), a listed Singapore-based company, and several of its listed Indonesian subsidiaries provides another example. APP and its listed units were audited by the Singapore and Jakarta offices of Arthur Andersen. APP became the subject of the largest emerging markets debt work out in history. It had around US$14 billion in debts by early 2002. Derivatives that led to US$220 million in losses went unnoticed in its audited accounts for three-and-a-half years and when they were finally noticed it took another five months before they were disclosed publicly. Even APP's chief financial officer said that the company's accounts, as audited by Arthur Andersen for the years 1997, 1998 and 1999, 'should not be relied upon'. Almost US$200 million was deposited by an Indonesian-based APP unit in a related-party bank that was misnamed in the audited accounts. And a billion dollars has been siphoned off by five mysterious British Virgin Islands companies that appear to be linked to Indonesia's Sinar Mas group which controls the company. The five companies, with names that almost no one has heard of, were responsible for almost a third of APP's 'sales' in 1999. By mid-2002, none of the money owing had been paid and the five companies had ceased operating. Disgruntled US bond and shareholders commenced legal proceedings in 2001 against Andersen auditors in relation to the audits of APP in Indonesia, Singapore and New York.

Sidharta, Sidharta & Harsono, the Indonesian version of KPMG, was pursued in 2002 by the US Securities and Exchange Commission (SEC) and the Justice Department, under the Foreign Corrupt Practices Act, for allegedly being the conduit through which a US$75,000 bribe was paid to an Indonesian tax official to provide a favourable tax assessment for US energy firm Baker Hughes. The matter only came to light after Baker Hughes' head office itself reported it to US authorities.

SGV, the Andersen affiliate in the Philippines, was reprimanded for 'unethical conduct' by the local accountant's professional body in 2000 after it unilaterally withdrew three years' worth of audit reports for a local listed firm, Victorias Milling Co., which later went bankrupt. Andersen-SGV had certified the inventory without actually checking it. The figures were later found to be massively fraudulent. In early 2002, SGV was ordered by the Central Bank of the Philippines to conduct 'tighter' bank audits after central bank officials disagreed with SGV's assessments.

It is not as if investors haven't had enough warning that all may not be well with auditing in Asia. In 1982, the collapse of the Carrian Group in Hong Kong led to a massive negligence action against Carrian's auditors and the prosecution of several members of its staff.

But is auditing in Asia worse than anywhere else? Auditing in Asia is not easy. There is a culture of secrecy, a suspicion of outsiders such as external auditors and a failure on the part of many majority owners to even understand their obligations once they list their companies on a local stock exchange. Too many fail to recognise that listing 'their' company means that it is no longer exactly that. The number of listed companies in Asia issuing annual reports in which their auditors express a qualified opinion or a fundamental uncertainty is rising. But, if anything, the numbers should probably be higher.

That even the local offices of the big international accounting firms are seen as potentially compromised was demonstrated best by the Indonesian government in the wake of Asia's economic crisis. Most of Indonesia's big conglomerates and nearly all its banks were technically insolvent by 1998. The government created the Indonesian Bank Restructuring Agency (IBRA) to help sort the mess out. The first task was to find out just how bad things were. But IBRA did not invite local auditors in to do the work. Instead they bypassed Jakarta and engaged auditors in the Australian and London offices of what was then the Big Five.

In Asia, perhaps more than anywhere else, listed companies habitually shop around for the most agreeable auditor. In the United States, a listed company's decision to change auditors is a decision not taken lightly – it rightfully begs the question of whether the company has something to hide. The same degree of apprehension is yet to develop in much of Asia.

Yet another complication rarely thought about is what happens to local affiliates when the world's major accounting firms merge? The 1987 merger of Klynveld Main Goedeler with Peat Marwick Mitchell to form KPMG Peat Marwick is one example. Once the merger occurs, it is assumed that all the obstacles must have been ironed out. That might well be the case as far as the key participants are concerned, but the merger between two major world accounting firms may mean that unfriendly local affiliates are dragged into the process as well. For example, when Price Waterhouse and Coopers & Lybrand merged in 1998 it meant that their Jakarta affiliates, Hadi, Susanto & Co and Sidharta & Sidharta, also had to merge. Too bad if the two firms have a long-standing rivalry and even hatred of one another. The problems can take years to sort out, as KPMG found after it was formed. Inappropriate mergers at the local level in Asia are simply asking for trouble.

There is no doubt that the big international accounting firms in Asia have been instrumental in exposing enormous corporate frauds and impropriety across Asia, but it should never be assumed that there is a single standard of quality across all branches in all countries. Nor should it be assumed that branches faithfully replicate those in, say, the United States. In many Asian countries, foreign accounting firms are required or have been encouraged to take local partners. Not all the marriages are seamless. Typically, these mixed marriages employ Western expatriates but rarely are they employed in the lucrative and sensitive auditing divisions. More usually, and particularly when it is the local partner that is ascendant, they are restricted to the taxation and consulting divisions.

When so much else has failed in Asia, be it government and stock market rules and regulations, or systems of internal corporate governance, it is too much to assume that auditing can pick up all this slack. It is also too much to expect that the professionalism of the sector can be maintained when so much of the environment in which it must operate has been so compromised when it comes to modern standards of ethics and corporate governance.

Conduct Unbecoming? Western Investment Banks in Asia

Investment banks are another source of corporate information. They have been useful in modernising corporate Asia, but there are limits to this usefulness. Many of the big investment banks have helped local firms to issue new shares and bonds and have assisted them with other services. They also offer investment advice to institutional and retail investors but rarely, if ever, do they declare the work that they have done, are doing, are bidding for or are likely to bid for in relation to the companies they analyse. What incentive does an investment bank have to rate the stock of a company from which it is earning millions of dollars in fees as a 'sell'? The lack of transparency relating to this practice and the perversions in advice that have resulted are every bit as unseemly as the worst corporate governance excesses in Asia.

Part of the problem is the Asian inability to brook any criticism whatsoever. The concept of 'face' has been so highly developed that many owners and senior managers see any criticism, no matter how minor, as major. Criticism is not seen merely as restricted to that practice being criticised but is seen as a general affront; an assault on their credibility, authority and standing. Thus research reports that report fairly on companies' good and bad points are simply unacceptable to many in corporate Asia and they habitually move their business accordingly.

Second-guessing the Investment Banks

1. Undertake the research yourself or commission some. All the statutory corporate filings need to be examined. Particular attention needs to be taken to related-party transactions.

2. Ask the investment bank or brokerage that has issued the research what, if any, commercial relationship it has with the company under research or that it expects to gain. View the efficacy of its research only in light of its answers to this question.

3. Take a lead from institutional investors. Generally, they have their own in-house research that is independent of the potential conflicts of interest of the research teams of brokerages and investment banks. If they are buying into an issue, presumably they see it as well priced.

Some Questions you should ask of Local Auditors

1. What commercial relationships do they have with the companies that you are interested in? Do they, for example, contract the company for any services, or rent any property from them?

2. In respect of accounting firms in Thailand, Indonesia, China and the Philippines, are there any Western expatriates who work in the auditing division or are all the staff local? If the company does employ Western expatriates, in what divisions are they and if there are none in auditing, why?

3. If the accounting firm is a member of the Big Four, is the local office a joint venture or is it operated outright by the Big Four firm?

4. Can the firm guarantee that none of its audit staff trade in the shares of the company in which you are interested?

Some Questions you should ask Local Business Consultants

1. If you are to commission a study from a local consulting company, ask for the names and CVs of all the staff who will work on the study. Is it possible to meet each of the staff? Who will be leading the research team? What are that person's qualifications?

2. Who are recent past clients? Would any be willing to discuss their experience of using the consulting firm's services?

3. Can the consulting company guarantee that it is not currently engaged by any competitors?

4. Can it guarantee that none of its research staff have family or any other links with competitors?

5. Who is the ultimate owner of the consulting company? Do any of the shareholders have any other businesses that might pose conflicts of interest for the work you wish to assign to the company?

6. Will the consulting firm be undertaking all the work or does it intend to subcontract all or part of the project? Does it guarantee that it will undertake all the work itself?

A Note on Consultants' Out-of-pocket Expenses

Consultants almost always charge for two items – their time and 'out-of-pocket expenses' (OPEs as they're called in the business). These are the costs they incur, such as travel expenses, data purchasing costs and so on, that are directly attributable to your project. Often the contract will include some sort of cap for OPEs such as 'OPEs will not be more than 20% of the total agreed professional fee without the written approval of the client'. If it does not, you should insist on it.

Clients rarely seem to question OPEs in Asia. They should. These are routinely padded out and become a back-door way for consultants to earn extra fees. One assignment undertaken for a major American client by a Southeast Asian office of one of the world's big accounting firms included US$58,000 for out-of-pocket expenses. The main consultant later admitted to one of the authors that the accounting firm had documentary evidence for less than US$5,000. The rest was padding. This is fraud. Clients do not accept these sorts of things in New York, Sydney or London, so why do they accept it in Asia?

You should *always* insist that out-of-pocket expenses are capped and that they will be paid upon receipt and verification of all the supporting documentation for the claim. Claims for expenses that cannot be verified or reasonably justified should not be honoured. Allowance will need to be made for those expenses for which supporting documentation cannot be obtained, such as unofficial payments to government officials for obtaining statistical information, but typically these should be relatively trivial.

Economising on Information

Information makes the difference, not simply between success and failure in Asia, but between success and losses that can be ruinous. Saving money on upfront research is a false economy.

There is no need to rush in to Asia. It will still be there tomorrow. Gains that might be won by getting in early and cheaply might be lost by having gone from a position of ignorance.

There are surprising differences between the nationalities of foreign investors when it comes to gathering information. Large and well-resourced American companies sometimes send in wave after wave of research teams. They keep them in-country for maybe three months at a time while they learn and conduct their research. It is expensive but better than using local consultants who might be an unknown quantity. The local consultants, if used at all, can be hired simply to set up local appointments. Many large companies find that this is a sensible division of labour.

When American companies, for example, commission local consultants to do research, they tend to ask few – too few – questions about how the research was conducted. Rarely do they test finalised research reports for their veracity, but they should.

Japanese firms often conduct their research in-house. When they do commission work from outside consultants, they are utterly meticulous in questioning the consultants about how the research was conducted, the appropriateness of the methodology, who undertook the research, their qualifications and so on. Nothing is taken at face value, nothing is trusted and everything is questioned. The contrast of this with the ease with which American managers accept the findings of externally produced research reports is startling.

UK firms tend to stick to the consultants they know. Names that they are comfortable with such as the EIU and the big accounting firms are used. Australian firms, being smaller and less well resourced, tend to economise on their research. They are not used to paying the big consultants' fees that American and European companies pay. They are more likely to hire expatriate Australian staff in Asia who come with on-the-ground experience. Such staff are used as a substitute for commissioning research reports.

Note

1   *Business Times,* 'Accounting firm helped to cook books: Xinhua', 21 August, 2001.

Network like a Local; Negotiate like a Westerner

Why do Relationships Matter?

There are three things that really matter when it comes to doing business in Asia. They are (in no particular order):

1. Relationships
2. Relationships
3. Relationships.

The US popstar Cyndi Lauper had a hit in the 1980s called *Money Changes Everything*. The Asian version could well have been 'Connections Change Everything'. They really do. Knowing the right people can solve most problems in much of Asia.

But why do connections and relationships matter? They matter because from China to Indonesia and much of what lies in between, legal protection is weak. And when laws are weak businesspeople need to find other ways to protect themselves. Typically, they do business only with those they trust and are comfortable with. So the first step to being Big in Asia is to develop good connections; a good local network. A general rule of thumb is that the weaker the local legal system, the more needed are well-founded local personal connections to trade and invest successfully. Thus, they are very necessary in Indonesia and China, less so in Malaysia and Korea, and less still in Singapore.

'At one time, *guanxi* was sufficient to win deals. Then it became necessary but not sufficient. Now we're between that phase and the time when *guanxi* will no longer be necessary.' So said telecoms consultant Duncan Clark in relation to winning contracts to manage telecom IPOs (initial public offerings) in China.[1] Having friends matters everywhere. But the path to economic modernity means that friendships and relationships become less important to doing business over time.

Having a wide network of friends and colleagues also provides the means for collecting information, and as we have said, much of Asia is an information-poor environment. Opportunities come and go but without a good network, you will simply never hear about them. Or if you do, you will often lack the means to access them.

Connections open doors and keep them open. By way of example, almost all expatriates who work in Indonesia do so officially in only one capacity, that of 'technical advisor'. The idea is that Indonesians should manage all businesses operating locally and the expatriates are there merely to advise. Of course, it is a farce and everyone knows it. There is a chronic shortage of human capital in Indonesia and outside managers are needed there perhaps more than any other country in the region.

The Ministries of Manpower and Immigration and the police are able to call in any expatriate and accuse them of acting beyond the limited confines of their work permits. At that point, exorbitant bribes might be demanded. But if the expatriate has connections higher up in any of these bodies, or is connected with someone who can intervene on their behalf, then the harassment can be stopped. If not, the expatriates can be thrown out of Indonesia, as has happened.

Connections help with solving day-to-day problems but they are necessary at every level of business. Having a lot of friends means having a wide set of potential business opportunities. Not having many friends can constrain the growth of a business. So social structures in Asia have developed to allow people to meet and greet easily, to circulate socially. Weddings tend to be big lavish affairs with thousands of guests. There is a lot of emphasis on eating out in restaurants and taking the whole family. Business after all is a family affair. Chambers of commerce are popular as are social clubs such as the Rotary and so on. All this allows people to catch up with each other, to maintain friendships and develop new ones. And with friendships comes business.

In a business environment that is defined by overlapping webs of personal connections and loyalties, who's who takes on vital importance. It is essential that newcomers to Asia get on top of who the big names are in the local corporate scene and how they all fit together. Whereas the business community in the West is a community of companies, the business community in Asia is a community of people. In the West, companies tend to do business with one another. In Asia, the deals are all done between personalities. So when, in 2000, Hong Kong's China Cyberport bought a stake in Kerry Group, it was not of itself big news. The real story was that Oei Hong Leong of Indonesia's billionaire Widjaya family had bought a stake in the private family holding company of billionaire trader Robert Kuok. That was the big news. It's a different mindset.

The people who own and run Asian firms determine the firms' integrity. Goodwill is attached to the owners rather than the firms themselves. Many businesspeople in Asia will even be unfamiliar with trading and company names because of this tendency to think more in terms of the people behind the companies rather than the companies themselves. Westerners, on the other hand, tend to recognise company names but have little idea who owns a company or the name of its CEO. Personalities and people matter in Asia, and so does news about them. Corporate gossip is everything. Often the media cannot be relied upon to convey accurately the latest corporate goings on in Asia. In countries such as Thailand, the Philippines and Indonesia, bad news is often kept out of the media by paying journalists and editors not to run it. Reliable credit checks and due diligence assessments are hard to come by, so good managers in Asia have little choice but to keep their ears to the ground; to stay attuned to whatever gossip is going around. Who is having problems meeting their orders, debts and other commitments is essential information but is only likely to be spread by word of mouth.

Not knowing the names and backgrounds of the people behind the big companies in New York, London or Sydney is, at best, barely necessary and, at worst, ignorance. In Asia, it's unforgivable. Who's who and who is doing what to whom is the lifeblood of conversation in Asian business circles, and for good reason. There's little point sending a business development manager to Asia who is not gregarious.

Can Non-Chinese Utilise Overseas Chinese Networks?

Can non-Chinese utilise the cross-border connections that many, although not all, overseas Chinese have? It's all very well hearing that the Chinese do business on the basis of personal connections or *guanxi*, a term that has become much overused, but what practical relevance to a non-Chinese are the networks of the overseas Chinese?

They can work for non-Chinese but, like everything in Asia, it takes time. Consider this example. One Perth-based businessman had been doing business for many years with a local ethnic Chinese timber importer. This man had lived in Australia for almost 20 years but was Malaysian by birth. The two had a business relationship of several years standing but had also become friends, not close but they did enjoy each other's company. The Australian businessman decided that he wanted to expand his business into a new area – importing children's clothing to Australia. He wanted to buy in Asia, probably Thailand, but didn't know how to go about it. One day he mentioned this in passing to his Chinese friend. 'I can help you', he said, and right away began making telephone calls to associates in Chiang Mai in northern Thailand. Everything was arranged after just three phone calls. The Australian would go to Chiang Mai where a local Chinese businessman, a friend of the Perth Chinese man, would meet him at the airport. This friend would take care of everything. The Australian didn't know what to expect but decided to go to Chiang Mai and just see what would happen.

He arrived in Chiang Mai and received a welcome that could not have been more effusive and helpful. He was taken around factories and shops and wined and dined. His host, the friend of his Chinese friend back in Australia, would not allow him to pay for a thing. He provided cars, guides and personally accompanied him as much as he could over the course of a week. The Australian was taken to factories all around northern Thailand and introduced to all the right people – everywhere doors opened. The locals even took care of the shipping and customs.

It was a successful trip to Thailand – stunningly so – and it was all due to cross-border Chinese connections. The non-Chinese Australian was given access to and benefited from these connections. However, the key to this story is that he had a long-standing relationship with the local Chinese businessman that was built on both business and friendship over several years. The Chiang Mai businessman was not doing the Australian a favour, rather he was doing it for his Chinese friend back in Australia.

Many people claim to have 'connections' or 'relationships' but it is their quality that matters rather than the quantity. Knowing someone in Asia or having had a few dinners with them does not constitute being strongly connected to them. It helps get one to the right door, but don't expect the door to swing open – at least not yet.

Culture Counts But Not That Much

How important to business success in Asia is an understanding of the local social etiquette? Contrary to popular belief, the answer is, probably not much. Business guides tend to overemphasise the cultural aspects of doing business in Asia. 'Don't touch Asians on the head', 'don't point with your feet', 'don't touch locals on the back' and so on – forget all that. Common sense is what matters – listen and be sensitive to the needs and reactions of others and you'll go a long way.

Everyone expects those from other cultures to get it wrong. Businessmen, Asian or otherwise, just want to make money. Million-dollar deals, or, for that matter, deals of any size, are not going to fall through because a visitor to a foreign country handed out his business card in the wrong way. Equally, no one is going to be a success in Asia simply because they have mastered all the local social mores and habits. All cultures make allowances for guests. Minor cultural trespasses are readily forgiven, if noticed at all. Businesspeople in Asia are no more unforgiving of minor cultural errors than Westerners are of them. Besides, if you are from the West, people can reasonably expect that you will behave like a Westerner – and Westerners are generally admired across Asia.

Of course, efforts to get it right are appreciated but at the end of the day making money is what counts. Small cultural errors are important between Asians and will be seen as the insult that they are probably intended to be. But it's a different story when they occur between Asians and visitors to the region. Western sensitivities to the minutiae of cross-cultural nuances derive more from political correctness trends at home than any codes of behaviour particularly demanded of foreigners in Asia. Of course Western businesspeople should not go to Asia and be loud, aggressive and backslapping, but then that sort of behaviour is not necessarily acceptable back home either.

In any event, times are changing and Asia's business elite increasingly are Western-educated and speak English, which is fast becoming Asia's language of business. Knowledge of Asia is rising in the West too. Both sides are becoming more comfortable with each other. It is the practicalities of doing business that really count rather than the vagaries of cultural nuances.

Developing Relationships and Connections in Asia

Having exchanged a business card with someone does not mean that you have a 'relationship' with them. It simply means that you have met. Similarly, having met a lot of people in Asia does not mean that you are well connected. Good relationships in Asia are something that should endure over the years and that means that they must be built on solid foundations.

There was once a conference on doing business in Asia that featured a session in which audience members were given 20 minutes to meet as many attendees as possible and, after the 20 minutes, the individual who had collected the most business cards was declared the winner. It sent out entirely the wrong message. Quantity of connections at the expense of quality is not the approach if you want to be Big in Asia.

There are no quick and easy rules to forging relationships in Asia. They take time if they are to be worth something. Similarly, simply because someone has spent a lot of time in Asia does not mean that they are well connected. Someone might have lived in Jakarta for 25 years, for example, but that does not mean that the locals respect that person or that they can open doors. Asia is full of long-term residents from the West who have not so much run to Asia as run from the West. If they had trouble making it in their own countries, what hope do they have in someone else's?

Asian and particularly ethnic Chinese businesspeople are always looking to forge new connections and relationships. But they don't do this with specific business goals in mind. The friendships are ends unto themselves. Networks of friendships are forged and then business opportunities are allowed to arise. It's an organic process, which does not happen the other way around – friendships are not developed to cover a specific business opportunity.

This confused many Americans during the 'Donorgate' scandal in which Indonesian Chinese businessman James Riady made illegal donations in respect of President Clinton's election campaigns. 'Why would the Riadys donate this money – they don't have many businesses in the United States', was a common theme in the media. But this was looking at it from a Western perspective. Businesspeople from Asia generally prefer to develop relationships first and then invest. They do not invest and then attempt to develop relationships to protect or enhance investments already made. India presents an exception to this rule. As mentioned earlier, Indians like clear upfront indications about the benefits that they can expect. 'Why should I see you? What will it mean for me?' might be a typical response in India. Once the answer to that is made clear, the relationship building can commence.

The most important rule for developing relationships in Asia is not to rush into business right away. Locals will understand that someone from a large American or British firm who is not based in Asia has only limited time and they may make some allowances for that. But it is still necessary to forge good relations where possible. Repeat visits and plenty of follow-up are important. Remember, people in Asia tend to see business as something that occurs between people rather than companies. It is the people who give the companies definition rather than the other way round. There is an element of that in Western business too but it is heightened in Asia. So, taking an interest in the local parties outside work is essential. Taking the trouble to learn about their personal interests and their families is a good idea.

How does an outsider know when they have been accepted in Asia and that associates are no longer just that but now part of their network? There's no easy answer. But one indication might be when the locals themselves suggest opportunities that could be embarked on together and when they personally invite you to functions and events that are important to them in their private lives.

Choosing a Local Partner: Some Basics

A local partner can make sense in those markets that are difficult, complex and lack transparency. In some sectors in some countries (such as accounting in Thailand and mining in Indonesia), a local partner might even be required by law. However, having a local partner is a not a universal panacea. In fact, it can prove a disaster. There are plenty of foreign companies who opted for local partners in China and Indonesia which led to the destruction of the venture when possibly the company might have performed better going it alone. So, if taking a local partner is necessary or seems sensible, it's worth the time and the expense to choose the right one. Here are some things to consider:[2]

■ *Make sure that you have similar objectives to your partner.* You might be looking to achieve market share but your partner might be interested in quick profits. Differing objectives are a common reason why joint ventures come unstuck.

- *Make sure that you have similar plans for the venture as your partner.* For example, you might intend the venture to stay focused, whereas your partner might want it to diversify; you might be planning for a single factory, but your partner might be hoping for six across the country.

- *Make sure that your partner isn't involved in other businesses that will present a conflict of interest for your venture.* You don't want to discover that your partner is reluctant to move into certain areas because he is already producing in that area, or is related to someone who is.

- *You need to feel comfortable with your partner.* To feel comfortable you need to know as much about them as possible. You must be able to trust your partner. You do not want to discover some time after agreeing to a joint venture that your local partner is actually a front for some general or a local politician's youngest son.

- *Your partner must be well thought of locally.* You need a partner who can deal with the local bureaucracy and speed things up. You do not want to be tarred by your partner's pre-existing business problems and bad blood with the local authorities or business community.

- *You need to consider how much information you will share with your partner and how safe it will be.* Asia is littered with examples of joint ventures in which the local side simply wanted to use the venture to gain technology transfer and other know-how and once this was gained, created a dispute with the foreign party so that they could be free of their contractual obligations to start up on their own.

- *You might want to consider paying for a due diligence check on your prospective partner.* What is their actual corporate structure? What related parties are there? What other joint ventures do they have and how have their other partners been treated? Who are all the equity participants and who are the real ultimate owners? What sort of general reputation do its principals enjoy, do they have criminal records, what are their outstanding tax obligations, their bank and other debts? What is its financial position? What are its sources of financing? Does it face any pending legal action? Has it been involved in any practices which, if continued, would lead to a possible contravention of the US Foreign Corrupt Practices Act or similar laws on the part of the foreign party? What is the structure of the family behind it and are there any internal family conflicts? Is there a myriad of cousins, half-brothers and half-sisters among whom trouble could flare in future? What are the other corporate activities of the immediate and the extended family? With whom are they close and who are their enemies? Are they politically neutral or politically aligned? How would a change of government affect their business prospects?

■ *Your partner should be able to add to the business.* It's always tempting to sign on with a local partner who is already in the business that you are in, simply because they know the business locally. It is far better if they can also bring to the business something that you do not have – such as a good distribution network, useful land holdings or good local access to raw materials.

The most important ingredient to finding the right local partner in Asia is time. It takes many visits if the entrant company does not have local representatives. All too often joint ventures are signed too early and thus between incompatible partners, simply because of pressure at home to deliver a signed and sealed joint venture in Asia. Too often, foreign firms in Asia sign joint venture agreements too early because of a need to be seen by head office to have made 'concrete' progress or improve someone's immediate career advancement prospects.

Even after a joint venture is established, sound relationships must be established between the staff on either side. The trust of the local staff must be gained and everyone must feel comfortable and able to share information and news, be it good or bad.

It is not uncommon to take two or three years to find a suitable local partner in Asia and then another year for the two partners to properly enmesh and the staff on both sides to establish good working relationships.

If negotiations fail and a joint venture does not materialise, all is not lost. What might well have been gained are useful relationships and they should not be discarded. Maintain them and they might prove to be helpful later. The Asian side at least will see such relationships as a positive outcome in themselves.

Negotiating in Asia: Some Suggestions

Typically, businesspeople will find that it is members of the owning family with whom they work when dealing with smaller overseas Chinese-owned firms. In larger overseas Chinese firms, initial negotiations will be with employees. Members of the controlling family will be introduced as negotiations proceed. At that point, negotiations will gather pace noticeably, or the fact that a family member has suddenly become involved signals that the local side believes that the negotiations are close to nearing completion.

Things can be a little different in India. Negotiations will be more formal than elsewhere and more regard will be paid to hierarchy and process. To quote one Western businessman who does business there:

> India is still a very class-ridden society. Determining each rank of the locals with whom negotiations are to be conducted is very important. I find it prudent to always ask for a list of the locals' names and their position in the company before the meetings begin. That also helps with working out the seating arrangements. Small things like who sits where can matter a lot in India. These things are less important in China and Southeast Asia. We are always expected to make the first presentation, which gives them the advantage of reading the situation better. They do not like surprises and always want briefings ahead of meetings.

When planning for negotiations in Asia, be it for trade or investment, the following should also be considered:[3]

- *Never economise on information and research.* Enter negotiations well briefed on the market that you are interested in and the people with whom you are to negotiate.
- *Never negotiate alone.* It is far better to have two main negotiators, but they must present a unified front and never disagree with each other in front of the opposite side. Disagreements can be handled during requested adjournments. Almost certainly the local side will outnumber the non-local side, and there might be some people in the room whose reason for being there is not obvious. Ask who they are and what their position is.
- *Keep the same negotiating team.* Negotiations can go on for months and sometimes even longer, so keep the same negotiating team. Relationship building and trust are important for both parties and negotiations can take longer when new negotiators are brought in because trust will need to be established with each new team member.
- *Do not send in the final decision maker,* or at least suggest that you need to refer decisions to some absent decision maker. The local side will always want to defer decisions up the line and you can do the same. This buys more time and allows for decisions to be made outside the room and not in the heat of the moment.
- *Negotiations in Asia take a lot of time.* This is partly strategic – single negotiation sessions might be drawn out for five or more hours in a deliberate attempt to wear down the opposite negotiating party. Things that you thought had been agreed might be reopened just when every-

thing looks clear cut. So sufficient time must be allowed. One way around shifting decisions is to keep records of all decisions and have both parties sign off on them, reconfirming them after they have been checked with the higher authority.

Negotiations can also take a lot of time because many in Asia typically are not direct. Issues can be raised with a great deal of preamble and the matter of contention is not always clear. Important matters might be raised in the most oblique ways, so it is important to listen very carefully and deal with each point at the time, one at a time. Be mindful also that if negotiations are to be conducted in English, for many Asian people that is their second language.

Discussion might be oblique but it might not always be polite. Some negotiators in mainland China tell of actually having been yelled at and abused by the opposite side – usually by just one individual in what looks like a rehearsed 'good guy, bad guy' routine. One response is to call for a temporary halt to proceedings and only agree to return to the negotiating table once the other side agrees to adopt a more civil and appropriate mode of behaviour.

Don't Dirty your Nest

The web of overlapping networks that define business in Asia mean that information is exchanged rapidly. This can mean that commercial in-confidence information once leaked can spread quickly. Similarly, news of a falling out between partners can spread quickly. The local business sector can close ranks and the party deemed to be at fault quickly frozen out. Thus, it is important that not only are relationships made in Asia but that they are kept. Failing that, when relationships end, care should be taken that all sides do not lose 'face' or that the relationship dissolves into acrimony. Because there is a tendency in Asia for everyone to be related to everyone else, falling out with a partner can have serious knock-on consequences.

When the impeachment trial of Philippines' President Joseph Estrada was before the Philippines' Senate in January 2001, one of the 22 senators was Miriam Defensor-Santiago. The previous year, her brother Benjamin Defensor was made head of the Philippines' air force. Her husband, Narciso, had been appointed interior undersecretary. Her sister, Peachy Defensor, was appointed environment undersecretary. Estrada is also the godfather of one of Senator Defensor-Santiago's adopted daughters. Asked if any of this would influence her vote, Senator Defensor-Santiago was reported in the media to have said, 'Of course not'.

Everyone knows that relationships are important to running a business in Asia, be it the presidency of the Philippines or more commonplace ventures. Many senior business figures in Asia are related to other prominent figures by blood or by marriage. The connections in Asia are often not obvious to outsiders but they can be a minefield for the unwary.

The mix of marriages and blood relations in Asia can make for some complex webs. Here are a few examples that involve some of Asia's biggest business names:

- Lee Kim Yew, Chairman of the Singapore food company Cerebos Pacific, is a brother of Singapore's Senior Minister and former Prime Minister Lee Kuan Yew. Lee Kim Yew's wife is Gloria Lee, the founder of one of Singapore's most prominent stock brokerages Kim Eng Securities. A third brother is Lee Suan Yew, a past director of Singapore's Hotel Properties Ltd. His wife, Pamelia Lee, has been a senior director at the Singapore Tourist Promotion Board. Kwa Soon Bee, the brother of Lee Kuan Yew's wife Kwa Geok Choo, is a former permanent secretary of health and a member of the Singapore Tourist Promotion Board. Lee Kuan Yew's sons Lee Hsien Loong and Lee Hsien Yang are deputy prime minister of Singapore and head of Singapore Telecom respectively. Lee Hsien Loong's wife, Ho Ching, is head of Temasek Holdings.

- The sister of the Gunawan brothers who founded Indonesia's Panin Bank is Suryawaty Lidya who married Mochtar Riady, the founder of Indonesia's Lippo Group. Mochtar Riady controls the Matahari department store chain, which was founded by Hari Darmawan. Hari is related by marriage to Ong Tjoe Kim who owns Singapore's Metro department store chain.

- Tony Tan, who built up Singapore's Parkway Holdings is a nephew of Malaysia's Tan Chin Nam who controls Malaysia's IGB Group.

- Edgar Chen of Singapore's Wing Tai Holdings is married to a daughter of the late Hong Kong shipping and property magnate Y.K. Pao.

- The Quek family of Malaysia and the Kwek family of Singapore who operate the Hong Leong groups in both countries are blood relatives. The Malaysian Queks are also related by marriage to the Whang family who are behind Singapore's Lam Soon food and beverages group.

- Edward Soeryadjaya of the Soeryadjaya Group (elder son of William Soeryadjaya, founder of the Astra Group), is married to Atilah Rapatriarti, whose brother is married to Sukmawati, a sister of Indonesia's

President Megawati Sukarnoputri. Soeryadjaya's late first wife was the adopted daughter of Megawati's father's third wife.

There are also plenty of linkages between companies. Firms routinely take equity stakes in one another and rarely is any company in Asia completely independent of other companies. Take the time to look at the notes to any annual report of a listed Asian firm and chances are you will see a whole raft of transactions with related parties – companies that you never knew existed. Asia's corporate scene is not so much a constellation of independent bodies as it is in the West but a tightly bound web in which everyone is linked to everyone else. And that has real implications as to how business should be approached in Asia.

Notes

1 As reported in *Asiaweek*, 29 December, 2000.
2 Some of the points in this section have been adapted from a speech given by John Coates, then General Manager Commercial for Amcor Fibre Packaging Asia, 'Amcor's direct investment experience in Indonesia', 31 August, 1995.
3 Adapted in part from a speech given by John Coates, ibid.

Strategy 7

Taking the
M&A Route?

White Knights and Vultures

'Foreigners to be allowed hostile M&As under revised law'

'Asian market slump sees bargain hunters move in'

'Buyout, merger explosion as result of turmoil'

'Rich pickings for the vultures'

The appearance of headlines such as these in the region's newspapers in the wake of the 1997–98 economic crisis accounts for the rise in M&A activity in Asia during the five years that followed. Foreign companies (not just

Western but those from other Asian countries too) had been shut out of whole categories of industries during the boom years. Now they found the door not just unlocked but, in some cases, wide open. However, the headlines also contained a warning, and, in some countries, the warning turned into a threat. As the reference to 'vultures' indicates, foreign investment was not universally welcome, and many of the 'bargains' were not what they seemed.

Yet despite the initial euphoria and the rush to acquire fire-sale assets so widely publicised, local fears of the foreign takeover of Asian markets and Western domination were not realised. A few high-profile deals went through but negotiations often dragged on for years, and many acquisitions failed to live up to their promise. Who have been the winners and losers and what made the difference?

Why M&As?

The Asian crash provided an unparalleled opportunity for multinationals to move into the region. Desperate for Western investment to save them from bankruptcy, governments in South Korea and the countries of Southeast Asia declared themselves open for business. For Western firms, outright acquisition seemed to offer the perfect way to bypass all the problems associated with minority shareholdings or joint ventures. Conditions seemed ideal, as pressure from the IMF forced countries in the region to promise privatisation and deregulation. When some of its most famous conglomerates began to restructure and put assets up for sale, foreign companies at last saw the opportunity to take real control of their Asian operations, rather than being at the mercy of a local partner.

There is no such thing as a bad asset – bad assets are simply ones that are overpriced. Reality was at last catching up with asset valuations in Asia. With valuations of companies at historic lows, Western managers were granted a once-in-a-lifetime opportunity to buy at bargain basement rates. In some sectors, such as hotels and cement, assets were actually trading at a significant discount to replacement values.

Under cover of those fashionable slogans, globalisation, liberalisation and privatisation, Western firms set up merger and acquisition task forces and began bidding; their moves were heralded with great fanfare in the local and international press, although in fact they often lacked in-depth preparation. International investor George Soros was an early entrant, being part of an American consortium to invest $650 million in a Thai steel company in March 1998.

Sometimes the intense competition between Western firms increased prices. One American manager recalled how the ethnic Chinese owner of a firm in the Philippines skilfully played his company off against a European competitor. The American firm thought it was close to a deal, and the US manager was about to leave for the airport to lead the due diligence team in the Philippines when a phone call told him that the Chinese owner had called it off. Three hours later it was on again, then off, and the US manager finally flew out the next day to join a team of 30 people ready to start work. They then sat around for a week while nothing happened, until the Chinese owner finally said the deal was dead. As they later learned, he had actually sold out to the European firm: 'He just used us to push the price up.'

Further north, meanwhile, the Ministry of Finance and Economy in hitherto xenophobic South Korea announced that foreigners would be allowed to make hostile M&As under a revised law. The country's *chaebol*, the huge conglomerates that had led South Korea's economic miracle, began a series of minuets as one potential foreign partner after another came forward to try and make a deal. Anything seemed possible when, in September 1999, the South Korean government signed an agreement to sell a controlling stake in Korea First Bank to Newbridge Capital Ltd, a US-based investment firm. Analysts hailed the US$525 million deal as the first step in President Kim Dae Jung's efforts to reform the economy. In fact, it was only finalised after Newbridge was indemnified against future debts, an issue over which other deals later faltered. For the moment, however, the party continued.

The M&A Frenzy

Figures on M&A activity in Asia between 1998–2000 illustrate both foreign investors' initial enthusiasm and their later disillusion. In 1998, US acquisitions reached a value of $8 billion, double that of the previous year. In 2000, the headline was 'Asia hits M&A record' with transactions worth $76.5 billion announced in the first quarter alone, although the figures were inflated by a couple of big telecoms deals.[1] But this turned out to be the peak year. In 2001, the value of announced deals was down 46% on the previous year and during the first two months of 2002, *M&A Asia* reported a 'tortoise-like pace' compared with the previous two years; the number of European deals was down two-thirds on the previous year, from 37 to 12.[2] The decline continued for the rest of the year, part of the global slump following the events of September 11 in the US. In the end, the volume of activity in Asia (excluding Japan) for 2002 fell 12.6% to US$100.6 billion.

The more cautious approach was also the result of mounting disillusionment among investors. Many potential deals foundered during the process of due diligence, as the real extent of companies' debts became clear. In January 2001, Casino, the French retailer, retreated from a deal to take over Uniwide, the Philippine discount hypermarket chain, citing its debt situation. Early in 2002, American International Group (AIG), the world's largest insurer, dropped out of a consortium planning to invest US$846 million in Hyundai Securities and two affiliates after 18 months of negotiation. This would have been the biggest ever transaction for South Korea's financial services industry, but the prospect of hidden debt traps in the end proved too risky a gamble for AIG to take. The company returned to South Korea in 2003 and finally gained control of Hanaro Telecom, but only after a long and bitter battle with the LG Group, Hanaro's biggest shareholder. Even then, LG said it might take action to try and nullify the shareholder vote in AIG's favour. Another high-profile victim was the US firm Micron Technology, which for six months pursued a possible $3.4 billion merger with Korea's Hynix Semiconductor. The deal would have created the world's largest chipmaker, but it turned out to be yet another long-running saga. Labour unions and minority shareholders held up the deal, which finally collapsed in May 2002.

By then, Western firms had been further discouraged by the lack of progress on restructuring in countries such as Indonesia and Thailand. The Indonesian Bank Restructuring Agency (IBRA) promised much, but became embroiled in scandal and lacked transparency. It also suffered from regular changes in its senior management – it had seven chairmen in four years – and only achieved one big sale, that of PT Astra International in March 2000.

Three years later, when IBRA finally got around to selling stakes in assets seized from other major conglomerates such as the Salim Group, or the Riady family's Lippo Bank, the sales were overshadowed by rumours that the original owners were in fact buying them back via proxy bidders, and at bargain prices. Not surprisingly, foreign investors were steering well clear of this apparently rigged auction.

Local opposition also played a part in preventing deals. When, in 1998, Cemex, the Mexican cement group, took a 25% equity stake in the Indonesian cement group, SMGR (Semen Gresik), it thought it had an agreement with the central government to increase its holding later to a 51% controlling share. However, the plan ran into tremendous opposition from the provincial governments involved, notably that of West Sumatra. The projected foreign takeover became part of the wider issue of independence from Jakarta, and to locals seemed to threaten a long-standing source of income and patronage. While the struggle went on, Cemex, unable to institute any reforms in the companies, watched its investment dwindle. Its only realistic hope was to wait for the results of the 2004 elections, which might lead to the emergence of a stronger leader who could enforce the Cemex claim. In Thailand and Korea, shareholders and unions combined to vilify foreign firms and defeat acquisition attempts in several industrial sectors. As one analyst observed: 'The Koreans don't see any of the deals as win–win. They think that if the foreigners get it, then Korea is losing.'

The sad truth is that the majority of M&A deals in Asia fall short of their promise and unravel. Some of the highest profile deals have become major disappointments for acquirers and their shareholders. Too often, the original forecasts have had to be drastically reduced, and what was touted as a new global contender, turns out to be something rather less. The high failure rate is not, however, just an Asian phenomenon; many M&A deals in the West also end in tears. According to research carried out by academics and consultants, 60–70% of *all* mergers fail, 67% of them in the first five years.[3] The DaimlerChrysler deal, for example, hailed as 'a marriage made in heaven' in 1998, seemed the perfect strategic fit – global reach and scale for Daimler-Benz, investment and technological know-how for Chrysler.[4] However, for numerous reasons – price, an overestimate of Chrysler's strength, the loss of key executives, poor integration and the failure to cut costs at a time when the market was deteriorating – the merger was judged a failure. In March 2001, a turnaround plan was announced for the company, by then in dire straits.

DaimlerChrysler's problems were further compounded by an Asian binge, in which it bought 10% of South Korea's Hyundai Motor for US$420 million in June 2000 and agreed on a joint bid for Daewoo, then estimated to be a mere $16 billion in debt. Two months earlier, it had purchased 34% of Mitsubishi Motors for $2.1 billion, a deal that again turned out to have hidden problems. These acquisitions were less strategically justifiable, being mainly guided by a desire to gain a foothold in Asia and start a truck business, with DaimlerChrysler supplying the technology and parts and Hyundai the distribution and production facilities. Unfortunately, out of ignorance, DaimlerChrysler negotiated badly, agreeing to accept only one seat on the board of Hyundai – still tightly controlled by the founding family – so leaving it impotent from the start. Neither did it take into account the huge cultural problems it would face.

Despite all these problems, in 2003 Western companies remained upbeat about the long-term prospects for the region as a whole, although in the short term their efforts tended to focus on the booming China markets. The magnet of the large and literate labour pool and unsaturated markets still attracts, but the problem for many is to know how to structure and time their expansion, and how to be sure of creating value from a merger.

A Seamless Process

Ideally, the acquisition process should be a seamless one, in which the end is foreseen and planned for from the beginning. From target to post-merger integration (PMI) should be one long process in which what is done before the deal is as important as what happens during any negotiations. What you do after – the PMI plan – should emerge, almost by osmosis, along the way. Doing one stage at a time with different sets of people involved works against the possibility of this happening. Unfortunately, due to time pressures or lack of people experienced in the acquisition process, it is the way many companies act.

Despite this, some multinationals have succeeded in making a good deal, and are busy implementing post-acquisition strategies to bring their new assets up to speed ready for the economic upturn. What did they do so right? What are the 'dos and don'ts' of making an acquisition? Where are the most common pitfalls?

The Pitfalls

A lack of clear vision – why are we doing this? Where is the strategic fit? What synergies do we expect from it? What do we want to gain – market share, a strategic foothold or economies of scale?

Without satisfactory answers to questions such as these, companies will be groping in the dark. The logic of going ahead with an acquisition must be clear and compelling. Along with this go realistic expectations about what can be achieved. This in turn implies careful planning to identify targets that fit into the company's overall strategy. Grabbing at an apparent bargain for the sake of it spells disaster from the start.

Inadequate due diligence – doing due diligence does not, of course, mean merely checking out the books, although in a region known for creative accounting (a PwC study found that South Korea, for example, had one of the most opaque standards of accounting and corporate governance of the 35 countries it surveyed) this is essential.[5] One experienced member of an international due diligence team remarked that he often had to go by instinct, backed by an assessment of the plant or businesses for sale, how much it would take to get factories up to speed, current market prices for products and so on. But sometimes, he said, 'You just shut your eyes and go for it.'

This is what the Singapore bank, DBS, appeared to do in its opportunistic takeover of the Thai bank, Thai Danu (TDB).[6] One of the region's largest financial institutions, DBS decided to take advantage of the Asian crisis to fulfil its ambition to expand outside Singapore. Offered the chance to increase its minority stake to a controlling share, DBS took the bait, even accepting TDB's request for 'a waiver of the full due diligence process', on condition that it conducted an independent audit of its accounts.

The deal went through at the end of 1997, but what DBS had seen as a rare opportunity in fact turned out to be a headache. With hindsight, analysts concluded that the Singapore bank went into Thailand too early, paid too much for TDB and was too slow in reacting to the problems of NPLs (non-paying loans) and integration. In 2000, reflecting on two years of painful restructuring of its acquisition, Jackson Thai, then the Chief Financial Officer and future CEO of DBS, believed that one of the most important lessons to come out of the TDB episode was the importance of conducting thorough due diligence to allow DBS to make a fair assessment of the banks it was trying to buy, and structure its bid accordingly.

Different valuations are another common reason for deals failing. During the ongoing negotiations between General Motors and Daewoo, when GM tried to reduce the price, the US partners reportedly complained that the Korean negotiators thought not of the company's present value, but how much they had invested in the past. The Koreans complained that the Americans were going to get valuable assets at far below equity. In fact Ford, the original preferred bidder for Daewoo, had already closed talks after a closer inspection of the books. But GM was convinced it had sound strategic reasons for the deal and pressed on. Negotiations on price between GM and Daewoo dragged out the deal for two years. There were rumours that the GM team had uncovered 2 trillion won of contingent debt, something denied by the Daewoo team, who accused GM of using the rumours as leverage to reduce the price. The deal was finally signed in April 2002, after both sides had made concessions.

Poor cultural due diligence – in Asia, due diligence must also include the cultural aspects of the deal – the human resources available to both sides, the management culture and the cultural fit. Is there likely to be a clash between the values and beliefs of the two sides that will cause problems? Will good staff stay to work for the new owners? Research has consistently underlined the crucial role of human resource issues in the outcome of the acquisition process. For example, an impression of opportunistic buying rather than a commitment to build something for the future will not help your cause. In 1998, Thailand's Bank of Asia reportedly chose ABN Amro as its new majority shareholder because it agreed to keep the bank's name and top executives and so, 'left it with its dignity intact'. Such cultural sensitivity can go a long way to give you the good publicity to clinch a negotiation and get off to a good start in the relationship.

In many companies, the process is spearheaded by the HR (human resource) division, which consolidates all the information on the target company and produces a list of key issues for due diligence. A useful move is for members of the due diligence team to study the local culture to learn what to say and how to act before they go into the company. For this, local consultants can be used.

A due diligence team is usually made up of experienced staff in systems, HR, finance, acquisitions, commercial, operations and administration, selected by head office. The key is to take the best from each area and fly them in for the time it takes (anything from a few weeks to 18 months) to carry out the procedure. The information collection should be a two-way process; the targeted company needs to learn about the acquirers – why it is interested in the company and what it hopes to achieve if and when it takes over.

The importance of cultural knowledge and sensitivity is illustrated by the following true story. One experienced due diligence finance director was sent out to Indonesia to finalise a deal. After a few hours on his first day at the potential acquisition firm, he left his team working to go and answer a call of nature. Following the signs down a series of narrow corridors, he came to what he assumed was the washroom. He looked through a door and saw that the room contained a pipe running round the wall, with holes at regular intervals through which passed running water into a gutter. He relieved himself and returned to work. When he arrived the next morning, it was to find that the workforce had called a huge demonstration, and that the owner was threatening to call off the deal because 'Someone had peed in the room where the Moslem workers wash before going to prayers'.

Poor integration – stemming from mistakes made at the beginning of the process. Perhaps the company did not take care to understand fully how the assets would fit, perhaps it bought at too high a price, perhaps early management contacts were hostile, in which case the post-acquisition phase will fail. To avoid this, work to a clear PMI strategy, covering all the key issues thrown up during the negotiating process, using your best and most experienced managers. The culmination should be the integration of the acquisition into your regional and global structures.

Finally, take a long-term – seven–ten years – Asian view of your investment. It will demonstrate that you are beginning to understand the culture.

What may pass unnoticed in all this emphasis on Western acquisitions is the amount of M&A activity that is taking place among Asian companies. New giants are being created in China, and domestic deals in many countries of the region are creating strong competitors for the future – both in Asian and Western markets. Western companies cannot afford to be left out, or continue making such a mess of their acquisitions. To help them, they might usefully study the following case study of how one European company made an acquisition that – up until today – seemed to work.

Lafarge Gets Big in Asia[7]

A Strategic Objective

In the aftermath of Asia's economic crisis, Lafarge, the French construction group, took part in an assault on cement manufacturing companies in the region, which had become the objects of a fierce acquisition battle between the largest Western cement producers. Lafarge had less exposure to emerging markets than its nearest competitors, such as the UK-based Blue Circle or the Swiss group, Holderbank (later Holcim). Consequently, how to be first in any acquisition spree that came along was a key preoccupation of the global strategists at the Lafarge headquarters in Paris.

The Preparation Period

Although it had been present in Southeast Asia since the 1980s when it opened an office in Singapore, the region's weight within the Lafarge portfolio remained minute. During the 1990s, with the industry growing at 10% annually, the company decided to step up its efforts there, setting up industrial facilities and opening sales offices. However, along with other multinational players, it had concluded that, pre-crisis, acquisitions were too expensive in ASEAN, and virtually impossible in northern Asia. The Southeast Asian cement manufacturers were doing so well that they had no reason to sell, or take a partner. Effectively shut out of these markets, Lafarge decided to focus on greenfield projects in Bangladesh and Indonesia. Its only acquisitions were an Indonesian manufacturer, Semen Andalas, and a Chinese firm, Chinefarge, bought in 1994 and 1995 respectively.

Information Gathering

During these years, the HQ strategy team kept a close eye on the region, studying the main players, building up a network of relationships and compiling a dossier on the dynamics of each market. Systematically, its managers gathered industry knowledge specific to each country – the intensity of the competition, the evolution of prices, whether they were controlled by the government (in which case deregulation might be an imminent possibility) and so on. They identified where the local industry was protected by import bans or tariffs, and made some preliminary calculations about how prices were likely to evolve. Finally, they ranked the countries of the region in order of attractiveness for investment.

As a result of all this research, Lafarge probably knew the region's markets far better than any of the local producers, who had no time for such careful calculations. They were revelling in the growth conditions that they were experiencing, busy counting their profits and expanding like there was no tomorrow with the help of huge bank loans. But Lafarge, always known for long-term strategic thinking and an old hand in the cement game, understood that the oversupply situation building up in the region would sooner or later lead to a collapse in prices. Its planners counted on making acquisitions during this counter-cycle.

In 1996, a new business development manager was sent to Singapore to study the markets in greater depth. He was not surprised to see acquaintances from every other big cement company setting up offices to carry out the same task. They all smelt big profits in the air, if only they could get access to the local markets.

When it arrived, the 1997–98 economic crisis made the overcapacity problem far more severe for the locals, and acquisition easier for foreign firms. In this case, events played straight into their hands.

Acquisition Mania

The regional economic crisis and subsequent downturn completely changed the game for foreign players such as Lafarge. The local producers found themselves caught in a trap of their own making. They had all borrowed heavily – mostly in dollars – in order to fund expansion. When the crisis came, they were hit by a triple whammy. Their hard currency debts exploded in local currency terms and yet most of their earnings were in local currencies. The sector had borrowed on the basis that it would continue to experience high growth but instead, it experienced a sharp contraction. And the local currency earnings themselves collapsed. Asia's cement firms had been walking a narrow path between growth and debt, and they now found themselves utterly overwhelmed by events that pushed most of them into insolvency. The only hope for most was to find a rich investor.

The usual outcome of this would be to allow foreign firms to pick up such failing companies for a song but, in fact, the intensity of the competition between the multinationals to complete deals while the window of opportunity was open led to far higher acquisition costs. And this despite the fact that cheap exports from neighbouring countries were flooding in, making overcapacity even worse. Taiwan and Japan were dumping their excess, China was pushing up its own cement production; it was a frenzied time. So although the region's economies were collapsing, the cement industry was at a standstill and prices were dropping like stones, there were no cheap bargains to be had.

Lafarge in Action

Its thorough study of the region had given Lafarge a very good idea of which companies it was really interested in. Its business development team had already identified those with the right fundamentals, that is, those with sound infrastructure and potential for growth when cement demand once more turned round.

So, once the crisis took effect, the team only had to get out the list, check the targets and see what was available. In fact, during the first months of panic, Lafarge had many calls from cement firms throughout the region, begging it to take a share or buy them out. But it neither made a move nor committed itself until the local company had been checked against its hit list, and several were rejected straight away. As soon as anyone called, the head of the Lafarge team knew who they were and whether he was interested in them or not.

In making its acquisitions, Lafarge used a variety of approaches, depending on the circumstances and the information in the dossiers it had built up. In some cases, it went for a strategic partnership with a company that wanted someone to share its debts, and took an equity stake. Alternatively, in the case of local companies that had only moved into cement as an opportunistic move, Lafarge bought them outright. There were different patterns and Lafarge adapted to each individual case.

Once Lafarge decided to move, its managers took care to handle negotiations as sensitively as possible. Since cement was a young industry in the region, many of the founding fathers were still in charge of the target companies. Having done their cultural due diligence, the Lafarge team was well aware of what it meant in terms of loss of face for such a family to sell out, so they treated them with appropriate deference and sensitivity. They spent time with the heads of these companies to talk through the deal and convince them of the wisdom of taking a strategic partner. In view of all the bad publicity in some countries about Westerners being sharks coming to gobble them up, this was very important. Lafarge argued that it was the only sensible decision to take, and especially emphasised the need to keep local managers in place, since they knew the market and its own managers did not. Its catch phrase was 'Let's build something together for the future.' Once the deal was done, the Lafarge managers moved very circumspectly, always leaving the local management to continue running the plants – as long as they were good.

The negotiations were run from the Lafarge office in Singapore, backed by the HQ team which followed progress from Paris. Lafarge had one local and three expatriate managers on the ground, but once the due diligence stage was reached, HQ sent in finance, human and legal resources to compile as complete a picture as possible of the target company within the time limit.

These people, too, were keenly aware that, in Asia, due diligence was another part of the relationship-building exercise, during which it was important to show that they understood the company. The team leader emphasised to those carrying out the due diligence process: 'This is a polite and culturally sensitive exercise, don't act like tax inspectors!' The Lafarge philosophy was that the success of the due diligence process depended as much on what you did before the deal as after – it was the culmination of all your efforts. So the time its managers spent getting to know the company and building up trust was not wasted and, of course, by doing it this way, they rarely missed anything.

Inevitably, there were some hard negotiations on price. The Lafarge valuation included a calculation of the quality of the plant – how expensive it would be to keep it going while it got production prices down and so on. Generally, the team had already identified where improvements could be made in its investment targets and these were packaged ready to hand on to the post-acquisition team. These were based on the objectives of reducing production costs and improving the quality of the asset, so the plant would be ready for action once demand rose again.

Since every Western firm was working in more or less the same way to the same end, within a surprisingly short time all the deals were done and the region was more or less sewn up between the big producers. In the Philippines, for example, of 19 local cement producers, 10 sold large equity stakes to foreign investors, including Lafarge. Consequently, around 80% of the country's cement production fell under the influence of the Western partners.

Profitability

The Lafarge strategy in the region was both aggressive and cautious, and followed the clear investment guidelines laid down by head office. The golden rule for this was, first and foremost, profitability. Lafarge has very stringent profitability criteria for any acquisition; it must be EVA (economic value added)-positive within three years. If the business development team did not believe this could be achieved, it would not make the deal. Thus Lafarge turned down possible acquisitions in Malaysia and Thailand because it did not meet this requirement. Lafarge was interested in expansion, but not at any price.

Its strategy was also guided by the need to participate in the consolidation of a market, which was being whittled down to a few major players, of whom Lafarge was clearly determined to be number one. But at the same time, those acquisitions had to provide synergies with positions it already held, synergies either within the local domestic market or through trading between various countries in order to produce best delivered costs. Finally, Lafarge looked for future growth possibilities – companies with good limestone reserves that would allow future low-cost expansion.

Knowing that the present oversupply situation in Asia would not vanish overnight, Lafarge planned to use the intervening time to make sure that the integration process went smoothly. The aim was to ensure that its new plants were running as efficiently as possible when the market picked up. Each country would recover in its own time. In the meantime, Lafarge continued to build up its assets in order to become Big in Asia.

Key Lessons

- Set a clear strategic direction
- Evaluate potential targets carefully
  - their business portfolio
  - their human resources
  - their potential profitability
- Define objectives
- Decide on negotiation strategy and tactics
- Fully brief the financial and cultural due diligence team
- Implement a seamless process, from target to post-merger integration.

Notes

1   *Financial Times*, 'Asia hits M&A record', 11 April, 2000, p18.
2   *M&A Asia*, 'Recent Deals & Joint Ventures', February 2002, pp16, 19.
3   *Financial Times*, 'Exposing the truth behind merger myths', 25 March, 2002, p30.
4   *The Economist*, 'Schrempp's last stand', 3 March, 2001, pp18–19.
5   *The Economist*, 'Korean murk', 31 March, 2001, pp89–90.
6   Taken from 'DBS' (A), (B) (C) and (D), series of case studies by Keeley Wilson and Professor Peter Williamson, 2000 INSEAD-EAC.
7   Taken from 'Lafarge in Asia', case study by Charlotte Butler and Professor Peter Williamson, 2001 INSEAD-EAC.

Managing the Partnership with the Southeast Asian Firm

Horror Stories

Whenever a group of Western managers with Asia experience gather together, talk almost invariably turns to horror stories about Asian firms they have known and the pitfalls of doing business with them. This is because, for many Western companies, managing business relationships in Southeast Asia proves to be a confusing, frustrating and mostly loss-making affair. Yet success in managing these relationships will be critical to the outcome of your Asian investment.

In great part, this attitude stems from the feeling of powerlessness that overcomes many Western businesspeople during their everyday transactions in Asia, whether they are dealing with joint venture partners, suppliers, distributors, local politicians or ministry officials, customs people or bankers. This helplessness in turn arises from their discomfort at operating in such a foreign environment. The best antidote to this is to forge your own competitive edge, one that will give you sufficient power to balance this otherwise unequal relationship. Unfortunately, this comes only after gaining a working knowledge of Asia's very different business culture. Before you can join with corporate Asia successfully, you must understand the firms and, most importantly, the people behind them.

Why a Partnership?

For most firms, their experience of managing relationships in Asia comes from being in some kind of strategic alliance or partnership with a local firm. Before the 1997–98 economic crisis, the most popular route to enter Asia was via a joint venture. In many countries, this was the only legal way open to foreign firms. More practically, it was the only way that gave any hope of gaining access to protected or difficult markets. Moving into such unknown territory, it made sense to take a local partner to spread the risk and provide the capabilities and resources lacking in the foreign firm. These capabilities included, most famously, access to the networks or *guanxi* – political and business – necessary to negotiate with local politicians or officials to gain licences or operating concessions, and to deal with what were often euphemistically termed 'speedy service' payments. A local partner could also provide access to marketing and distribution networks and the workers and managers to run them. In return, Asian companies usually sought access to technology and an injection of financial resources, although in theory the financial burden was shared by the partners. In summary, Western firms provided the cash and the locals the connections.

Such partnerships had the advantage of providing a learning curve for the foreign company involved. Over the years they would build up experience of the business environment and, once they had learned the ropes, they could either branch out on their own with a wholly owned operation or perhaps buy the partnership out, so taking over a going concern they knew well.

However, this theory rarely worked in practice. Many partnerships fell short of their promise; research shows that over 70% ended in failure within ten years. The most common reason for failure was a mismatch between the foreign investor and the local partner or, as a Japanese saying puts it more picturesquely, because the two partners found themselves 'lying in the same bed but dreaming different dreams'.

For the majority of Western companies entering Southeast Asia, the partner dreaming different dreams was one of the local Chinese family-owned and managed firms that accounted for between half and three-quarters of all listed companies on the stock exchanges in Hong Kong, Taiwan and Southeast Asia. The unique nature of these firms was beyond the experience of most Western businesspeople, and the secretive way in which they operated militated against any balanced relationship between the partners from the start. Building up the trust and commitment required for a successful relationship required a different mindset in order to understand this very different business model. Unfortunately, by the time most foreign firms grasped this essential fact, it was too late and the relationship had irretrievably broken down. Therefore an understanding of how these firms operate, both pre-crisis and since, is important to any firm hoping to become Big in Asia.

Understanding the Chinese Family Firm

The founders of most of the sprawling conglomerates that dominated business in Southeast Asia were ethnic Chinese entrepreneurs. Starting out as traders with very little during the 1970s or earlier, they built up diversified empires assisted by strong *guanxi* – the close political and business connections that brought them opportunities and sometimes even concessions and monopolies.

Power in these conglomerates was firmly centralised in the hands of the founder. Surrounding him, the senior management ranks were the preserve of close family members (sons and daughters, brothers and nephews) or old friends. The latter group was usually there not by virtue of any particular management skills, but because they had been with the patriarch from the early days, when life was hard, and had been part of the early struggles when the founder was making the deals that helped to make his fortune. This shared history as schoolmates or fellow traders guaranteed them a place in the sun for life, part of the trusted inner clan.

As Western managers would eventually discover to their great frustration, however powerful they might be in their own milieu, rarely could they be part of this magic circle. They would always be heard with courtesy, but would never be able to influence key decisions. Any close relationship would have to be built up slowly, over time, as Douglas Daft, Chairman of Coca-Cola explained when speaking of his relationship with

Robert Kuok, former Chairman of Hong Kong-based Kerry Holdings, which was one of Coke's major bottling partners in China:

> We had a lot of common ground and, I think, liked each other. That led to the ability to discuss and develop a business relationship. Essentially that relationship was on trust ... without that relationship it would have been months of dialogue between parties at different levels to reach an agreement on the way the business would be structured. [1]

However, to reach that level of trust required a heavy investment of time and effort that few Western managers were able to make.

The autocratic and centralised leadership style also came as a rude surprise to many Western managers. Business meetings, for example, tended to be not so much open discussions of financial forecasts or strategic issues than the occasion for rubber stamping a decision already taken by the inner circle. One Western businessman recalled his shock at the sheer terror inspired by one patriarch at meetings, even to discuss relatively non-contentious issues. Bullies are not unknown in Western business circles, but the atmosphere of fear around the table, he recalled, was palpable. The local managers were so intimidated that they did not dare to tell the truth about the progress of a project, or the fact that the target date for completion might be missed. Another time, there was complete silence, nobody spoke until the chief had made his own opinion clear, after which everyone rushed to agree with it. Alternatively, when the head of the firm tried the tactic of waiting to speak last in a debate so as not to influence the decision, everyone could see the knuckles of his hand going white with the effort to stop interrupting. On one occasion, everyone turned up for an 8am meeting but the chief was delayed. Nobody dared move until 1pm, when the meeting was finally cancelled.

Another characteristic that could mislead Western firms was the lack of ostentation showed by many of the most successful founders. In the West, success tends to be obvious, with expensive offices, perhaps even a corporate jet; in Asia, many of the richest men in the region often keep a low profile. This is because coming from poor backgrounds and being a minority in countries where they have often been scapegoats and subject to violence when the hard times came – as occurred in Indonesia at the fall of Soeharto – they have learned to be discreet about parading their wealth, so that foreign firms can be deceived about the true extent of their resources.

For many years one very powerful and successful ethnic Chinese entrepreneur kept his head office in a rundown part of town. Its anonymous entrance was in a busy commercial street, above a grocery store. To reach the offices, visitors were forced to climb a rickety, uneven staircase, and frequently found themselves tripping on steps added in at random to avoid the total number of stairs amounting to an unlucky number. A walk through a narrow passage led to a bare meeting room, whose decoration reflected utility rather than gloss, and through whose thin partition walls could be heard the clack of typewriters and shouting. Tea was served by people who could occasionally be seen shuffling round in carpet slippers.

Such an alien context prevented several would-be investors accepting a partnership with the entrepreneur. But such cultural dissonance is part and parcel of Asia, and can cause opportunities to be missed. Lacking the cultural reference to assess such a context, Westerners tend to judge on external appearance alone, and so they severely underestimated the substance behind the rundown office. As the entrepreneur observed, 'They never understood how things are done in our part of the world'. Cynically, he added that later, when his entourage had moved into a brand new plaza, built by himself in the central part of town, the queue of applicants for a partnership was a long one. Still, none of this need imply that Western businesspeople are necessarily inept. When corporate transparency is poor, the state of a company's offices might become a proxy for its creditworthiness, albeit an obviously poor one.

The culture of secrecy that characterises the ethnic Chinese firms is another hurdle that Westerners have had to face. It meant that the key facet of the relationship would be ignorance on the part of the foreign investor about the local partner's businesses, particularly his financial affairs and the true extent of his business interests. Often, the original stake on which the founder's fortune was based came from trading deals, made quickly with money borrowed from family or friends. Money came in and went out, and only the founder knew how many deals were cooking at a time. This habit of not letting the left hand know what the right was doing died hard, and made it almost impossible for foreign investors to track the route of any investment meant for a joint venture operation, even in companies known for their integrity. As one Western banker observed of such companies:

> they could lose anything anywhere, and you could drive yourself nuts trying to follow investment A through to B via C and D, not to mention E and F.

However, the two most worrying practices for Westerners have been the cronyism and nepotism associated with their way of doing business. The practice of giving contracts, jobs or easy loans to friends, associates and other well-connected individuals is again something foreign firms have found hard to accept in their partners. Post-crisis, these practices were condemned, and much has been written about the need to reform the Asian way of doing business. The new emphasis is on restructuring, focus and professional management, transparency and corporate governance.

A New Generation

For the implementation of these desirable outcomes, many put their faith in the new generation beginning to take over from their founding fathers, or creating their own empires. Educated in Europe and the US, usually with MBA qualifications, foreign partners have generally found them easier to deal with, since they share a common vocabulary and tend to be more open.

However, the instincts of many of these younger men, just like their fathers, are still to trust school friends and family members. In 2002 Fred Ma was appointed group chief financial officer of PCCW, founded by Richard Li, second son of Li Ka-Shing. Ma, who joined the company in May 2001, replaced one of the most senior men to stay on after the takeover of C&W in August 2000. A Hong Kong native, Ma attended the University of Hong Kong at the same time as Anthony Leung, Hong Kong's financial secretary. The two are still friends and golf partners, together with Canning Fok, group MD at Li's father's company, Hutchison Whampoa.

Moreover, in many cases, although their fathers have 'retired' from business, deference to age means that the old patriarch still exerts great influence. In one sense, they never retire – the culture in which they operate prohibits it. Robert Kuok, the Malaysian-Chinese tycoon and founder of Hong Kong-based Kerry Holdings has an empire that includes the international hotel chain, Shangri-La. An international trader in commodities, the group also has interests in the media, property development and a manufacturing base in China. In theory, Kuok retired and handed over key businesses to his two sons, two nephews and a nephew-in-law. However, he remains head of the steering committee which watches over the group. Li Ka-shing, founder of Hong Kong's Cheung Kong Holdings, has appointed his son Victor to succeed him, but nobody doubts that he will remain the guiding power as long as he lives. The head of the Thai agribusiness colossus, Charoen Pokphand, still dominates the two businesses, cable TV and telecoms, which, theoretically, he has given to his two sons to head and develop.

Contracts can still be blocked by cronyism, things still get done through relationships, just as the old school tie connects managers in the UK or the meritocracy of the *grandes écoles* executives in France. Asian businessmen still use their connections to achieve their goals, and trust only their family and a close circle of old friends.

So despite the sale of some assets and superficial restructuring, many of the same patterns of doing business are still discernible, even post-1997. The pressure of the old guard, however discredited, is still immense, as the slowing or reversal of reform attempts in Indonesia or Thailand demonstrates. Prachai Leophairatana, the founder of Thai Petro-chemical Industries (TPI), resisted the financial restructuring of his empire, in debt to the tune of $3.7 billion and declared insolvent in 2000, every step of way. When the Western accountant met 3,000 of his employees to explain the restructuring plan, he discovered that the micro-phone had been turned off and, when he did speak, he was heckled. Before a meeting of the TPI creditors, thousands of TPI employees turned up, waving banners castigating 'Norman the bloodsucker'.[2] In October 2003, three years later, Prachai was still battling to keep control of the cement company and fiercely resisting pressure to sell a stake to a foreign partner. Building a positive relationship with such determined business-people is not easy.

So, once you have understood the rules of the game, how do you build a more equal and lasting partnership in the future? One of the keys is to select the right partner in the first place.

Partners to Avoid

Experience has shown that, in Southeast Asia, partnership with state-run companies, or with powerful political or military figures can be time-wasting and unexpectedly costly. The former can also bring problems that you may be unable to resolve, such as a corporate culture that is simply too different from yours. The latter will always have the upper hand, and may mobilise regulatory, legislative and even judicial enforcement against you should the relationship deteriorate seriously. Moreover, political alle-giances may change and you could easily find yourself tied in with the wrong side.

Similarly, it can be safer to avoid government projects. Governments and their agencies are often only interested in gaining access to technolog-ical expertise, and may drop you as soon as it becomes convenient, or may break undertakings if under financial pressure, as has been the case in Indonesia (see Strategy 21 for more on this.)

By and large, the safest strategy is to maintain good relations with the host government of the country you are in but, if you have the choice, never enter into a joint venture with it or its agencies.

Know the Key Players

Take time to look at the key players in the region. The best approach by far when it comes to forging the right links in Southeast Asia is either to link up with someone who has real business strength and a genuine interest in making the relationship work or, alternatively, with someone who may be an up-and-coming power and has a small but strategic business. If you get in early with such budding entrepreneurs, you will have a friend for life and grow with them.

Knowing who the key players are in the region is the first step in selecting a suitable partner. This is not always easy. Many are notoriously publicity shy. Successful Western businesspeople might write books and give interviews to the media, but you will be unlikely to pick up Li Ka-shing's top ten business tips at WHSmith in Singapore's Changi Airport.

Therefore, collecting good information on any potential partner and the business context is essential (see Strategy 1). Look at the skill base of its managers, its relationship with the government (which may be a positive or negative factor) its financial credibility and so on. Talk to bankers, suppliers, customers, competitors and other foreign investors as much as you can. Such preparation will pay off, as Tesco found when it entered the Thai food retail market via a partnership with the Charoen Pokphand (CP) Group. Tesco took the stake only after it had sent out four teams to explore opportunities in Thailand, Taiwan, Malaysia and South Korea.

Much of this information will, of course, be circumstantial and difficult to verify, given the secretive nature of the beast. The only financial accounts that you can trust will be those of any publicly listed companies, which tend to be newly established and so 'clean'. But remember that the boundary between public and private assets is blurred, and that the most profitable companies in any group typically will be wholly under family control. However, what will be public knowledge is their past record in conducting relationships with foreign partners. If you find a company that has successfully sustained a number of long-standing joint ventures and has built up the business of both themselves and their partner, it is surely a safer bet than most. Two better known groups that have managed relationships successfully with outside firms for many years are Thailand's Charoen Pokphand and Indonesia's PT Astra International.

The Charoen Pokphand Group

The Thai civil service rankings are known as C levels, with C1 being the lowest, then C2 up to C11. After C11, it is said, comes CP – Charoen

Pokphand, the biggest conglomerate in Thailand.[3] That joke circulated after yet another government official left the Thai civil service to join CP, and illustrates the nature of the group's excellent array of connections, which brought CP the contacts and benefits that enabled it to expand its core agri-business to become the undisputed agro-industrial leader in Asia, and the world's largest feed producer.

Through joint venture partnerships, CP has expanded to Southeast Asia, Taiwan and China, where it was first through the door that swung open in 1979.[4] It also entered Portugal (although it later withdrew) and Turkey. In 1993, CP was invited by the president of Vietnam to set up there. CP has used joint ventures 'to develop our capability' and, in the process, managing partnerships with foreign firms has actually become a key CP competence.

CP, run by Dhanin Chearavanont, son of one of founding brothers, is the master of the joint venture. Both the Thai and Chinese Governments have regularly made it offers which it couldn't refuse, asking it to diversify into industries that were deemed important to the country's economic growth. These included petrochemicals, motorcycle manufacture and telecoms. CP always accepted, but then brought in the best partner it could to supply the expertise it lacked. Its key strengths lay in its core agribusiness and so, for new businesses, it found the best foreign partner available, preferably the leader in its field.

CP's move into telecoms in 1990, for example, was at the request of the Thai Government. It won a concession to install two million fixed lines in Bangkok and took the US giant Nynex (later Bell Atlantic) as its strategic partner to provide technical and operational support. Nynex took an 18.2% stake, its first step into Asia, and after a shaky start the partnership flourished, the listed TelecomAsia becoming Bangkok's largest provider of multimedia network and cable TV. The two undertook several projects together in Thailand and overseas.

CP was hyperactive in China, where by 1996 it was the biggest individual foreign investor with 130 joint ventures in all but two provinces. These included a three-way venture with Heineken and the Chinese government when it entered the brewing business. There was also a motorcycle manufacturing business (the largest in the country), banking and cosmetics. Asked by local governments to start businesses to help poorer areas, CP even ventured into the tea business in Sichuan Province.

The group was one of the few to restructure thoroughly in the wake of the 1997–98 economic crisis. It sold many of its non-core business stakes to its partners, leaving it free to concentrate once more on its core chicken business. Thus the UK food retailer, Tesco, bought a stake in Lotus Super-centres. The partnership worked well; Tesco helped CP to develop a competence in food processing, Tesco got the marketing and distribution for its superstores business. Everyone gained, which is how joint ventures should work, but rarely do.

PT Astra International

In Indonesia, a long preferred joint venture partner has been Indonesia's PT Astra. In the murky political and business environment of that country, Astra, with its marketing and distribution expertise, has shone like a beacon for many foreign firms seeking to enter the country. Astra also had the advantage of a professional management, trained in both Japanese and Western business methods. It has long been one of Southeast Asia's most admired companies.[5]

Known for keeping its distance from the government circle, Astra grew to be the second biggest conglomerate in Indonesia through long-running joint ventures with Japanese firms such as Toyota, Honda, Komatsu, Daihatsu, Fuji and Xerox, plus the North American-based GE Credit Corporation and Digital Corporation, all the main European auto manufacturers, Taiwanese and South Korean firms. For anyone contemplating a partnership in Indonesia, Astra was the first port of call.

Like CP, Astra chose its partners carefully, selecting the best one for the industry it wished to enter and learn about. Its skill in conducting these relationships was demonstrated by the fact that although many of the ventures began in the 1970s, they were still going strong over 30 years later, despite the political ups and downs of both the company and the country. The group also had long-standing and excellent relations with foreign bankers such as Citibank, Chase Manhattan, Société Générale, Nomura Securities, and was consistently singled out as the only company they could trust and do business with. Post-crisis, a stake in Astra that had been seized from delinquent debtors was the first big sale actually completed by IBRA, a 23% slice going to Singapore's Cycle & Carriage Ltd. The strength of the company was demonstrated by the fact that there were several consortia of bidders, all eager to buy a group with such a good record and strong business partnerships. It was, and remains, Indonesia's only genuinely blue-chip, private sector company; its flagship Toyota and Honda ventures still dominating the auto and motorcycle markets and, in 2003, attracting substantial investment from them.

Key Factors in a Partnership

Clear Objectives

Before entering any partnership, it is important to know exactly what you hope to gain from it. Is it a short-term opportunistic move, or a long-term investment to build a position in the market? Is it a preparatory stage for an acquisition or expansion, do you hope to buy out the partner eventually and take over, or sell your stake at a profit?

The answer will determine both the size of your investment and the strategy you adopt. Westerners tend to think primarily in financial terms. They have their shareholders to please and so usually their key measure for success is how long it will take to achieve profitability. Few can afford to lose money over a long period if a partnership turns out badly. So decide how big a gamble to make at the beginning, and have an exit strategy prepared if it all goes wrong.

Control

This is one of the most difficult issues and one that can cause most friction with a Southeast Asian partner. Someone who has spent a lifetime being in total control and respected by everyone around them is not likely to share it willingly. This fact alone tends to make Southeast Asian family companies difficult joint venture partners. Rarely do they have a culture of sharing control.

Therefore it is important to determine from the beginning who is responsible for what. Partnerships are supposedly about complementary skills not competition, so if your strength is technological expertise and your partner's is distribution, a division of responsibilities should be easy. If you are the more experienced partner in a new venture, then make sure you are able to exercise control.

Another important point is to make sure that you are kept fully informed by putting in key people, for example a finance manager or a good production manager, to report on what is happening. Make sure that senior people make regular visits and, most importantly, check that the composition of the board gives you real power and that you will not merely be a cipher. And remember, never equate control with any legal power you might think you have. As many discover too late, a strong equity share, seats on the board and even government promises by no means guarantee control. They all help, but might not be enough.

Leverage your Power

Southeast Asian firms are like businesses elsewhere – they do not enter into joint ventures or business partnerships out of altruism. Ideally, they would prefer to keep the business in the family. They need you for a reason. This power that you have is there to be exploited.

So decide where your power lies – in brand names (which are becoming increasingly important in the region), technology or access to international markets – and leverage it to the full. Use it to negotiate very hard on partnership issues, especially when it comes to control. For example, during their highly successful operations in partnership with PT Astra, neither Toyota nor Honda ever transferred state-of-the-art technology, but drip fed the Astra subsidiaries with older technology, despite the company's wish to go into production on its own account. By so doing, the two Japanese companies kept the upper hand in the relationship.

Build up Trust and Commitment

Trust and mutual respect are the basis of any successful partnership. In Asia, it comes from long-term relationships, not only by working together, but by giving assistance with family matters. For example, you might be asked for help in sending children abroad for education, or looking after relatives visiting abroad for the first time. A positive response to any such requests will be greatly appreciated and will help to cement the relationship. The UK company Inchcape plc, which had many partnerships in Asia and other parts of the world, kept a list of half-term holiday dates for main schools at which its partners had children, and made sure they were looked after. It was a gesture that paid off in forging strong relationships.

Trust also comes from shared adversity as well as success. Asians do not like people who 'take away the umbrella when it rains' any more than anyone else, so staying in through the bad times as well as the good will show that you are committed to making the partnership work – and will not be forgotten. In any business, changing market conditions will require additional resources, probably financial but also perhaps in terms of personnel. Discussing such issues and showing that you are willing to give something extra will also help to establish the partnership.

Don't try to run the venture at arm's length. The more you discuss and manage problems together, the stronger the bond will be. Send in good people to work with them on a permanent basis, not technical or production staff who fly in and out. This will be taken as a sign of commitment.

Make sure that your interests in other markets don't impinge and spoil this partnership. Virgin Group's mobile phone business in Asia, for example, was launched in partnership with Singtel, while Singapore Airlines (SIA) took a 49% stake in Virgin Atlantic. However, the relationship became strained when SIA's Australian partner, Ansett, collapsed, partly due to competition from Virgin Blue, an Australian domestic airline set up by the Virgin Group.

Know When to Withdraw

Even in the euphoria of signing the contract, have an exit strategy prepared and make sure that, if you threaten to withdraw, you really mean it and can get out with bearable losses, with at least a store of experience and knowledge which you can use the next time.

Key Lessons

The secret of managing a good partnership in Southeast Asia is:

- Find the right partner to start with
- Understand his business model
- Have a clear idea of what you expect from the partnership
- Build commitment and trust
- Lay down clear rules on control
- Keep a close eye on operations
- Have a good, pre-prepared exit strategy.

Notes

1 *Far Eastern Economic Review*, 'Coke's New Formula', 20 April 2000, pp64–5.
2 *Business Week*, 'Fixing the debt mess', 12 February, 2001, p18.
3 Taken from 'De-mythologising Charoen Pokphand: an interpretive picture of the CP Group's growth and diversification' by Paul Handley.
4 Taken from 'CP Group: From Seeds to 'Kitchen of the World', case study by Keeley Wilson and Professor Peter Williamson, 2001 INSEAD-EAC.
5 See 'Dare to Do: The Story of William Soeryadjaya and PT Astra International' by Charlotte Butler, McGraw-Hill Education (Asia) 2002.

Managing Partnerships with Japanese and South Korean Firms

The Model

The economies of Japan and South Korea are each dominated by distinct forms of business organisation – in Japan the *keiretsu* and in South Korea the *chaebol*. One of the unique features of these business models is that they were born out of a centrally directed industrialisation policy, so that for decades, the strong government backing and protection they received made them practically invincible in their home markets. However, buffeted by economic downturn and the pressures of globalisation, times are changing, opening up opportunities for outsiders to enter and grow even in these most difficult of Asian markets.

Japan

Writing in 1993, a business school professor noted that:

> As a market, Japan is still perceived by many foreign firms as a nightmare rather than as an opportunity, despite 120 million affluent customers. The rules appear to be different and rigged against them.

In fact, the Japanese way of doing business has several unique features that are usually held responsible for the difficulties foreign firms have experienced in penetrating Japan's markets. Notably, these include the role played by government ministries in directing national economic policy and the perceived collusion between the main corporate groupings, or *keiretsu* networks, in order to repel outside competition.

MITI and the *Keiretsu*

Universally acknowledged as the driving force behind Japan's industrial and economic success in the 1970s and 80s, the Ministry of International Trade and Industry (MITI), together with the powerful Ministry of Finance, was long seen as one of the villains of the piece because of its control of Japanese companies through what it euphemistically called 'administrative guidance'. Having chosen certain industries for nurture and development, it then set goals and 'encouraged' growth along the lines it had selected. Although theoretically free to accept or ignore this guidance, the threat of 'undesirable outcomes' ensured that MITI's advice was usually followed.

MITI's weaponry also included various policies seemingly designed to exclude foreign enterprises from the domestic market. These included informal rules such as not allowing foreigners more than a 50% share in joint ventures, restricting the number and voting rights of foreigners on the boards of Japanese firms and, in the last resort, excluding any foreign participation that had not obtained its permission.

The offspring of MITI's work were the *keiretsu*, a term mainly associated with bank-centred financial groupings. The big six that came into being in the 1950s were those based on the Fuji, Sanwa, Mitsubishi, Mitsui, Dai Ichi and Sumitomo banks. In accordance with MITI policies at that time, each bank group acquired or created within it a range of companies covering all the government-designated growth industries. A typical group would consist of several firms operating in different industries, centred on a main bank, a main manufacturer and a general trading company.

The overall strategy of the *keiretsu* was growth. The bank played the critical role in expansion by providing capital for the group members. It owned a significant number of shares in the group firms and often took part in management. To protect the *keiretsu* firms from hostile takeovers or unfriendly shareholders, cross-shareholdings between group members was common. The shares were held long term, leaving few to be traded on the open market. This stable shareholding structure enabled the companies to concentrate on developing new products and markets rather than worrying about short-term dividends.

The intra-firm relationships and alleged willingness of *keiretsu* to cooperate led non-Japanese competitors to portray them as representing a barrier to entry into Japanese markets and a major reason for high prices there. But, in fact, a high degree of competition existed between *keiretsu*, which were keen rivals in individual industries, where the leading firms were of more or less equal size, and totally committed to winning and keeping market leadership. What is not disputable, however, is the way that this very particular business environment made it difficult for Western firms to compete successfully there.

Cultural Obstacles

Another barrier to entry has been the distinctive Japanese business culture, which represents a blend of all the cultural and religious influences guiding Japan over centuries. From Shintoism comes the ideas of harmony and ritual, from Buddha, the concept of space and not offending, from Confucius, the idea of roles and place, from *Nemawashi* the idea of informal canvassing for support before a meeting, and from the US business guru, Deming, the idea of continual improvement. Such a culture makes the negotiation and decision-making process in Japan very different from the Western norm. As Coca-Cola President, Douglas Daft, discovered during his time in Japan, the negotiating table is not the place where minds can be changed. 'Before the Japanese have reached a consensus', he noted, 'they can't negotiate. After consensus is attained on the other side, there is nothing to negotiate.' Over time, Daft learned how to communicate in Japan:

> and I don't mean speak Japanese. For example if I want to have a meeting with the chairman of a company, first of all someone goes and talks through what the meeting will be all about. By the time we get there, both parties know if there are any controversial issues and what the outcome of the meeting will be.[1]

Not every Western manager or indeed other Asian managers had the time to understand and adapt to such a different environment.

Another particular feature of the business culture was the belief in lifetime employment; that meant Japanese managers regarded the company they first joined as their only company, and an extension of their family. This strong bond made it difficult for local managers to transfer their loyalty to another company, even if it was Japanese. Being taken over by a foreign firm was unthinkable and seen as a great loss of face. Foreign firms therefore found it hard to attract good locals to work for them, to sack workers in companies they acquired, or to sell off poor performing divisions. Even recently, asked if he was prepared to consider forming an alliance with a non-Japanese bank, one senior Japanese banker reportedly replied: 'I do not want to become a subsidiary of the Americans.'[2]

The Japanese Consumer

Apart from these structural and cultural obstacles, Western companies were also handicapped by their failure to understand the notoriously difficult Japanese consumer. Discerning and demanding, Japanese customers insist on extremely high standards of quality and service that many Western firms find difficult to meet. In addition, foreign entrants found themselves operating in fiercely competitive markets, where it was difficult to differentiate their products from those of domestic players. After that loomed another very high hurdle; getting their products on the shelves given the tight local distribution networks. To all these problems, the obvious solution was to take a local partner. Unfortunately, few joint ventures between foreign and Japanese firms lasted long, largely due to disagreements over control. Add to all this the high property prices and living costs that meant companies trying to enter Japan needed deep pockets, and it is not surprising that the convenient excuse, 'Japan is too difficult, too different', was readily employed by Western firms to excuse their failure.

Failure

Recent high-profile failures of Western retailers who tried to do all the right things, in vain, seem to indicate that this view is still valid. In 1999, Boots plc, the UK health and beauty retailer, formed a joint venture with the trading house, Mitsubishi. Boots usually spends two years preparing entry into a new market but, for Japan, it took over three until it felt it had found the right partner. This potentially powerful ally, it believed, would give an unknown foreign entrant credibility, besides supplying government and legal contacts, advising on adaptation to the local market and providing logistical help.

In Japan, opening up in the right area is critical and, with Mitsubishi's help, Boots opened four stores in prime locations. It also reformulated over 2,000 products to gain a Japanese licence and changed the packaging of its products to cater to the Japanese preference for fancier wrapping, as well as introducing seating at its cosmetics counter. 'Japanese customers are extremely demanding', noted the president of Boots Japan in October 2000.[3] 'You have to get things more right in Japan than anywhere else. You need to have patience, you need to rethink every aspect of your business.' Yet despite its meticulous preparation and cautious approach, the venture failed and Boots withdrew in July 2001. The French perfume and cosmetics chain Sephora (a subsidiary of LVMH) also withdrew after a similar experience.

But Some Successes

And yet American firms, such as Coca-Cola and IBM, and French luxury goods companies, such as Cartier and LVMH, have had a long and profitable presence in Japan, as have many pharmaceutical firms. Japan is the most important market in Asia for foreign pharmaceutical companies, being second in size to that of the US. In the past, the government's support for a strong domestic drugs industry put high hurdles in the way of foreign entrants, including regulatory requirements that made it hard for foreign firms to license medicines and sell them. Despite this, the US pharmaceutical firm American Home Products Corp. has been present for 50 years and Pfizer is the largest pharmaceuticals firm operating in Japan, albeit with a market share of only 3.3%. Novartis and Merck have also been successful, although on a much smaller scale than they would normally expect.

By 2000, all the signs were that the market was slowly opening up, and that foreign firms were gaining approval more quickly and easily. However, when AstraZeneca, tried to launch a new cancer treatment in June 2002, it 'shot itself in the foot' by not giving enough information on side effects, resulting in screaming headlines calling the drug 'a killer', following reports of death from side affects among people taking the treatment. Observers judged that AstraZeneca had 'failed to take account of the peculiarities of the Japanese market, and marketed the drug too aggressively to doctors not used to prescribing this type of medicine'.[4] Although the drug was later approved, the episode was a PR disaster for AstraZeneca.

Despite such episodes, globalisation and international pressure to normalise its markets are slowly bringing change to Japan. A decade of stagnation since the bursting of the economic bubble has brought down costs and made markets more accessible, and even hiring local staff has become easier. Having seen their elders laid off in the recession, the younger generation are more prepared to look to Western companies where they can progress more quickly than under the old seniority system. Even the power of MITI has diminished with deregulation, as the global firms it created have moved beyond its sphere of influence.

A New Model?

As Japan continues to open up, and encouraged by the success of partnerships such as Renault–Nissan, Western companies are again looking at its markets more seriously. The pioneering Renault–Nissan alliance was seen as 'mission impossible' when it was signed in March 1999. A tie-up with Nissan had already been rejected by Ford and Daimler in the belief that 'only a mad Frenchman would do this sort of thing'. Yet the partnership has confounded every pessimistic forecast that it would be defeated by cultural clashes and strong opposition from the Japanese workforce.

In fact, both sides had a lot to gain. The ailing Nissan needed Renault to survive and the French firm, faced by the rapid consolidation and globalisation of the car industry, needed to be part of a larger group to ensure its long-term sustainability. The alliance covered manufacturing, procurement and sales, which meant the two firms were deeply integrated only at the operational level, sharing production facilities, jointly procuring parts and sharing platforms (the building blocks of car) and exchanging best practices. This brought both companies the mutual benefits of new skills and technology, reduced costs, improved marketing and distribution and greater geographical coverage, while avoiding the danger of cultural clashes that a merger would have brought. After just three years, Nissan announced a record net profit and the decision was taken to deepen the alliance by increasing their stakes in each other, while still avoiding a full merger.

Other examples of tie-ups that bring genuine benefit to both sides indicate that this may become the model for other firms in the future. In April 2002, Ericsson, the Swedish telecoms equipment maker, was discussing a joint venture mobile phone operation with Sony of Japan. The deal was labelled 'a dream combination of Ericsson's technology and Sony's consumer electronics know-how, brand and marketing skills'. Another recent example is the partnership between Germany's Leica Cameras and Matsushita Electric Industrial to develop digital cameras, announced in July 2001. Despite the impression of a David and Goliath alliance, both have technological advantages to offer and Leica's reputation gives it influence beyond its size.

In December 2001, Roche Group, the Swiss drug maker, announced the acquisition in a friendly merger of Chugai, Japan's tenth largest pharmaceuticals company, which will become the fifth largest in the country. The evidence suggests that Western companies are sensing a weakening of resistance to the entry of foreign firms into Japan. Perhaps at last it is time to be Big in Japan. Certainly, this seems to be the Wal-Mart view. In January 2003, the company announced it was making a big push into the market via a controlling stake in its Japanese partner, Seiyu. The challenge was described as 'how to find a way to meet the fastidious Japanese consumer expectations for service and quality while maintaining their streamlined cost structure, despite high labour costs and a multi-layered distribution system'.[5] Quite.

Sumitomo 3M[6]

Among the shipwrecks of innumerable attempts over decades to operate joint ventures between US and Japanese firms, Sumitomo 3M has stood out in both duration and results. Having lasted for over 40 years, it is one of the most successful in the country. The story of its development illustrates perfectly the importance of learning from your partner if you want to succeed in Japan.

Formed in 1960, Sumitomo 3M was a joint venture between Minnesota-based 3M and two members of the Sumitomo Group; Sumitomo Electric Industries Ltd (SEI) and NEC Corporation. For 3M, the challenge was to adapt to a totally foreign environment and launch its products onto markets that operated in ways diametrically opposed to all its previous experience, while maintaining a measure of control over its businesses and the transfer of its technologies.

The partners

From the beginning, clear ground rules for the division of authority between the partners were laid down:

> The role of 3M is to provide technology, operational direction, the sense of family and new products. The role of Sumitomo partners is to provide the local presidents, the sense of local community, and their share of the funding.

This stance effectively reduced the role of NEC and SEI to that of investors, for although they alternately provided the president, he was only responsible for labour and personnel relations and government contacts. 3M would actually run the company via the managing director appointed by its headquarters in St Paul, Minnesota. Two other key posts were held by American managers: the technical director and the engineering and staff manufacturing director. According to Ron Baukol, Vice President for 3M Asia-Pacific in the 1990s: 'It was very important in the early days for this understanding to be reached to ensure that the goals were compatible.'

However, this did not mean that Sumitomo 3M was directed from St Paul. It was an independent subsidiary and, from the start, 3M was determined that it would work within the Japanese system. The attitude was 'Just tell us the rules and we'll play by them'. As Baukol noted, this was in contrast to other US companies, which tended to complain to their government about unfair treatment. Neither did 3M swamp the nascent company with expatriates, but merely sent a few of its manufacturing people over 'to get it started'. Apart from the three key posts filled by 'true 3M-ers', 95% of its employees were Japanese.

... Mutually learn from each other ...

In the early days, 3M was, on the whole, open to advice from its partners about how to build its businesses in Japan. According to retired CEO Lewis Lehr: 'we learnt a lot from NEC about how to distribute and sell goods in Japan the way the Japanese expected, as opposed to trying to impose the US system on them'.

However, despite the hands-off approach of St Paul, it still took some time for US managers to appreciate how different selling in this market was. Lewis Lehr recalled a duplicating product that:

> we took to Japan, and said we are going to sell it in Japan like in the US. We are going to set up our own distributors, not do it the way they recommend. I don't think that product lasted a year in Japan, and we never went back with it again.

3M CEO Jacobson remembered another notable failure, a tape gun that 'the Japanese wouldn't use because it was shaped like a weapon'. Examples such as this taught him 'to pay more attention to those who are closest to the local markets'.

During the first 20 years, the venture experienced phenomenal growth. By 1970, Sumitomo 3M's sales exceeded ¥10 billion and by 1980, they stood at almost ¥40 billion. Despite this, there was a feeling within Sumitomo 3M of missed opportunity, that although the company had done well, it could have done even better and, to many, the reason for this lay in quality problems.

The 'quality crisis'

For Mr Okuda, who became president in 1981, the most crucial issue concerned the quality of 3M products relative to local needs and compared with those of competing manufacturers: 'the product was suitable, but its quality was not up to standard'. Although this problem was evident for many years, the Japanese management was unable to convince those in St Paul that it represented a serious handicap to the company's growth. As Mr Nishina, then responsible for the electrical group, recalled, 'we had many arguments about quality. It was not that 3M USA products were poor, but that their standards were different. 3M was slow to understand this.'

As he discovered:

> It was very difficult to make the US office understand the exacting attitude of the Japanese end user. If a product was advertised to contain 100 pieces, for example, then it had to contain exactly that number. The US did not understand that they must check the exact number every time. Some of the St Paul divisions felt that our Japanese standards were unrealistic.

Such episodes, he believed, demonstrated, 'more a country than a culture gap'. Managers at 3M USA also failed to appreciate the prejudice of local consumers against foreign goods that had to be overcome. Observed Mr Nishina: 'There was always the thought in the consumers' minds that "foreign products are no good because they are different."'

Long-serving Sumitomo 3M managers had similar stories of products that failed to satisfy the Japanese consumers, whose exacting standards even extended to the packaging. According to Mr Sato, head of public relations, if this wasn't absolutely perfect, for example if the writing on the label was crooked, it was assumed that the inside would be equally imperfect and customers would not buy the product.

By the late 1980s, Mr Okuda felt it was a priority to tackle the growing gap in quality standards and, in particular, win back business from one of Sumitomo 3M's parent companies, NEC. It was a great surprise to him, however, when he found that 3M was not open to the ideas for improvement that he took for granted: 'The specification came from St Paul, and any deviation was not acceptable.'

To resolve the problem, Okuda spent a lot of time in Sumitomo 3M's plants, trying to find ways of improving and adapting 3M US products. He also visited the US factories to explain the problem and see what could be done at that end to improve quality. As a result, a regular interchange of manufacturing people began: 'They came over from the US to see us for a few weeks, and vice versa. This was especially important when a new product or process was being transferred.'

> Our people work on multiple levels, [said Okuda] so it is important that they learn the technology in a US environment, and then return to Japan with colleagues from the US to see how we can make it work in Japan. They cannot just bring in technology from the US and make it work, but to be able to modify it, they must understand it. Then we can keep the core technology, but adapt the product to our different markets and quality standards. Once the US understood our needs with regard to quality and delivery, improvement really took off.

Soon, Sumitomo was manufacturing its products to the highest local quality standards and as a result, NEC returned to the fold. Okuda's original ambition had been to double sales within five years. In fact, he recalled, 'we did it in four years'.

Communications

Where Okuda had identified quality issues as the main cause of friction between Japan and St Paul, Dr Gastaldo, who became MD in 1990, felt that the real roots of the problem lay in the decision-making process. This, he believed, had long been bedevilled by mistrust and poor communications between US and local managers.

Gastaldo concluded that, despite years of meeting each other, the two sides had rarely spoken frankly:

> People from the US feel intimidated when they come to Japan. They are over-defensive and over-nice to the people they meet. Once they are back among their American colleagues, then they complain about the Japanese.

On the Japanese side, Okuda commented that:

> We Japanese are not comfortable with confrontation. When a visitor arrives from the US, we are reluctant to speak up and contradict, as this is not polite. We do not have the courage to say 'we need to change'. This confidence is only just beginning to develop.

Gastaldo and Okuda both saw the need for a greater degree of leadership from St Paul. This implied more visits from the chairman to give the company a greater sense of 3M's overall direction, and longer stays from St Paul executives, rather than just 'parachuting in and out'. Subsequently, visits increased to speed the spread of the 3M culture and technological ideas, and strengthen the ties between the two countries.

Eight years later, the joint venture was still going strong and, in 2001, contributed more than 10% of 3M's total profits. Why did this particular joint venture succeed? Kenzo Tanabe, the second president of Sumitomo, underlined the importance of flexibility and compromise:

> What matters most in a joint venture is mutual understanding. Instead of clinging to our own position, we must understand and respect the opinions of our partners ... The key to success in international business is finding how to harmonize those things international with those things national.

South Korea

The economic change that lifted South Korea from poverty to affluence in one generation, making it the world's 11th largest trading nation and, in 1996, the first Asian tiger to join the rich man's club, the OECD (Organization for Economic Co-operation and Development), was led by its family-owned business groups or *chaebol*. Their initiator, General Park, who ran the country until his assassination in 1979, based his economic policy on the Japanese model.

The *Chaebol*

Through a series of five-year plans, Park built national champions or *chaebol* who entered selected industrial sectors. In the 1970s, for example, Daewoo, a *chaebol* then specialising in textiles, was ordered to take over a machine-tool maker and a shipyard, besides entering the automotive sector.

Park's strategy was based on encouraging the growth of heavy industry, at first steel and shipbuilding, together with an export orientation to supplement the small domestic market. In the 1970s, the focus was on metals, machinery and chemicals industries, but the next decade saw a move for companies to develop their own technology and market their brands outside Korea. The state rewarded firms investing in these areas by giving them cheap loans and other subsidies. The strategy resulted in growth of 10% a year and an economy dominated by five big, family-run *chaebol* – Hyundai, Samsung, LG, Daewoo and Sunkyong. By 1998, they accounted for over a third of the country's entire sales and almost half of all exports. Their tentacles reached into every business from shipbuilding and car making to semiconductors, consumer electronics and satellite broadcasting.

Like Japan, South Korean firms had a particular business culture, characterised by a quasi-militaristic organisation and a paternalistic management style that demanded a high degree of loyalty and obedience from its workers. Promoted according to seniority, they worked long hours in return for lifetime employment. After 1987, the growing power of the trade unions gave the country a reputation for labour militancy.

The cosy arrangement between the *chaebol*, the politicians and the bureaucracy resulted in a market that Western firms found almost impossible to enter. Moreover, in Korea, the cultural heritage led to the development of a much more overtly hostile business environment, in which the *chaebol* became synonymous with a nationalistic, almost xenophobic outlook.

Foreign firms who did try to enter the market were faced by government restrictions on their owning controlling stakes in joint ventures in 'strategic industries'. Those that did take minority partnerships found that the *chaebol* were prone to use their investment either to prop up weak subsidiaries, or to increase market share. Either way, there were few dividends for investors. An EIU survey found that, in 1996, wholly owned foreign firms reported more than double the operating profit of joint ventures.[7] Perhaps not surprisingly, analysts noted that the usual lifespan of a Korean joint venture was four to seven years, compared with several decades in other countries.

In December 1992, the newly elected President Kim Young Sam refocused the attention of the *chaebol* on *segyewha* or globalisation. Ever obedient to the government's wish, the largest *chaebol* issued almost daily announcements of the establishment of overseas plants, alliances and takeovers as they invested in North America, Europe and neighbouring countries in the Asia-Pacific region. The pace of investment was fast; by the first half of 1996, investments abroad amounted to US$9.5 billion, of which $1.7 billion was destined for Asia and half of that for the fast-growing China market.

The economic crisis of 1997 saw an abrupt halt to this spending. Their traditionally high gearing, with debts sometimes averaging four times their equity, had long put a question mark over the financial stability of the *chaebol*. Now, the crisis revealed a history of reckless borrowing, excess and an abuse of corporate governance that surprised even their fiercest critics. Subsequently, the IMF rescue package of $58 billion, signed by new President Kim Dae Jung in 1998, imposed a wide range of reforms on the corporate and banking sectors. Daewoo was allowed to collapse in 1999 and Hyundai, once the largest group, was dismantled into five mini-groups. As a result of the opening of the capital markets to foreigners, over half the stock in companies such as Samsung Electronics was bought by foreign investors, who by 2001 also held 30% of shares traded on the Korean stock exchange.

Many rejoiced at the apparent demise of the *chaebol*, anticipating it would open up the economy and allow small and medium-sized, more entrepreneurial companies to emerge. South Korea itself won wide praise for making one of the fastest recoveries from the 1997 crisis, having paid off its loan three years ahead of schedule.

However, five years after the crisis, the depth of the restructuring of the *chaebol*, and the bad-loan-ridden banks from whom they borrowed, was still not clear. Recent signs seem to indicate that the changes are only skin deep: at the start of 2002, the top 30 groups still had 617 affiliates, and lack of transparency in accounting remained a serious problem. This was underlined in March 2003 when ten executives of SK Group, the third largest conglomerate, were charged with accounting fraud. Its vice chairman was later jailed for three years. Other conglomerates, such as Hyundai and Samsung, were thought to be similarly vulnerable.

So for foreign firms seeking to acquire or form a partnership with a South Korean company, the legacy of the *chaebol* years, the threat of opposition from the powerful workforce, a hostile press and cronyism still represent considerable obstacles to their ambitions to enter this highly attractive market. To these factors must be added the Korean culture and the way that it influences how local managers conduct their business.

A Different Culture

The influence of Confucianism in South Korea means that Koreans place a heavy emphasis on duty and harmony, based on respect for hierarchical relationships and obedience to authority. This is reflected in their negotiating stance: Koreans tend to present themselves in a team organised vertically by rank and gender, and it is important to identify the leader from the start. The need to maintain harmony is a crucial goal throughout any negotiations. However, this has not stopped the Koreans from gaining a reputation as extremely tough negotiators. One of their favourite tactics is to go over the detail of any proposition over and over again in order to wear down the opposition. 'The Korean culture', remarked one veteran negotiator, 'doesn't allow for a win-win situation. It's kill or be killed.'

This attitude arises out of the mental scars caused by South Korea's long history of foreign invasion and occupation that has left its people with an 'us and them' mentality that equates foreign ownership with imperialism. There is an ingrained attitude that Korea will only succeed by keeping foreigners out, hence the strong antipathy towards selling to outsiders. Among the reactions after the IMF bailout, for example, was the staging of public burning of foreign goods, the vandalism of foreign cars and a boycott of foreign imports in favour of 'Buy Korean'. As soon as foreigners show any interest in buying into a business or making an acquisition, the Koreans believe that they are selling it too cheaply.

Against this background, the many foreign firms that entered South Korea after 1997 looking to pick up a bargain have had a hard time finding one. Even after identifying a possible partner, the lack of transparency, and the hostility and threats from the labour unions have made any negotiation a protracted and sometimes unpleasant process. HSBC, Deutsche Bank and Ford all invested a lot of time and money to make deals with supposedly debt-laden and desperate local companies, only to withdraw, defeated by the complexity of the deals and the difficulty of gauging the true extent of the company's indebtedness. Other companies found their efforts strangled in red tape. In 1998, the US-based Dow Corning decided to give up its plan for a $2.8 billion silicone plant, which would have been the largest foreign project in Korea, and build it in Malaysia instead. Even foreign companies that do persevere have not found that the situation improves with time. GM negotiated long and hard to take over part of Daewoo Motor Co. and by early 2003, felt that its investment was paying off (see Chapter 7). But in September that year it was forced to give its workers a 14.8% pay rise to avert a strike that would have jeopardised all its plans for the future.

Another stumbling block has been the mismatch in expectations between venture partners. In 1996 the US firm GE Capital went ahead with a joint venture with Sindoh Ricoh, which makes copiers and fax machines. GE planned to expand later and move into financial services but, unfortunately, its 51% stakeholding partner did not want to step outside its known consumer business. The venture broke down.

Similarly, a US investment bank which entered into a securities joint venture with a Korean *chaebol* discovered very quickly that the two were a long way apart when it came to their understanding of what the business entailed. Among the factors that led to the breakdown, the most telling was the experience of the US manager drafted in from New York to head the venture. In his first week, he was surprised to learn that one of his Korean staff had been sacked for losing $2 million on a deal. The US manager protested that in such a high-risk business this was considered peanuts, and was by no means a sacking offence. The same person could lose $2 million today but might make $8 million tomorrow – such losses were part of the game. His argument was not accepted. Within a few months the venture was dissolved; the gap in the understanding of the two sides about the meaning of risk proved unbridgeable.

The failure of so many projected deals in 2001–02, between Hynix and Micron, between AIG and Hyundai Securities, and the two years it took to finalise the deal between GM and Daewoo, demonstrate how difficult it is even to get to the starting block of building a relationship in South Korea. However, the situation is not all gloom and doom. Slowly, South Korea, too, is changing, as a younger, talented generation realise that lifetime employment is no longer on offer. There is a move towards a more flexible labour market in which people change jobs and are willing to work for foreign firms that offer better career prospects.

Finally, a story to demonstrate that it is possible to manage a successful partnership with a Korean firm. Dongsuh, a joint venture that began in 1984, illustrates some of the key points to watch in order to build up a harmonious, enduring relationship.

The British Frog in the Field[8]

Dongsuh Industrial Company Ltd was the offspring of the British automotive components group T&N and Yoo Sung Enterprise Co. Ltd, a piston ring and cylinder liner producer. The South Korean firm was a well-respected mini-conglomerate, founded by Mr Hong Woo Ryu in 1960 to produce cylinder kits for the nascent South Korean automotive industry. By 1996, the group consisted of six companies, all producing component parts for domestic car makers. Of these, Dongsuh was the jewel in Mr Ryu's crown. Despite his 72 years, Mr Ryu was still the active chairman of Dongsuh. One of his five sons, Si-Hoon, had just been promoted to managing director and was being groomed to take over on the retirement of the then President, Mr W.K. (Simon) Min.

The 50/50 joint venture to make pistons was signed on 13 December, 1984. The name of the new company, 'Dongsuh' was chosen by Mr Ryu to illustrate that the venture would be a marriage between the East (Dong) and the West (Suh). In 1984, Dongsuh's board was composed of two directors from each side, plus Mr Ryu as chairman with the casting vote. By

1997, the board was made up of Mr Ryu, his two sons and Simon Min for the Korean side with three representatives (one of them a finance director) representing T&N. The board met twice a year.

As Simon Min recalled, from the start there was a gentleman's agreement that management should be the responsibility of the Koreans, while the British firm would restrict itself to technical support. For the first three years, a UK engineer was located almost permanently at Dongsuh to provide support to the production engineering side, especially during visits to customers. This close contact continued.

The company operated from a site on a new industrial estate outside Seoul and, from the very first day, 'everything went like a dream'. As the South Korean car industry grew, so Dongsuh grew with it, to become an enormous success story. After making a loss in the first two years, the company broke even in the third year and, from then on, its profits increased steadily to provide a 15% dividend annually. In the 12 years of operations, sales expanded twenty times (enough to pay royalties and fund all its subsequent growth and new machinery) and T&N, whose initial investment was US$1.4 million, had 'never put in a bean since'.

According to Simon Min, apart from labour disputes, Dongsuh had encountered no major problems, nor had there been any tensions in the relationship with T&N. He attributed this to the excellent understanding and friendship that developed over the years between Mr Ryu and Sandy Barr, the T&N director of licensing and joint ventures responsible for handling the Anglo-Korean relationship until 1992.

The growth of Dongsuh

When it was established, Dongsuh produced only 20,000 pistons a month. By 1996, it had grown 25 times and was producing 500,000 pistons a month, or 6.5 million pistons a year. Of this total, 2.8 million pistons were for diesel and 3.7 million for gasoline passenger cars. It also produced 3 million gudgeon pins for Hyundai.

In 1997, Dongsuh was the number one piston manufacturer in South Korea, with a 40% share of a market dominated by four companies. Its nearest competitor, Dong Yang (in which Mahle GmbH had a 45% share), had 30% of the market and the other two companies shared the balance. Dongsuh's products were distributed through three main channels to its four principal customers: Hyundai, Daewoo, Kia and YPR. Demand, observed Simon Min, had never been a problem for Dongsuh, rather, the difficulty had been to meet it.

Technology

Technology transfer, a frequent cause of friction in many joint venture relationships, has never been an issue. At the outset, 11 British engineers worked alongside their Korean colleagues and 'made every effort to transfer technology as quickly as possible and make sure everything was understood'. Fortunately, recalled Mr Min, 'the learning curve was very sharp and so we could go very fast. This experience formed an unbreakable trust between us and T&N, and again gave us confidence.'

Indeed, the years have seen a reverse technology transfer take place, for which Si-Hoon was given much of the credit. He had worked closely with a UK engineer in overseeing the automation of Dongsuh and, under his guidance, Dongsuh developed its own innovative production engineering processes. These so impressed T&N that they had been deployed in their other operations round the world.

Relationships

T&N's strategy towards all its joint ventures was to treat them, as far as possible, like wholly owned subsidiaries. While exercising fairly strict financial control by requiring monthly statements and regular full accounts, T&N was always concerned not to appear to usurp authority but, instead, exercise control or influence through building good relationships. It was a delicate line to tread but in Dongsuh, thanks mainly to Sandy Barr's close affinity with Mr Ryu and Simon Min, it had been achieved. Brian Ruddy, who took over Barr's role, noted that: 'At T&N, we worry a lot about our relationships.'

When trying to explain why the relationship had been so successful, Mr Min placed a heavy emphasis on the word 'trust'. 'We established trust between us through good communications. When two partners are a long distance from each other, small things can quickly become big problems. But both partners made every effort to avoid this.' As Min spoke both English and German, communications were never a problem and, he recalled:

> We would telex each other two or three times a day at the beginning and telephone every evening. I reported every little thing that happened, just to keep Sandy informed. He visited us twice a month at first, and we quickly became the best of friends. Whenever we had a problem, he would try to solve it for us. Even if he didn't succeed, we knew he had done his best.

In a video made to celebrate Sandy Barr's retirement, Min calculated that Barr's travels to and from Dongsuh amounted to circumnavigating the globe seven and a half times, 'and in those days, the trip was not so easy'. In turn, Mr Min made regular visits to the UK.

Si-Hoon explained the difference in outlook he had noted between the British and YPR's Japanese joint venture partners:

> We have a saying that the Japanese approach is like a frog in a well. All it sees is the sky in a round shape. The British are more like frogs in the field, they see the total view and they are more open. That is why we have confidence in them.

Key Lessons

Setting up and running joint ventures in Japan and South Korea requires patience and commitment.

◼ In Japan:

- Don't simply try to transfer Western models
- Always keep local management and listen to them
- Study the customer and remember: quality, quality, quality – from the product to the packaging and beyond.

◼ In South Korea:

- Go for a majority share or wholly owned venture
- When drawing up the contract, insert clauses to absolve you from responsibility for future debt that may be uncovered
- Put in a good finance director you can trust.

Notes

1 *Far Eastern Economic Review*, 'Coke's New Formula', 20 April, 2000, pp64–5.
2 *Financial Times*, 'Culture clashes prove biggest hurdle to international links', 24 January, 2002, p15.
3 *Financial Times*, 'The Japanese Face of Boots', 4 October, 2000.
4 *Financial Times*, 'Hard Lessons from Japan's Drugs Market', 24 June, 2003, p11.
5 *Financial Times*, 'Retailers Set Sights on Japan', 13 December, 2002, p24.
6 All quotes in this section about Sumitomo 3M are taken from the case studies 'Sumitomo 3M' (A) and (B) by Charlotte Butler and Professor Daniel Muzyka, 1997 INSEAD-EAC.
7 *The Economist*, 'Look before you leap', 14 March, 1998, p78.
8 Taken from the case study 'Dongsuh Industrial Co. Ltd.' by Charlotte Butler and Professor Henri-Claude de Bettignies, 1997 INSEAD-EAC.

Avoid Post-acquisition Trauma

Beyond the Point of No Return

So, you have made your acquisitions and are now part of the Asian business scene. Perhaps you have bought a company outright, perhaps you are the majority owner of one or more companies. Maybe you paid a little too much, maybe you got a bargain – or think you did. But now it is time to make the investment pay back and, for most, that means serious planning and thought about how to manage and organise these new operations. And this in turn means making changes.

This is not to say that multinationals and other smaller investors are necessarily making poor investment decisions. In most cases, the business they buy into is a good one with potential. The company is perhaps the market leader or one of the top three in its industry, and has probably turned in improved results annually before the 1997–98 economic crisis. On the other hand, often deals are signed quickly in the heat of the competitive situation or to take advantage of preferential tax situations. Due diligence is done as well as possible, and the market research looks promising. But, as we have seen, information about these areas can never be 100% reliable and faults are almost bound to appear later.

In all cases, with an eye to the future, Western companies will invariably aim for greater efficiency to improve the results and competitiveness of their Asian possessions via an injection of Western business methods and technical know-how. Maintaining the status quo is not an option. If you want to be Big in Asia, that probably indicates the need for big changes. But how you manage those changes in order to integrate your acquisition successfully will be vital to the success or failure of your investment. Siemens Corporation, the German electrical engineering and electronics firm, has a wide experience of cross-border acquisitions. Interviewed in 2002, its CEO, Heinrich von Pierer, declared that:

> To fully integrate the companies that we have in our portfolio is the decisive factor in the success of an acquisition. This boosts productivity and optimises the new unit's potential together with our own competencies. Integration teams usually start structuring the acquisition process, but the real work comes in the postmerger period.[1]

Of course, in a perfect world, you will have made the right acquisition at the right price for the right reasons and will have a detailed integration plan ready to put into effect – no fears for your future. However, in real life, nothing is perfect, and the figures for disappointment or withdrawal by companies that have failed to make their acquisitions pay are chastening. In which case, a few hints on what to do and what not to do may be useful in avoiding that awful state of post-acquisition *tristesse*.

What Type of Changes?

The type and depth of the changes necessary will vary from one country and one industry sector to another. At one end of the spectrum, taking over a mainland Chinese state-owned enterprise, used to operating within a planned economy and all that that entails, means taking over a largely unskilled workforce imbued with a 'featherbedded' culture of lifetime employment and no sense of personal involvement in issues such as quality or productivity. The barriers to change in such a company are daunting and can take years to break down, so be prepared for the long haul.

At the other end of the scale, an acquisition in, say, Malaysia will have a head start in terms of trained workers who are good English speakers and used to maintaining relatively high operating standards. In between, Thailand, Indonesia and Hong Kong offer a range of cultural and business environments that may throw up greater or fewer obstacles to growth. Of course, buying out a local partner will give you the benefit of advance knowledge of a firm and a pool of managers who have built up contacts with their local colleagues. Their experience will make it easier to bridge the change of ownership, but does not necessarily mean that there will be fewer changes to make.

The Post-merger Integration Process

Following the acquisition, experienced companies move straight away to implement a post-merger integration (PMI) plan. This plan is based on reports from everyone who participated in the acquisition process but, primarily, from the work of the due diligence team. These reports normally contain an assessment of the new possession and a list of proposed areas for improvement. During the next stage, these reports are analysed and combined in a single document by a specially constituted PMI committee, whose membership includes corporate strategists, business development planners, Asian experts, financial, operational and product managers. The single document that emerges from this operation is then circulated among senior executives and any problems identified are benchmarked against the company's own operations. If it appears that the acquired company has a better method of doing something, the difference can be noted and adopted to the benefit of the rest of the company.

In a parallel phase, the PMI plan sets targets for the acquisition, based on its present and future capabilities, and the company's objectives for its Asian investment. These objectives should also fit within the company's overall global strategy. The outcome should include a fairly detailed business plan for the short and medium term, targets for production, which products for which markets and so on.

Once this framework has been established and the list of improvements and the business plan finalised, then operational teams – even if only two or three people – can be despatched to begin the process of change. In the past, some Western firms have been content to let local managers continue to run their Asian operations, merely sending out technical advisors on short-term missions to transfer technology, and a senior executive to attend board meetings. But trying to run an Asian acquisition (or even a joint venture) at arm's length is one of the surest ways to ruin. Western companies must send in their own 'best' people to lead the company and control crucial functions such as finance. 'Best' in this sense means people who possess both excellent business and management skills, and are also attuned to the cultural sensitivities of the host country. Their task is to bridge the gaps between the two companies, to blend the different organisations and cultures to achieve enhanced performance, which requires a high degree of skill.

Sending in new people definitely does not imply a clear-out of the existing management team. Good local managers will be vital to the future and, in any case, it is hardly motivating to acquired firms if their people feel threatened or unappreciated by the new owners, especially if they are foreign. Again the PMI plan should have identified their strengths and weaknesses and indicated where management needs to be improved. So the long-term aim of the Western team is to introduce training programmes where necessary to improve staff skills, raise standards in administration and production and, the biggest challenge of all, change the prevailing culture to match that of the new owners. Only then will there be a good chance of implementing the business plan successfully. The advantage for a company that develops such a procedure is that the teams are able to work quickly to turn the company around. Of course, this does presuppose a high-quality team, with experience of managing change in different cultures – unfortunately quite a rarity, even in sophisticated multinationals.

The usual areas targeted for improvement are human resources, transparency, product quality and efficiency. However, success in changing these depends very much on how well the post-acquisition team is able to begin changing the corporate culture and induce the troops to accept new ways of working.

Cultural Change

To implement cultural change is difficult even within a mature market context – think of the potential problems arising from a French acquisition of an English company. Then think of what it means for a Western firm to try and introduce change into an Asian acquisition, whose local managers are used to deferring utterly to seniority and hierarchy, have developed their own close-knit networks and might operate in a culture where bribery is a fact of life. To alter Confucian social structures and habits of obedience and respect for authority which have been entrenched for the last 2,500 years could well be classed as the thirteenth Herculean labour.

Real change – as opposed to superficial lip-service – means shattering the status quo and replacing it by a new culture marked by very un-Asian characteristics such as individualism, self-assertiveness, initiative and personal responsibility. Most of all, Western companies talk about implementing a winning culture, one that is competitive and with a strong will to win. They aim for global strategies and the spread of global best practices, but many of these sit very uncomfortably with Asian habits and ways of thinking. To introduce such a changed mindset is a long process, requiring great skill on the part of the management and needing continual reinforcement. However, unless it is tackled with some success, tensions between the two cultures will severely impede the development of the company. The subject is dealt with in greater detail in Strategy 11.

One way of getting staff to think differently about their company may be through changing its image. A rebranding exercise, based on the known strengths of the investing firm, can bring great benefits both in changing customer perceptions and giving staff a new pride in their company. After ABN Amro acquired Thailand's Bank of Asia, its first step was to undertake a thorough rebranding exercise. While this was a delicate and sensitive issue to handle, it paid off within a year. Being allied to a foreign and 'trustworthy' bank was appreciated by its employees, which helped the bank to increase its market share.

If changing the local management culture is an enormous hurdle, managing the ordinary factory workers is perhaps an even greater challenge. Just as in Europe, huge cultural differences exist between the local populations of the different countries in Asia.

These cultural differences can radically affect the training process, as one British expatriate, who had been happily teaching machine operators in Malaysia, found. The Malay workers had some engineering experience and were familiar with the basic language and technical skills necessary, so were easy to train. When he moved to a plant in Indonesia, he found a totally different proposition. There he was faced by high school graduates with little foundation on which he could build. Working on a site in Kalimantan, all went well until a group of Bataks from Sumatra arrived. They were better trained, but their high-handed attitude towards the locals caused tensions. Their more aggressive approach disrupted workplace harmony to the point where the situation erupted in rioting.

Workplaces with different cultures that may prove antagonistic to one another need careful managers who understand the different cultures and know how to get things done. This is not usually the case with the expatriates sent in to head the company and fill key posts. Therefore, to ensure that orders are carried out and that factories run smoothly, multinationals must have a good middle layer of managers, supervisors and team bosses. In addition to local managers already in place, some companies recruit Indian or Filipino expats to fill these roles. Less expensive than their Western counterparts, they are often highly qualified. However, even here there can be problems.

Many firms have found that South African managers are the best solution. Their home experience in managing employees from different tribal groups gives them a distinct advantage, plus the fact that they tend to be more comfortable than many US or European managers with the concept of being a 'father' figure to the workers. Many have a long working experience in South Africa, but left their home country for political reasons and are seeking short-term contracts to fill in the years up to their retirement. This factor is another plus for companies hiring them. Since age is respected in Asia, local workers often find change easier to accept from a senior figure than a brash young manager in a hurry.

In the long term, the extent of cultural change and the ability to manage local workers is a major determinant in the success or failure of an acquisition. However, the trick is to know what can be altered or levelled up, and which parts to leave alone so that the acquired company feels it has some autonomy left. As Heinrich von Pierer noted:

> I think it's important that the buying company does not try to overrun and completely change the corporate culture in the acquired company. We at Siemens always strive to establish ourselves as good corporate citizens in all our local markets ... Whilst a rigorous, success-oriented culture throughout the company is important for big corporations like us, it's equally important to give individual units entrepreneurial freedom in their daily operations.[2]

If there is a discernible trend towards improvement, some diversity in practice is not serious, and a happy workforce is more likely to deliver the desired results. One of the key factors here will be communication between management and employees – why you are making the changes, how this will make them part of a winning team and why this is a useful aim.

Human Resource Issues

Human resources can make or break an acquisition; in every survey on key M&A issues for Western companies moving into Asia, they top the list of problems they face. Downsizing, finding good quality people and staff development are crucial issues and potentially the biggest barriers to growth if not dealt with effectively.

Downsizing

Before the economic crisis, of course, staff retention was the important issue, since the too few good people were easily enticed away by higher paying competitors. After 1997, the situation changed dramatically; for example Marks & Spencer, the UK retailer, found that its annual staff losses dropped from 30% in 1995 to almost zero post-crisis. Since then, the problem has been how to lay off staff without provoking demonstrations, bad feelings or even violence, since rejection is often taken personally. Following the economic downturn, the suicide rate increased in Japan and Korea, while the murder rate rose dramatically in Thailand where at least one manager was murdered by a sacked employee. It has been said that 'When a Korean loses his job he kills himself. When a Thai loses his job, he kills his wife.' Glib though this might seem, it does suggest the degree to which employment is linked with self-worth in Asia.

Compared with Western staffing levels, most Asian companies are over-resourced, and one of the first aims of a company making an acquisition is to reduce the headcount. However, any downsizing needs to be carefully managed, according to local labour laws and through negotiation with regional or local governments. This applies especially to China and Indonesia, which have particularly strict labour laws.

The process has become easier since so many Asian companies have themselves been forced to lay off staff since 1997. However, many have tried out halfway solutions to avoid social unrest. Some began with just a pay cut or loss of bonus. PT Astra, the Indonesian conglomerate, told its workers to stay at home so they could save on factory running costs and canteen facilities. The company was reluctant to lose trained workers and so continued to pay them for as long as possible.

One Thai owner found a way to cut down his distribution and sales force for one business from 100 to just 5 people that mixed Western 'rationalism' with Asian 'paternalism':

First of all I sat down with them and gave them the facts and figures. They saw that we just weren't able to go on because we were dealing with imported products and with the devaluation of the baht, we couldn't sell them at the high prices we got before. They understood, and we paid them all compensation. We parted amicably. Some workers I was able to move to other parts of the business, some I have let have a van to run a small business themselves. They pay us the cost of running the van and we source essential foods such as rice or fish sauce for them. These are all easy to sell from a van, and most are making a living.[3]

However, one Western expatriate who tried to get rid of an unsatisfactory finance director in a culturally sensitive way did not find it so easy. First he tried promoting the manager way beyond his capabilities in the hope that, overwhelmed by his new responsibilities, he would lose face and resign. In fact, although clearly under stress, the manager merely avoided meetings at which he might be exposed and showed no sign of leaving. The MD then promoted someone else who was well qualified and actually did the work, hoping that the rest of the finance team would see this as unfair and put pressure on the first manager to leave. However, when asked, they said that they were 'happy to work round him'.

Examples such as these demonstrate what a sensitive issue this is and why it must be handled carefully. Few ordinary workers would believe that a rich Western firm did not have the financial resources to keep workers on, so downsizing merely confirms Western firms' reputations for being uncaring and ruthless. Perhaps the most effective way to deal with lay-offs is to work with local managers to map out a strategy for any lay-offs, and try to keep the news quiet for as long as possible, to avoid sparking protests and riots. Generous compensation complying with, or even exceeding, the legal limits is a must. Some companies try to cushion the blow by hiring outside firms to give counselling and help in writing CVs so that workers can find other jobs. This approach will protect the firm's reputation and make it easier to attract workers back later.

Finding Quality Management

The other side of the coin is finding the skilled, well-trained local staff needed to run your acquisition. Quality staff are always in demand and, even with the downturn, there is a lack of well-qualified, professional managers in the region, especially engineers and IT specialists. Indian managers have long been especially prized for their engineering and IT skills, but companies have gone as far afield as Laos and Vietnam in search of people who can be trained. Headlines in an *Asiaweek* survey in May 2001 suggested that there were 100 jobs for every computer science graduate in China and that South Korea forecast 210,000 unstaffed IT posts by 2005.[4]

This gap means that hijacking or poaching is the most frequent way of hiring professional staff. It also means that retaining talent once they are trained is equally difficult. Many Western firms have used performance targets and bonuses for individual performance to motivate and retain staff. Following its entry into Thailand, Tesco quickly realised that its ambitious five-year expansion plan would not be achieved, given the 40% turnover rate of staff in the Lotus supermarket chain it had acquired. Tesco discovered that many were leaving to find jobs with similar wages in factories. Further research found that a prime reason was that shop-floor workers disliked the degree of deference they had to give to customers, who might even be younger than themselves – not a problem in factories. Consequently, Tesco reviewed its recruitment process to identify candidates most suitable for working on the shop floor. It also introduced a range of HRM techniques used in its operations elsewhere, but with Thailand-specific cultural sensitivities factored in.[5]

In the past, Citibank and IBM proved great training grounds for many ambitious Asians. However, once they hit the glass ceilings in these multinationals, they moved over to local conglomerates, taking their finely tuned skills and valuable insider knowledge with them. Although this caused some pain to the firms they left, on the other hand it helped to spread the Western culture within local companies. PT Astra, for example, was once headed by Rini Soewandi, a graduate of Wellesley College in the US and from a well-connected Indonesian family. But her early career was spent in Citibank, from where she and Michel Ruslim, later head of the finance division, joined Astra in the late 1980s.

The attrition rate of trained workers is still high even in the years after the economic crisis. In February 2001, a scenario in the *Far Eastern Economic Review* suggested that a local firm in India's Silicon Valley might be increasing its workforce by 20–40% a year, while losing 25% of existing employees to local competitors, multinationals or even small dotcoms.[6] The Taiwanese group Acer recently began offering stock options and bonus schemes to retain staff, while the Canadian telecoms company Nortel continued to pay its Asian workers full salaries throughout the crisis to ensure that its workers remained. Any firm wishing to keep its good staff will have to follow similar strategies.

Staff Development

In view of the staff shortage, staff development is becoming more important. Those who have been trained and encouraged are more likely to remain loyal and, if they see promotion possibilities, remain with the company. Training is also the way for a company to build the competencies and capabilities that will enable the acquisition to achieve its targets. Some multinationals are changing their recruitment approach in favour of introducing new tools to identify and nurture talent early on. To some extent, these new methods aim to make up for deficiencies in the educational system common to many Asian countries. This tends to concentrate on memory, rote learning and following rules rather than developing the more creative, autonomous attitude favoured by Western companies.

Shell, the Dutch oil company, spent US$60,000 on an internal psychological study profiling its existing Chinese managers and entry-level management trainees.[7] Competence profiling is another approach used by Unilever in India. It's a process which involves employers listing the competence that recruits must have and then focusing on their behavioural responses to certain situations, rather than experience. The emphasis is on attitude and personality as much as technical skills, developing the ability to deal with uncertainties in the workplace and cope with stressful situations.

However, such ambitious schemes need to be introduced slowly in the Asian context. Asian staff tend to prefer set routines, and situations which avoid the possibility of anyone losing face. The idea of moving around or being flexible is also disturbing to many. One Western MD found that his attempts to promote promising staff sometimes misfired badly. For example, he wanted to encourage one of the secretaries, whom he believed had the potential to become a top-level PA, to gain experience by working in different parts of the company. His suggestion that she might begin by applying for a vacant post with the deputy manager was interpreted as a sign that her work was unacceptable, and that she was being asked to leave.

Technical training remains a priority where operational standards need to be improved. The problem is how to do it. Do you send in technical staff from the home base to spend two or three months in the factory, or do you bring promising locals back to be trained on the spot and also, hopefully, absorb some different cultural notions? On their return, they can then act as mentors to their colleagues and spread ideas on production and safety standards. Either way is expensive and throws up problems of communication, and the possibility of homesick Asians or Westerners struggling in an alien work culture. But it must be done.

Today, a new generation of Asian managers either have MBAs or were educated in the US, and so share the business vocabulary of Western firms. Not surprisingly, multinationals often prefer to hire them to run their Asian operations. Another coveted source has been among the American-born Chinese community. American in culture and outlook, many of them now wish to have some experience of their ancestral home and work in the new China. But there are risks, as always. One US firm hired a US-Chinese, MBA-trained manager to run its operations in China, hoping that in this way they could finesse the problems associated with communications, cultural differences and managing local staff. But as the British expatriate manager sent to head the regional operation found when he visited the Chinese company, the American-Chinese had in fact surrounded himself with members of his family to help run the business, none of whom were remotely qualified for the job, and some of whom were managing non-existent projects. An experienced Asia hand, he was not surprised on a later night visit to the office to find commercially sensitive documents left on the photocopier, and faxes showing that the information had been going to a competitor. Caveat emptor.

Transparency

Despite due diligence, companies can never be sure of what exactly they are buying into in Asia. They can only hope that the cupboard does not contain too many skeletons. Gaining control of financial data and bringing more transparency into the company's finances is almost always the number one priority once they have deciphered the balance sheet. Only then can they go forward with confidence. An expatriate finance manager, able to install and maintain strict systems and processes, is the swiftest and surest solution. In the long term, it is a cultural issue that time and training will change, as managers used to working in the Asian way get used to the idea of openness and accountability.

One example illustrates how fraught an issue this can be. A Scottish managing director with 30 years' experience, mostly in Malaysia, was hired to identify the problems of a newly acquired, badly performing agri-business division in Indonesia and turn it around.[8] He quickly decided that the accounting system needed a complete overhaul. Although the division produced numerous sets of figures from the units, none of them made sense.

An outside accountant's report confirmed that the system needed to be changed completely, and a new one was drafted. A memo was circulated, calling for a meeting of all division managers in order to present the new accounting format and the rationale for change. Both the finance manager and the heads of the individual agribusinesses were present. Within a few minutes, the Scottish manager knew that he was facing a solid block of resistance – nobody was going to accept the new format. Exchanges became quite heated, as the managers refused to accept his arguments and accused him of being a one-man show, not consulting them and so on.

The Scottish manager called a five-minute break to allow tempers to cool, then began again, patiently explaining why the system had to be changed and answering all criticisms. He also said he would not give in, that whether it took an hour or 24 hours, the meeting would not end until the new format was accepted. In an ever more hostile atmosphere, one manager finally rose to his feet and, in what the Scottish manager afterwards realised was probably the only time in his life he had given an honest opinion in a meeting with his boss, actually shouted: 'We do not want this. Don't you realise that if we change, people can understand our figures? We want no one to understand our figures.'

Processes and Systems

These are at the heart of change and vital to the success of the integration process. First and foremost is the need to ensure that the acquired company's production processes are in line with those of the investing firm. Technological incompatibility, of IT platforms for example, can be a particularly thorny issue that needs to be sorted out straight away. Delays are likely to lead to more expense later on, so it is better to make the investment in the early days while the change process is in full swing.

Ideally, the due diligence process will have itemised all the areas in the product process that need to be changed, committed the necessary resources for training and the replacement or updating of equipment. This is important where equipment, originally of good quality and technically sophisticated, has been badly installed and poorly maintained during its life. Improving production will almost inevitably mean new management, since often plant managers will have been long established and surrounded by employees who are friends or relatives.

Another frequent obstacle to change is the manufacturing culture in Asia. Any attempt to talk of increased production to meet changed economic circumstances, a keener competitive environment or future challenges is likely to be met by blank incomprehension. As far as existing managers and workers might be concerned, the factory has increased output over the years and that is quite sufficient. There may also be a strong union presence. To get workers to accept new practices or feel able to suggest ways of improving systems will take time and patience. Again, the key is training; taking a few key people for special courses and then cascading the new processes down.

A useful approach is to lead by example and work directly with the workforce. One European manager trying to improve production at a factory in China gained the respect and interest of the workforce by working alongside them, 'getting his hands dirty'. It also meant he could keep an eye on what they were doing. Another experienced Dutch expatriate found himself pulling on cables in the rain and mud on a factory site in Indonesia but, again, he found that it was the best way of demonstrating how to do the job. Yet another, senior Australian manager, who had been more or less office-bound for many years, was surprised to find himself hanging upside down from the roof joists, doing electrical work to keep the newly acquired factory going. It's usually more important for expatriate Western managers to be seen doing such tasks than it is for local Asian managers.

Quality Improvement

ISO 9000 registration is becoming increasingly sought after in Asia. However, it is often difficult to get local managers to take working towards it seriously, since it means a lot of documentation work or written procedures that are alien. A faster first step is to set up a quality control department staffed by trained workers. Previously, many factories either lacked such a department or it functioned badly.

Coordination Mechanisms

Once a company has several acquisitions in different countries in the region, it faces the problem of how to organise the relationship between them in order to leverage value. An extension of this is how to organise the relationship between the Asian subsidiaries and the home base. The problem is how to strike a balance between too loose a rein, which can result in subsidiaries wasting resources competing with each other and fighting turf wars, and too strict a mechanism that merely adds a further layer of bureaucracy with expensive overheads. Out of the various formal coordinating mechanisms tried in the past, the two most popular solutions have been regional headquarters and country managers.

During the 1990s, regional headquarters (RHQs), usually based in Hong Kong or Singapore, became fashionable. Through them, companies hoped to capture synergies and square the circle of the ongoing battle between geography, function and product. This frequently resulted in hostilities, when the demands of global product managers clashed with those of local managers more attuned to the sensitivities of their particular markets. However, there were advantages. Having a senior manager based out in the region, it was argued, would send a strong signal that the company was committed to its Asian investment. In addition, the regional base could act as a funnel for continued information collection and begin to formulate a regional strategy to increase the pace of growth.

Unfortunately, many of these RHQs only added an extra layer to the organisational and administrative hierarchy out in the region, an unwelcome development for hard-pressed subsidiary heads. Regional directors, moreover, ended up spending a vast amount of time in the air, either between the subsidiaries or flying back to home base for meetings. Generally, these structures proved neither successful in becoming a focus for investment in the region, nor in resolving the local/product manager clash.

With the Asian currency crisis, many of them were closed down. Three years later there was a move to reopen RHQs, but this time in Hong Kong rather than Singapore, a sign of the changing direction in Asian investment. But by 2003, the pull of China was proving irresistible and the next round of moves left Hong Kong losing out to Shanghai and Beijing.

The appointment of country managers, tasked to look after geographical and political dimensions, was another attempt by multinationals to ensure that local responsiveness was not swamped by the emphasis on globalisation. However, as several companies found when they tried the experiment, in any fight involving product and geography, product won hands down, and the hapless country managers, lacking any real authority, found themselves quite powerless and irrelevant.

In the end, the verdict on attempts to impose a coordinating mechanism across subsidiaries in Asia seems to be that, while it is important to make sure that managers in a region meet to get to know each other and exchange information, imposing a formal structure is not necessarily the most effective, and certainly not the cheapest, way to do so. Regular meetings in subgroups or in task forces and workshops, in the presence of senior managers from the centre who are there to listen as much as advise, seem to be a better first step to building a mechanism that can actually deliver something of value and help bed down new acquisitions.

Key Lessons

- Have a clear, well-designed PMI plan
- Send out the best people you can to implement it
- Communicate what you are doing and why
- Mobilise the commitment and resources for change
- Be patient. Remember the Japanese proverb: 'It takes ten years to grow a tree, but it takes a century to educate people.'

Notes

1 Interview by M. Javidan, 'Siemens CEO Heinrich von Pierer on cross-border acquisitions', *Academy of Management Executive*, 2002, 16(1).
2 Ibid.
3 Taken from 'Champaca Survives?', case study by Charlotte Butler, 1999 INSEAD-EAC.
4 *Asiaweek*, 'IT Crunch Time', May 2001, pp24–9.
5 *EIU Business Asia*, 'Stemming the flow', 6 March, 2000, pp3–4.
6 *Far Eastern Economic Review*, 'The Battle to Retain IT Talent', 15 February, 2001, p70.
7 *EIU Business China*, 'China on the couch', 28 September, 1998, pp2–3.
8 Taken from 'Changing the Figures', case study by Charlotte Butler and Professor Henri-Claude de Bettignies, 1994 INSEAD-EAC.

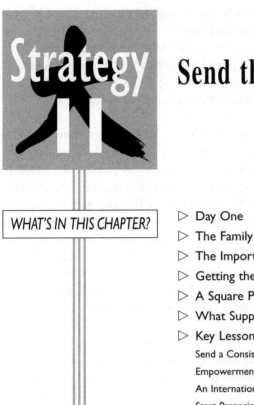

Strategy 11

Send the Right People

Day One

So here you are on your first day of your posting, installed in an office which could be in a tower block in downtown Jakarta or Central District in Hong Kong, in a special economic zone near Shanghai, a portakabin on a building site in Sumatra or perhaps overlooking a factory floor on a new industrial estate on the edge of Bangkok. If you really drew the short straw, your office might be in a run-down, formerly state-owned enterprise building on the banks of the Yangtse, with the smell of the rubbish drifting by and an overflowing spittoon in the corner of the meeting room – a sign of a long-standing local habit which you may or may not get used to.

Whatever the case, it certainly isn't home. You flew in with your family yesterday, and the heat and smells hit you forcefully as you climbed into the limousine at the airport, and the landscape as you drove into town was definitely not European or American. You are excited about the challenge as the job was presented, but now that reality kicks in, you are feeling rather isolated and daunted. If this is your first time in Asia, so you should be.

Perhaps your company has just acquired a local firm or transformed a long-standing joint venture into a wholly owned subsidiary and sent you out to lead the integration process; your job is to change the culture, expand production and generally make it more of a strategic fit. Perhaps you are taking over a joint venture that is not delivering and are there to 'sort it out', or maybe you are taking over from another colleague on a three-year rotational assignment in an Asian subsidiary. Whatever the case, responsibility for your home company's investment is now yours alone – the business development team and due diligence experts have moved their caravanserai on to the next target, the human resources director and the head of Asian operations who sent you there are far away back at headquarters.

Of course, you have the long-term corporate strategy to guide you, and within it your own particular mission and targets plus spreadsheets showing financial growth projections for the next five years. But what looked to be a straightforward, clearly structured business development plan back at head office or in the sanitised surroundings of regional head-quarters in Singapore can take on a very different picture once you are actually in place, and it is implementation time. Now you have to make the projected figures turn into the actual profits that will help to make your company Big in Asia.

At the micro-level, how its Asian operations are managed will be the key to the return that a company obtains on its investment there. Yet it is remarkable how poorly prepared are most expatriate managers sent out to run them. This is because appointments are generally made in a hurry, with time for only a minimal briefing. The lucky ones might get a trip out to visit the company before deciding whether or not to accept a posting to Asia but, in the days of budget cuts, this is becoming less and less likely. Some multinationals make an attempt to give their managers information about the country and the job – perhaps even sending them on a cultural course – but the reality of what it will mean to manage in such a very different cultural context is not easily conveyed in a classroom. Often there is little overlap between the departing expatriate and the new arrival, so there is no time for a proper handover. The new manager inherits an unknown situation and then has to spend the next 12 months on a voyage of discovery – whom to trust, what to do, how to go about it; all a terrible waste of a highly expensive resource.

The Family

Another dimension that is often ignored in sending someone off on a foreign posting is the effect on their family. Spouses are suddenly transported into a new environment, cut off from all their familiar support systems and finding themselves coping alone, with a partner who is working long days. Of course, for some, the expatriate lifestyle can be luxurious compared with conditions at home, especially for those based in Hong Kong or Singapore. Those benefiting from contracts stipulating large apartments, club membership and so on can have a wonderful time and, for most spouses, the perks of Asia include a nice apartment or a house with a pool, an amah for the children and even a cook and a driver.

But even these can turn out to be flawed. In all probability, the kitchen is overrun with cockroaches, stomach upsets are rife and the amah is spoiling the children. A young mother cannot take her baby out for a walk in Bangkok or Jakarta – even if there was a pavement it would be impossible to manoeuvre a pram along it and the air, polluted by fumes from a thousand exhausts, will soon give the baby a nasty cough. Often there is little scope for spouses who might want to work and, in the resulting vacuum, boredom and loneliness can put a heavy strain on a marriage. Alternatively, spouses who move to remote locations in the forests of Indonesia or Thailand may find themselves living in rudimentary accommodation on a factory site, where watching TV is a challenge as the generator usually breaks down several times a day. And if you become ill, the hospital is some distance away.

More than ever before, therefore, it is important for multinationals to consider carefully which people to choose for a posting to Asia and what sort of preparation to give them beforehand. Beyond that, they must also think about another critical but often neglected side of managing in Asia, how to organise the relationship between the multinational head office and its expatriate managers once they are in place. Unfortunately, in the excitement of planning and implementing strategies for growth in Asia, these issues are usually somewhat neglected, with negative consequences for the success of the posting for both sides.

The Importance of Being an Expatriate

In the past, as we have seen, Asia has not been high on the list of investment targets for Western multinationals. Even during the boom years of the 1990s, firms were at first slow to understand the growth possibilities of the region, and later held exaggerated expectations. Their emphasis was on gaining a foothold to keep up with their competitors and making short-term profits, rather than building up a good cadre of managers with Asian expertise who could run the business for long-term growth and solidly based prosperity. Those expatriate managers sent to Asia often found themselves overwhelmed by the number of VIP visitors from headquarters – main board members, corporate strategists, even the chairman – demanding a guided tour of 'our Asian interests'.

In the wake of the currency crisis of 1997, the instinct of many Western multinationals was to withdraw until the better times came round again, perhaps leaving a lone manager in charge of a scaled-down operation. Others saw the crisis as providing unparalleled acquisition opportunities at bargain basement prices. But as many of them now realise, having read it so often in the business press, making an acquisition is only the opening paragraph of the story. If they are not to lose the plot, but achieve the sort of returns on these investments that their shareholders require, they will have to manage their Asian operations much more effectively than ever they have in the past.

This means exerting a measure of control and introducing new management methods to integrate these acquisitions into their global empire. To accomplish this vital task, they need to send in expatriate managers whose multifaceted task includes the introduction of organisational and cultural change, retraining the locals, straightening out the finances and making quality improvements in production. Then once the industry picks up again, their operations would be ready to work at maximum efficiency. For their investment to deliver, a lot will depend on the ability of these expatriate managers – most of them inexperienced in running Asian operations – to manage a sensitive relationship, especially in countries where foreign buyers are characterised as 'vultures' in the local press.

Clearly then, whether a company is supporting a lone representative in a scaled-down operation, sending out an expatriate manager to integrate an acquisition, or marking time while waiting for the door to China to open, the message for its senior corporate team is the same; a crucial factor in the success or failure of your investment will be the calibre of your expatriate managers on the ground. The importance of being an expatriate in Asia has never been so crucial.

Getting the Best

Unfortunately, HR departments have not, in the past, been spoilt for choice when selecting candidates for an Asian posting. Given the ambivalent attitude of Western multinationals towards their regional operations over recent years, this is not really surprising. Taking their cue from head office, neither corporate HR departments nor ambitious young managers have seen Asia as a plum job, a chance to perform in a highly strategic part of the corporate empire.

Rather, it has been a road to nowhere – less a case of making your mark than of blowing your future in some forgotten country few can readily find on a map. The success of Douglas Daft, who took over as CEO of Coca-Cola after 20 years developing its operations in Asia, beginning in Indonesia in the 1970s, is still an exception rather than the rule. More likely is the reaction experienced by a young manager sent out to South Korea early in 2000, who was asked by his neighbour on the plane out to Seoul: 'Where did you screw up in your last job?' One oil company refused to let its executives take familiarisation trips, on the grounds that 'If the manager knew where he was going, he would never take the job'.

More often, a posting to Asia has been seen as an opportunity to get rid of someone considered a maverick, someone who 'doesn't fit in', or even as a punishment. In the 1980s and early 1990s, many companies sent young, inexperienced managers who were considered dispensable or, at the other end of the age scale, people who were approaching retirement, to while away their last working years. Only in the middle to late 1990s did potential high-flyers begin to take an interest in an Asian posting, a trend that quickly died down again with the Asian crash.

This is because for many multinationals, despite their much vaunted claims to be global, Asia still represents only a small percentage of their portfolio. The weight of their interests and therefore the perceived glory lies in the US or Europe, and even Eastern Europe or Latin America are viewed as higher up the corporate wish list by ambitious managers. Not unnaturally, therefore, they focus their hopes on a tour of duty where their efforts are most likely to bring them to the attention of top management. Asian operations are still a long way from the centre of power at headquarters, and managers sent there fear being forgotten in some small outpost in Vietnam or China. Perhaps they have too often seen returnees fail to reintegrate successfully, or even be paid off as 'there is nothing for you here', to want to copy them.

Of course, some expatriate managers do catch the 'Asia virus' and settle in so thoroughly that they do not want to return to their home base but, since to go native is not seen as desirable either, fast-track promotion is again not readily associated with time spent managing there, as many of the old Asia hands to be found in the clubs and bars of the region testify.

However, in the future, companies will not be able to leave things to chance. If they wish to take advantage of the next upturn in investment in Asia, when the competition will be even keener, they must begin now to make a positive effort to train and develop managers to send there. Equally, they must give out the right signals about the priority attached to an Asian posting so that only the best apply. But, even before this, they need to identify the particular qualities that will make a manager most suited to this very particular environment.

A Square Peg for a Square Hole

So what skills are needed to be an effective manager in Asia? If you are the HR director of a large multinational, what factors should you keep in mind when choosing who should run your operations there? Too often in the past, head office selectors have failed to appreciate that not everyone can adapt to a new culture, and that the qualities that make for a good manager in the aggressive markets of the US or Europe will not necessarily be appropriate or effective in the more consensual environment of Asia.

As many expatriate managers have discovered, in Asia none of their usual standards apply when it comes to assessing market potential or financial worth, and as for managing local people, all their previous experience counts for nothing. Those used to working within formal structures that give security, or who in the past relied on the strict application of financial ratios before making a decision, must learn to operate in an ambiguous and volatile environment. In Asia, hard information is difficult if not impossible to come by, events can change rapidly and risk-taking is a natural part of doing business. Someone who manages by the rule book, has a strong individual streak or is an aggressive exponent of Western management concepts is unlikely to thrive in such a different environment, or to have more than a temporary success.

Nowhere else are political and negotiating skills so vital. Life in Asia, observed one seasoned expatriate, is 'one long negotiation'. This will include negotiating with local politicians, city or regional government representatives and officials at every level from ministries to foreign investment boards or trade councils, through unions and local suppliers down to the customs officer, not counting the daily negotiations needed to manage the workforce, its local managers and perhaps the joint venture partner. And remember, this must be done via an interpreter whom you must trust to convey the exact sense of your words. Chances are you will be unable to communicate directly with anyone except your personal secretary and most senior managers, and you cannot rely on the local newspaper to find out what is happening or what is being written about your company.

Any list of qualities and skills necessary for managing in Asia would probably include the following; resourceful, entrepreneurial, gregarious, patient and tolerant, a creative attitude to systems, a team player with good communication, negotiating and political skills, self-reliant, able to cope with high stress levels, build consensus, think on your feet, establish trust, and convince people to act in a way that is radically different from their previous habits in their working lives. Not an easy profile to fulfil.

And all this is only to be able to deal with the local environment; an equally heavy strain may be connected with the demands of the home base. For the expatriate is in place not just to manage a company but also to fulfil the targets and expectations of the corporate centre. These will probably encompass a variety of dimensions from increased production, improved quality and faster delivery to cutting costs or manpower while expanding the business and, of course, increasing profits, all in the shortest possible time. But London or Houston will probably have little under-standing of the reality of the business environment in which you are competing, or the true potential of its local company. Thus these targets may be ill-conceived or unrealistic and almost certainly will fail to take into account the long-term view that building a business in Asia requires, since the expectations of the home stock market and its shareholders will not allow it such a luxury. Little wonder that expatriates often find them-selves torn in two as they try to satisfy the interests of such diametrically opposed stakeholders, to be a success in headquarters' terms at the same time as they are themselves adapting to a new culture and struggling to come to grips with a foreign business environment.

To avoid such conflicts, headquarters need to ensure effective commun-ications between themselves and their overseas managers. No longer is it enough to send them off with a cheery wave and a 'See you in three years' time'. They need to be in regular and close contact to ensure that their demands are based on a true evaluation of the situation. This means giving careful consideration to what sort of information they collect and analyse before setting targets for their Asian subsidiaries, and to the back-up that they provide to help their expatriates do their jobs in good and bad times.

What kind of support systems should head office put in place to ensure smooth communications between itself and its overseas managers?

What Support Systems?

The ideal, real support effort supplied by headquarters would probably include a specific coordination team at the centre, headed by an 'Asian champion' who has pull at the highest level and consisting of people familiar with the business and cultural context. This team would be ready and able to, for example, respond quickly to faxes, appeals for help or information, perhaps negotiate with product groupings to arrange any special prices needed, send out any technical advisors necessary, supply training requests and, of course, boost the morale of those in the field. Such a system would be an expatriate's dream. Unfortunately, it rarely exists.

More typical is the experience of one German manager who found himself based in a factory in a small outpost in China, where he was at odds with his Japanese and Chinese joint venture partners over vital resource decisions and had little real power. Daily meetings deteriorated to a shouting match – albeit slowly due to the need for three-way interpreters. Often he went back to his hotel room in tears of frustration to drown his sorrows with Tsingtao beer in the empty hotel bar, knowing that his feelings about what should be done were not shared back at head office.

It is generally accepted that a company's attitude to managing its overseas subsidiaries reflects what has become known as its 'administrative heritage'; how it organised itself in the past. This can either be a source of key competencies or represent a brake on the company's ability to change, and tends to be identified with the centralisation/decentralisation debate. Companies favouring the former try to maintain strict control over what their subsidiaries are doing via control of capital expenditure (cap ex) and budgets, those following the latter adopt a more laissez-faire attitude, whereby local chairmen are given a fair amount of autonomy over how they run their operations. Neither one is ideal, and carried to extremes can be damaging.

British-based Inchcape and Unilever, for example, both historically took a decentralised approach, encouraging a culture of strong, local, self-sufficient operations overseas. This gave both groups great strength in terms of local responsiveness and knowledge, their managers had wide scope to act within the overall corporate plan and were able to take decisions quickly. Consequently, both saw a rapid expansion of their Asian interests due to the entrepreneurial efforts of their managers. In both groups, managers needed to have overseas experience to climb the company ladder and a posting to Asia was favourably viewed. Unilever attempted to build up a regional cadre of managers, while Inchcape left its managers in place for most of their careers, bringing them back to head office at a senior level where they could use their experience to coordinate communications between London and the countries where they had worked.

Wella, the German hair products company, also built up a strong position in Asia way ahead of other rivals such as L'Oréal due to the entrepreneurial efforts of one expatriate manager. He went out to Japan in 1969 with just US$20,000 to be used to develop a business in Japan 'because it was a big market'. In the event, this sum proved inadequate for the task and he was forced to use his own money but, within a short time, he had successfully broken into this supposedly closed market. He then supervised Wella's expansion throughout the region to give it a head start on the rest of the European competition. On the other hand, unfettered entrepreneurialism can be dangerous if it leads to the building of fiefdoms, run by managers who take no notice of the centre and destroy value by acting unilaterally against the wider interests of the group.

Centralisation implies a much greater restriction on the freedom of local expatriate managers to act in this entrepreneurial manner. It is usually associated with excessive bureaucracy at the centre, and phrases such as 'finance driven' and 'risk averse' to describe senior management. In particular, it implies the imposition of strict controls (especially of finance) and formal systems, manifested by an emphasis on regular requests for information and weekly or monthly form-filling to produce short-term targets with a heavy emphasis on rates of return.

Such a culture is often not applicable in an Asian context. Where local managers are so constrained by having to refer back every decision and wait for an answer, their frustration can be immense. 'If death came from Spain, we should all be immortal' was the famous remark made concerning Philip II of Spain's notorious inability to prioritise and give a swift reply to his ambassadors abroad. Managers waiting for urgent answers to faxes demanding permission to do deals or spend beyond a cap-ex level set so low as to be excessively restrictive know exactly how they felt. If a response is swift and demonstrates an understanding of the situation, well and good, but, as one Unilever manager remarked, 'the windows of opportunity in Asia are small and close up very quickly', so waiting for permission might mean the loss of a golden chance.

A senior Inchcape manager put the view more succinctly: 'I find it hard to understand how somebody sitting in London can second guess the guys who are in the market every day, 2,000 miles away.' He was not the only one. Many of its managers believed that it was the imposition of central control via global business streaming that led to the destruction of Inchcape's greatest skill, its historic ability to operate as a local player, and that this in turn contributed to the eventual decline of the group.

Key Lessons

Send a Consistent Message

If a company is serious about becoming bigger in Asia, it is vital that everyone in the company, the shareholders and the stock markets all receive this message and understand its implications. Investment in Asia is long term and entails the expenditure of much patience and financial resources with no fast payback – in fact in all probability it will mean taking a loss for the first few years.

This message must be sent loudly and consistently, and backed up by actions to demonstrate that, for example, a posting in Asia is not a second-class appointment. This implies that corporate HR directors must ensure that career plans include re-entry strategies for managers coming back from Asia, signalling that such experience is considered important for future promotion. This may mean quite a change in the culture at the centre to get high-flying managers to apply to go there, and to work it needs powerful business units to forsake their usual markets and invest in a region usually seen as high risk. This is easier said than done; if they did not invest when the region was booming, how can they be convinced when it is in the doldrums? One way, tried by the oil company BP, was to set up a target of 'x' per cent of assets in the region within five years for its business units, which at least served to concentrate minds. Where strong business units go, then ambitious managers will generally follow.

Other companies have emphasised the competitive dimension: we cannot afford to be left out if everyone else is established there, and those with the longest relationships do get the favoured deals and so on. Another way is to appoint a group of respected senior managers to spread the word and act as drivers for Asian investment; yet another is to send business unit chiefs on seminars to inform them about opportunities, or hold workshops in the region to showcase what can be achieved. Of course, the strongest signal would be to put an Asian manager on the board, but few companies have dared to go this far – yet.

Empowerment

Empowerment is not the same as leaving managers to sink or swim alone in their Asian postings. Rather, it means a recognition that a degree of autonomy is important in the countries of the region, local contacts and knowledge count far more than in other parts of the world and therefore a certain latitude in decision making must be left to the man on the spot, even though this might impinge on the interests of the global products division. It also implies putting in a structure and back-up systems, with experienced people in place at the centre able both to respond to requests, and supply help or informed advice as needed. Local managers can find themselves quite isolated at times, and in case of trouble need to know that there are reliable allies back home.

An International Cadre

One step further on from this might be the development of an international cadre of managers, experienced in different cultures and able to act quickly and effectively, while avoiding the extremes of going native or remaining stuck in their own cultural habits. Some companies, such as Unilever and Lafarge, have already tried this; Lafarge has developed an entry level for managers when they reach 35–40 years to train and take on an international role. Unilever, finding that many local managers in Asia were reluctant to move out of the region, concentrated on giving them the opportunity to change jobs within neighbouring countries, so developing a regional cadre.

Start Preparing Now

No company that wants to be global can afford to ignore Asia even in the years since the Asian economic crisis. However, when the next upswing comes, the pickings will not be as easy as before. Everyone is wiser all round. In this tighter competitive arena, a crucial factor in distinguishing winners from losers will be the ability of their people to manage in Asia, and of the corporate centre to give the right support in terms of human, financial and organisational resources. Start training your managers and spreading the right message now.

How 'ready' is your company to send staff to Asia?

1. Is Asia considered a good ladder to promotion?

2. Is commitment to the region clear?

3. Is there an attempt to spread enthusiasm for Asia within the company?

4. Are support systems at the corporate centre well adapted to ensure mutual confidence?

5. Are there informal and formal networks for spreading information about Asia?

6. Do HR directors have re-entry strategies for career planning for those returning from Asian postings?

7. Is there an attempt to spread knowledge and experience of Asia within the company?

8. Is managing in Asia a component of executive training programmes?

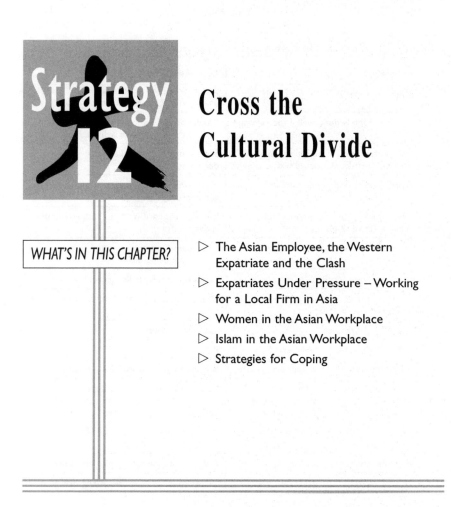

Strategy 12

Cross the Cultural Divide

The Asian Employee, the Western Expatriate and the Clash

Managing local staff and their expectations is a key to being Big in Asia. If you're an expatriate, managing a team that is outside your own culture might well be one of the hardest things you will ever do in your career. Many who have worked as expatriates in Asia say that their time there was among the most rewarding of their careers. Their time may not have always been happy, and was probably often frustrating, but most would agree that it was always interesting.

Stereotypes are not always accurate but they do contain more than a grain of truth, which is why they arise. Table 12.1 shows a comparison

Table 12.1 Comparison between local employees and Western expatriates

The Asian Employee	The Western Expatriate
Is most comfortable if there are strict orders to follow	Sees strict orders as insulting and undermining of personal integrity
Works to rule – a job is done well if the rules are followed	Results driven – a job is done well if the desired goals have been achieved
Prefers strict instructions, close supervision and unlikely to take the risks associated with creativity	Self-starting, likes to take initiative and demonstrate creativity
Views orders as commands to be followed	Views orders as suggestions to be modified and improved upon
Believes that loyalty to one's superiors and the firm counts above all else	Believes that hard work and honesty count above all else
Prefers teamwork and a lot of supervision	Prefers small or no teams and as little supervision as possible
Views the employer as a 'father'	Views the employer as a colleague
Prefers either no performance-based pay or only if it is averaged across the team	Likes performance-based pay to be linked to own efforts
Prefer little or no work travel	Likes work travel
Prefers lots of small vacation leave periods	Prefers few but long vacation leave periods
Will resign rather than air a workplace grievance	Is quick to voice workplace grievances
Will rarely voice an opinion in a meeting, particularly in front of local work colleagues – meetings are to hear what superiors have to say	Likes the dynamism and debate of work meetings – meetings are an opportunity for input and voicing concerns
Accepts boredom in the workplace if it is a consequence of following superior's orders	Would rather resign than be bored
Output must be monitored closely for quality	Able to self-monitor output for quality
Able to operate with only partial knowledge about the company	Wants to be privy to everything that goes on in the firm
Has difficulty delivering bad news or complaints to superiors even if it means telling half-truths	Happy to deliver bad news to anyone in the interests of transparency

between common attributes of locals and Westerners in Asia in their roles as employees. Few workplaces in Asia where locals and Westerners are employed are as harmonious as they could be.

Workplace Factions

The workplace might split into factions when relations between locals and expatriate employees are not carefully managed, with local employees on one side and expatriates on the other. This can happen particularly when there are frustrations on either side – the expatriates might be viewed by the locals as apt to look down on them and the expatriates might have developed a poor regard for the skills of the locals and, as a result, are frustrated.

The salary and promotion expectations of local employees require careful management. Often in countries such as Indonesia, Vietnam and Thailand local employees do not appreciate the gap between their technical skills and those of the typical Asian or Western expatriate. Consequently, the expatriates might seem overpaid to the local staff who do not recognise the relative extent of the expatriates' skills. A view might develop that the expatriates are paid more simply because they are expatriates, American, 'white' or whatever. This is a potentially dangerous workplace issue that must be handled carefully and sensitively.

Hiring new and very good local staff members can help. If they are good, the expatriates will gravitate to them, demonstrating that the issue that might be at the heart of the expatriate's dissatisfaction is skills related and not race related. Occasionally, disharmony between foreign and local staff can be the result of one or a few local staff agitating against the expatriate staff, stirring up concern among the locals. Managers need to identify who the agitators are and work out the best way to neutralise their activities. Access to training opportunities is one way of closing the skills gap, rewarding good local employees and developing a more dynamic and harmonious working environment.

Bad News

How information is shared is a big issue in Asian firms. It is one of the most important commodities in the workplace, so managers must be careful to have in place structures to facilitate its circulation. Bad news brings blame and loss of face, so it is the most difficult form of information to have delivered in a timely fashion. Often the rot will set in, more junior staff will know about it but don't feel able to tell anyone about it. It's usually only discovered after the damage has been done.

Bringing bad news can cause a loss of face. It can be seen as confronting a superior even though the messenger might only be just that – the carrier of the message. Consequently, shooting the messenger is a common practice in Asia. 'Why would you tell me this if you did not believe it yourself?' It's an unfortunate bind. The messenger acts out of loyalty, but his actions are interpreted as disloyalty.

Anonymous poison-pen letters are one way in which local staff might voice their concerns. But rarely will it be the excellent employees who resort to this technique. The letters are usually slanderous. Their anonymity adds to the general lack of transparency rather than helps it.

Local Labour Departments

One big surprise for many outsiders who come to Asia is that labour laws in most countries are not nearly as liberal as the Western media portrays them to be. While trade unions may not be powerful, local labour laws can be highly restrictive. Indonesia's are among the most restrictive in Asia. The Department of Manpower frequently intervenes on behalf of local employees, particularly if it is an obviously wealthy Western firm that is the employer. Overzealous labour ministry officials might be seeking bribes to halt their harassment. It happens. The best way to deal with these issues is to appoint a trusted local member of staff to manage relations with the labour ministry. That person's responsibilities include the need to develop good relations with officials, keep abreast of all new regulations to ensure that they are not contravened and learn about the structure of the ministry so that the company can protect itself particularly, say, if vexatious former employees wish to mobilise the ministry to cause trouble for their former employers.

Expatriates Under Pressure – Working for a Local Firm in Asia

There are four types of professional in Asia. There are locals who are educated locally and those who are Western-educated. There are Westerners who work in the Asian offices of Western firms, and there are the Western expatriates who work in Asian firms.

The latter group is ignored by almost all the literature on management in Asia. Almost all guides on how to cope as a Western expatriate in Asia assume that you will be working for a Western company. The difficulties faced by expatriates who work for a local firm in Asia are little appreciated and understood.

Many leave for Asia expecting the good life of an expatriate and assuming that they will be valued employees in an organisation eager to modernise and utilise their skills. Most are disappointed, while many return home bewildered, disappointed and angry.

Why should this be so? Outside Japan and mainland China, most firms in Asia – big or small – are owned and managed by families, and the companies are run as extensions of the families. Western expatriates in Asian firms face the problem that, while they are employees and probably highly paid ones, they will almost always be viewed as outsiders. Their seniority will be judged not by any formal internal organisation chart but by their perceived closeness to the controlling family.

Rarely will they command the trust and respect in these companies that is commensurate with their level and position, as compared with working back home. For many it is a rude shock. Management at home is participative. But in the Asian firm they must get used to following orders, never really knowing what's going on and get used to not trying to find out. Many Western expatriates in Asian firms soon discover that they are grossly overpaid, given their lack of empowerment.

Many find that when they first arrive, the more junior local employees are appropriately deferential. But after some time, and if it becomes clear that they do not enjoy the full confidence of the controlling family, their position in the unofficial hierarchy starts to slide. They might even find themselves a target for anti-expatriate or anti-Western feeling when it becomes clear that they lack a powerful patron within the organisation. Many an expatriate responds by working harder, feeling that their increased work effort will win the day. But they've missed the point. A valued employee is not one who is necessarily productive. It's loyalty to the controlling family that counts rather than to the firm or the other shareholders.

Added complications come from the lack of transparency within the firm. Asian firms often do not have formal internal codes of conduct and written rules. Everything depends on the whim of senior management and the founding family. Written rules mean inflexibility and a ceding of control – and Asian corporate patriarchs usually have little desire to share power with a rule book.

A newspaper column by one of the authors of *Big in Asia* on the difficulties of working as a Western expatriate for local firms in Asia drew many responses from readers who wanted to share their experiences. Nearly all spoke of feeling 'disempowered' in their jobs in Asia and the deep frustration and distress that caused.

Asian employees are comfortable with a higher degree of workplace supervision than are Westerners. The paradox of the Asian workplace is that absolute loyalty above all else is demanded of employees by management and yet that demand for loyalty does not translate into the workplace being a high-trust environment. Everything must be micro-managed and initiative is discouraged.

One former expatriate in Hong Kong who had been working for a local firm said that after returning to a job in the West she was shown the stationery cupboard at her new workplace and told to help herself. 'I nearly burst into tears', she said. 'The previous job [in Asia] had me fill out a form for every pen and I was told that I was showing disloyalty to the company for using three writing pads over four months to the total value of US$2.50.' She felt undervalued and underutilised for much of her time in Asia. Big achievements were ignored and instead she felt that she was measured on little things such as her stationery use. She reported that occasionally she would get together with other former expatriates and they would discuss their experiences over a drink but she abandoned this. It was 'too emotionally draining'. She, like other Western expatriates who had spent time in Asia working for local firms, was still too angry to relive the experiences.

Another former expatriate who had worked for a local firm in Japan described the experience as 'feudal' and the managers as 'bureaucrats rather than managers'. He felt undervalued, not trusted and valued not as a potential long-term employee but merely for his short-term, 'stop-gap' capabilities. In that regard, another former expatriate described having been employed by a local firm in Hong Kong to help it to restructure. The changes that he suggested should be made were used as an excuse to fire eight staff and with that the expatriate's usefulness evaporated, he was starved of work and he resigned to flee the boredom.

Many expatriates talk of the importance of trust. It seems their productivity is never doubted. But it's not all about gaining the trust of management only. Many Western expatriates find that they must battle on two fronts – above and beneath them. Said another former expatriate:

> Expats are not trusted because of their short-term contribution, which lends itself to a self-reinforcing cycle. The power rests with those who stay in the company, have developed links with the more junior staff and thus gain their loyalty. Locals who are Western educated understand this and adapt accordingly.

Expatriates in local firms in Asia tend to either resign early or stay because of the financial benefits and because typically their title is more superior than what they could achieve at home, and they want to 'leverage' it for a better job next time around. Rarely, however, are Western expatriates in Asian firms happy. So why do so many Asian firms bother hiring expensive Western expatriates but then don't bother to get the best out of them?

Expatriate staff are often used for their stopgap capabilities. They can go in, tread on the toes that need to be trodden on in a way that hierarchy-aware locals won't dare to and then be dispensed with. This makes them ideal for troubleshooting. But also it makes them short-term employees. Again, there is a mismatch of expectations. They expect that the reforms they make will see them rewarded but instead they might be shown the door. Their job is done and with them can go the blame for the inevitable unpleasantness that change in the workplace brings.

At other times they are hired by Asian firms to provide prestige or present a Western face when it's time to seek loans from Western banks or deal with Western fund managers. In this case, they need not be terribly productive at all. Their job really is to be corporate window-dressing. Their job is to make the Asian firm look modern, professionally run and sophisticated. They might not be empowered and it might still be the controlling family that calls all the shots but it's the mirage that counts.

Whatever the case, rarely are the Western expatriates who go to work for Asian firms in Asia prepared for the mental maze of their new workplaces. Some have a very fulfilling time but many leave Asia feeling that their skills and time have been wasted. Their experience is often completely different from the typical Western expatriate who goes to Asia to work for the local branch of a Western company.

Women in the Asian Workplace

Women play a significant role in the Asian workplace and nowhere is that more true than in East Asia's two main Islamic countries, Indonesia and Malaysia. This might seem counterintuitive to some outsiders who equate Islam with the subjugation with women. There are even some ethnic groups that are matrilineal. It is the women who are the decision makers and it is the daughters who inherit the property, leaving the sons with nothing. For example, the Minangkabau people who originate in West Sumatra in Indonesia and Malaysia's Negri Sembilan State are matrilineal.

Women play a role that is both full and prominent in Malaysia and Indonesia. It is common to see women in senior management positions in both the civil service and the private sectors in these countries.

In the professional and managerial category in Malaysia's federal public sector, almost 43% of officers are women. Given that women do take time out to have babies and raise young children when men don't, such a high figure is extraordinary. There are also several women who serve as secretary-generals of ministries. In higher education, the number of female students at the institutions of higher learning is more than 50% of the total enrolment. Affirmative action policies for women might be needed in the United States but clearly not in Malaysia.

Then Malaysian Prime Minister Mahathir Mohamed appointed Zeti Akhtar Aziz as the governor of Bank Negara, Malaysia's central bank in early 2001. The fact that she was a women barely rated a mention in the Malaysian media, and yet it is one of the few occasions on which a woman has been appointed to head her country's central bank. It hasn't happened in the United States, Australia or the United Kingdom, but it did happen in largely Islamic Malaysia.

Meanwhile in Indonesia – the world's largest Islamic country – a woman, Rini Soewandi, was made CEO of car assembler Astra International in 1998. Astra is one of that country's largest listed companies. It was no sinecure – her first task was to fire 25,000 people. She was removed from the job in February 2001 but that had nothing to do with her sex. The government-controlled restructuring agency IBRA demanded it after she refused to hand over information that she deemed too sensitive and her actions helped to block the sale of a controlling stake in Astra to US interests. Soewandi was later appointed Indonesia's minister for trade.

Women play substantial roles in commerce and public administration in Singapore and the Philippines. Women are less visible in Korea and Japan where society is more male and macho-oriented. The big drinking culture of business socialising in those two countries also discourages women's effective participation in the workforce at a professional level.

One reason why women in Asia can be found in senior professional roles, often at a relatively young age, is because home help is cheap and there are few labour law restrictions on it. Maids and nannies free up local professional women so that the breaks in their careers when they have children need not be as great as they are for many women in the West where home help can be prohibitively expensive.

Islam in the Asian Workplace

Where do most of the world's Muslims live? The Middle East? Wrong. The answer is Asia. The countries with the four largest Islamic populations are all in Asia. They are Indonesia (with about 210 million Muslims), Pakistan (134 million), India (120 million) and Bangladesh (109 million). The biggest Muslim populations in the Middle East are to be found in Iran and Egypt, each with about 65 million Muslims. Other countries such as Libya which has a population of just 5.2 million – almost all of whom are Muslim – might be good at grabbing press headlines but they are tiny in comparison.

With a Muslim population of around 32.5 million, there are more Muslims in China than there are in Saudi Arabia, Lebanon, Libya, Bahrain and the United Arab Emirates put together. About 60% of Malaysia's population is Muslim and there are Muslims in Singapore, Brunei, the southern Philippines, southern Thailand and western Myanmar. Many of the Indians in Malaysia are Muslims too. Locally, they are known as the 'Mamak' people.

There are five prescribed prayer times each day for observant Muslims. Many companies in Malaysia and Indonesia provide a small prayer room for this, rather than have their employees leave the premises to pray.

Ramadan – the Islamic fasting month – has a lot of significance for Muslims, even if they are not regular mosque goers. Many who are not still choose to fast. The fasting involves not eating, drinking, smoking or having sexual relations during the daylight hours. Ill people, menstruating women and travellers are exempted from fasting for that period of the fasting month that they are affected but time lost should be made up for later. The abstinence is to teach self-discipline and develop empathy with the poor.

Inevitably, fasting has a serious impact on employee productivity. Employees who at other times of the year are happy to miss prayers may become more devout during the month and pray five times each day. It is a time of the year that requires considerable forbearance on the part of employers, as many staff are irritable, productivity is low and for the first few days at least it is not uncommon to see staff practically collapsed on their desks by mid to late afternoon. Headaches cannot be relieved by aspirin because that would mean eating.

Despite the fasting, food consumption rises during Ramadan and cold-storage companies in Indonesia, Malaysia and Brunei usually carry excess capacity throughout the year so that they can cope with the huge rise in demand for space during Ramadan. How is this so? Each night during the month, many Muslims break the fast together after sundown and do so in a festive atmosphere that involves consuming a great deal of food. People take it in turns to hold an open house at which large trays of pre-prepared food are offered to friends and relatives. It provides an excellent networking opportunity and local Chinese and even some Western expatriates often turn up at their Muslim business partners and colleagues' homes to break the fast with them. The open nature of the festivities means that many use it as an opportunity to drop in on senior business figures or government officials whom ordinarily they cannot get to see.

Ramadan ends with a celebration known as Hari Raya in Malaysia and Idul Fitri in Indonesia. It is a time when Muslims first spend time with their families and then go visiting friends and other relatives. Almost all Muslim employees will want time off for this period, which is Islam's most important holiday.

Deepavali (also known as Diwali in northern India) is the most significant religious holiday for Hindus. It is celebrated on the new moon of the seventh month of the Hindu calendar – October or November). So companies that employ Hindu Indian staff, be they in Malaysia, Hong Kong, Indonesia or elsewhere, will need to take account of the likely desire of those staff to want to take holidays at this time. Deepavali is a time for new beginnings. Many Hindus see it as an auspicious time to begin a new enterprise or open a new bank savings account. And on the first day of Deepavali, most Hindus wear a complete set of new clothes.

Similarly, the most important date on the Chinese calendar is Chinese or Lunar New Year. Most Chinese employees will want to go home to spend the week with their parents – so Malaysian Chinese employees working in Singapore will want to go back to Malaysia and so on. It is a time that is spent with the family and is analogous to Christmas.

Strategies for Coping

■ As a Western expatriate in a local firm in Asia:

- Greatly lower your expectations about what you will achieve. This is the most important rule.

- Think carefully about the real reasons why you have been brought in and then operate with those in mind.

- Be prepared to sacrifice productivity for shows of loyalty. Opt for loyalty if there is a conflict between the two. Ultimately those who are trusted will be able to achieve more.

- Identify the locals who are the 'power centres' in the hierarchy both beneath and above you and attempt to form visibly good relations with them.

- Learn to be a team player and share your skills.

- Try not to mix only with other expatriates in the workplace.

- Don't expect that all severance conditions will be honoured without a fight even if they are contractual.

■ As a manager of local employees in Asia:

- Adopt a paternalistic, caring attitude, but remain aloof. Generally, you will not be able to be good friends with your local staff and also be their manager. In most of Asia, it's one or the other.

- Deliver bad news or orders that are likely to be viewed negatively within the framework of your concern for the employee. ('We have decided to move you to this new position so that you will have fewer responsibilities, which we thought would allow you to spend more time with your family', is better than 'we're downgrading your position because you are not delivering'.)

- Try not to allow local employees to lose face in front of their local colleagues. Deliver admonishments in private and in a caring, paternal manner.

- Set very clear tasks, with measurable milestones on the way to achieving the final goal. Remember to check back on those milestones.

- Singling out high-performing staff for praise might be counterproductive. It might be interpreted as an attack on everyone else and the singled out staff might feel to blame rather than proud. Try to congratulate a team, even if it means that some in the team are not deserving.

- Bad news rarely travels up, so look carefully for clues about staff dissatisfaction. Don't expect staff to complain about other local staff and managers even if they have a real grievance, and even when they are taken aside and given full opportunity to voice their concerns in private. They might still deny that there is a problem.

- Treat unexplained resignations in any particular area as a possible sign that there are management problems in that area and that staff are unhappy. Investigate carefully.

- Be prepared to set aside more time than you would prefer to monitor staff output. Be sure to give feedback – praise where it is warranted and suggestions for improvement.

- Be aware of all the local religious holidays and the obligations that these might impose on staff.

- If local staff must be fired, try to arrange for the severance to be as friendly as possible. Aggrieved ex-employees in Asia tend to be more interested in revenge than in the West.

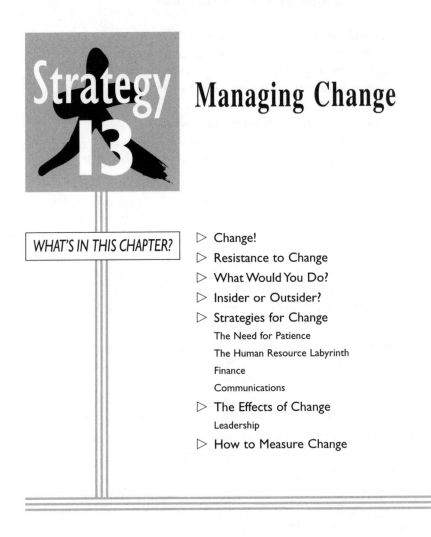

Managing Change

Change!

As we have seen, the *raison d'être* of Western multinationals making an acquisition or entering into a joint venture in the region is the opportunity it gives them to enter new markets and increase profits. Even before the deal is struck, the due diligence teams assessing the value of the targeted company will have signposted levers for change – ways to lower costs through efficiencies of scale, increase and expand production, improve quality, speed up distribution systems and so on. Where politically and socially acceptable, cutting down the workforce may also be on the agenda. Such moves will in turn be linked to the introduction of organisational, strategic and, the biggest challenge of all, cultural change.

Once the deal is done, therefore, Western multinationals will want to send in a general manager (plus possibly financial, technical or marketing experts) to look after their interests and introduce Western management concepts and operating methods. The endgame, of course, will be to integrate the Asian firm into their global organisation, enabling them to benchmark and transfer best practices across national boundaries. Consequently, for most expatriates sent out to Asia, managing a local company will mean managing change.

Resistance to Change

Change management has become a specialised branch of management; as one expatriate whose experience covered both Asia and Africa observed: 'Managing change is not an underrated skill, but it is an infrequent one.' In the past Western multinationals have discovered, to their cost, that not every manager has the skills to implement change and transform entrenched patterns of behaviour in a firm. Even more difficult is ensuring that any changes made are permanent.

In the recent past, attempts to introduce Western management methods have not always been either welcome or successful in the region; there has long been a debate in the business media about the extent to which Asia is 'different' when it comes to management. Many Asian observers have argued that Confucian values make uncomfortable bedfellows with 'management by objectives' or the hire and fire culture of Western firms. In their view, such practices are not easily transferable and run counter to the customary Asian view of the paternal relationship between employer and employee. In any case, it was frequently said, since Asian companies were doing well without their influence, their introduction was unnecessary. The events of 1997 and its aftermath rather undermined this argument, but while Asian companies have since learned the mantras of focus and corporate governance and made statements about the need to change their ways and become more transparent, deep down there is still strong resistance to such concepts. As many Western companies have found, when looking more deeply into the finances and assets of a newly 'restructured' Asian firm they might consider buying, any change is likely to be only skin-deep.

Change is never popular and in Asia can be a way of making enemies; Western managers run the risk of violence from disgruntled employees, and have occasionally been the target of death threats. Resistance –

passive or active – from those within a company to outsiders trying to change their ways is inevitable, and if well enough coordinated can effectively block or halt attempts at reform, even at the highest level.

Rana Talwar, for example, was appointed chief executive at Standard Chartered bank in a high-profile move to improve the bank's performance and revamp its old colonial image. Having targeted the usual suspects – strategy and culture – for change, he instituted a sweeping programme of reform. Among measures he implemented was the promotion of local African, Indian and Hong Kong managers to positions traditionally reserved for British expatriates. These and other measures made Talwar many enemies within the higher ranks of Standard Chartered, where his modernising efforts were not appreciated. Eventually he paid the price and, despite the support of the bank's executive directors, was ousted after only three years at the helm.

In truth, the challenge of operating in a radically different operating context, a society where both the work ethic and the cultural norms are completely different from those prevailing in the West, is enormous. That many expatriate managers have tried and failed to make any impact during their time in Asia is a matter of record, and in large part the fault of the Western firms themselves. Focused on the need for immediate productivity improvements rather than deep-seated structural or cultural change, they have tended to send in technical advisers rather than senior managers with experience of the change process. At sea in an alien culture and unable to exercise the influence that would result in any radical transformation, the poor technical managers not surprisingly chose to take the line of least resistance and concentrate on incremental productivity improvements. These delivered respectable results, but left the status quo unchanged.

For their part, the local managers took the cynical view that the expatriates would only last two to three years, and then return home. In the worst-case situation, if someone really made an effort to introduce serious change, they just battened down the hatches and waited for them to leave. They then resumed business as usual, their working practices remaining unaltered. As one veteran expatriate noted: 'Local managers in Asia are no slouches at this game. They can stitch up any manager they wish. They control all the information flows.'

In the future, this scenario will no longer be viable. Western firms wishing to be Big in Asia must send out people who can effect a deep transformation of the company, one that is measurable and that endures. This involves both structural innovation – the introduction of new systems and processes – and radical cultural change. But first know your enemy – what aspects of the Asian business culture are Western managers likely to find most difficult to deal with?

A Different Business Culture

Consider the following comments made by expatriate managers about the business culture prevailing in various countries in Southeast Asia.

'The loyalty of local employees', observed one, 'is directed towards their classmates from school and university, rather than the company that employs them. This means that they have no idea of confidentiality or secrecy about the company's business.' He was shocked to find that managers would 'quite cheerfully tell their classmates all the company's plans, with no sense of betrayal'. Working in Thailand during the booming economic climate of the mid-1990s, he quickly discovered that every worker carried a CEO's baton in his or her briefcase, and was busy building up another business of their own on the side, perhaps even at a tangent to the company that paid their wages. This might even involve rebranding materials and goods taken from your company stores, and then undercutting the price to sell it to your clients. Working for a Western firm might be a temporary expedient or a convenient way to get started. It also meant that, 'They would have a personal interest in whatever deal was going down ... Business life was a cosy environment of relationships based on longstanding arrangements and mutual friends.'

Two months after his arrival to manage an acquisition in Bangkok, he was asked to sign a pre-prepared letter (in Thai) that set out the salary bonuses for that year because 'You need to announce them soon'. When he sought clarification, he was told that it was that year's performance. His objections that it was only November were brushed aside with 'Well, we more or less know what it is'. The bonus, he learned, was 2.5 months' salary. When he asked for the basis for this calculation, he was told: 'Well, we budgeted for that'. The criterion for this budget, he further learned, was 'management discretion'. His refusal to go along with the letter caused astonishment, even consternation. Finally, after a deal of bluster, it was reduced to less than two months.

Another commented on the 'iron rice bowl' mentality that he found in Indonesia: 'Life in the company was so easy that turnover was small. Nobody had a service record of less than five years – and all of them expected to be with the company for life.' He too remarked on the cosy relationships between his staff. 'The relatively small pool of skilled managers with the required technical background for the job meant that managers in the industry all knew each other. Most had graduated from the same university so it was a mafia, a very pleasant social club in which everyone knew everyone else.' The company was overresourced and nobody worked a full day – 'how could they run their private businesses if

I expected them to work for me for so many hours?' Staff making visits outside the company were invariably non-contactable.

There is general agreement that the operating style in Asian companies relies on historic practice. Nothing is written down, so there can be no accountability. Commercially, this means that there are no criteria laid down for setting commercial terms, giving discounts and so on. Rarely is there anything that Westerners would recognise as a marketing effort – all sales take place on the basis of price only. Also, not just managers, but suppliers and dealers all know each other from school; reciprocity is the name of the game, with information the prime trading commodity. In this situation, there is insufficient control for an audit to take place – so it is odds on that the company is leaking money.

Another expatriate manager recalled finding a grossly overstaffed finance department. However, as he quickly appreciated, 'This was because the finance manager knew his countrymen, and their ways of fiddling money. So he had insisted on having all these pieces of paper that had to be signed in order to try and stop it happening. But this just ended up as a hopelessly inefficient and bureaucratic system.'

Being wise to the scams going on, noted another long-time observer of Asian companies, and stopping them, is an almost impossible task when you are handicapped by a lack of language or inside knowledge. A colleague working on a mill site in Indonesia, he recalled, was puzzled by the disparity between the constant deliveries of cement, wood and lime and so on needed to keep the factory running and the actual amounts in stock.[1]

He decided to focus on deliveries of an estimated 20,000 tons of cement, needed to repair a water treatment lagoon. Ordered from a local supplier, 20,000 sacks had been duly delivered according to the log. The trucks entered the site at five-minute intervals, drove onto the weighbridge to register their load, continued round to the warehouse for unloading and then exited by the same gate, returning an hour later with another load. However, to his experienced eye, the amount of concrete delivered seemed inadequate for the repair job.

In fact, as he finally discovered from talking to his driver, instead of unloading at the warehouse, the trucks had exited with their loads intact, returning later with the same load. To disguise the shortfall, the proportion of cement used to mix the concrete had been cut by 50% – the implications for the repair job of this weak mixture were horrendous.

He then asked his civil manager, a South American expatriate, to investigate collusion between the supplier, warehouse manager and batching plant supervisor responsible for overseeing the cement mix. His report said there was no evidence of fraud and that only about 800 out of 20,000 sacks had been lost – an insignificant percentage easily accounted for. Nobody was to blame but, 'like flour when it was sifted for a cake mixture, the cement had simply blown away in the wind'.

What Would You Do?

To make an impact on such an environment involves the exercise of highly sensitive political and managerial skills. Generally speaking, no MBA or executive training course will have prepared you for scenarios such as those that follow.

During your first week, you discover that your PA is a 'minor wife' of one of the senior local managers in the company. Such a connection will clearly make confidentiality questionable, but can you risk alienating one of your senior managers by getting rid of her, and what message will that send through the company? What, if anything, should you do about the situation? Do you act quickly, or do you take your time?

Next take the organisation you have inherited, which is your target for change. The organisation is typical of the region, no better or worse than many other multinational Asian subsidiaries; all the senior managers have been with the firm since its foundation, and have developed a line management system involving about 80 more junior managers waiting around to be told what to do by them. When any Western manager is around, at least one or two senior managers – including the finance director – block the system, ensuring that no meaningful information goes up or down the organisation.

The whole system needs to be cleaned up and made more transparent. But implementation of any change to this structure will be a problem, since the managers will say 'yes' to your face and then go away and do nothing. What do you do about the blockers? How can you keep a discreet check on where people are and what they are doing, without acting like a heavy-handed policeman – even supposing you had the resources to do so? You must put in some means of control, and get the message over to your staff that change is definitely coming, you understand what they have been doing and it has to stop. The Chinese call this 'killing the chicken to scare the tiger'. But where do you begin to change the system without arousing strong resistance? And how do you find out who you can trust to carry out your wishes?

If you try to recruit new managers, you will probably find that they are related to those already in place. You will not be able to tell the difference. How can you avoid this situation and break the circle of nepotism? How can you attract the more outward-looking, quality people you need? What key appointments do you need to make? Should they be locals or should you ask for back-up from head office? And where in the organisation should you put them?

Insider or Outsider?

To deal with such daunting situations, companies need to put in people who are strong enough to push change through in this inhospitable environment. For this there are two basic requirements; that the manager knows the business very well and is able to tread the very fine line between cultural understanding and cultural acceptance.

The two extreme ends of the spectrum here are that either expatriates stick firmly to their own culture, make no concessions to local sensitivities and risk alienating the workforce, or they 'go native' and try to understand and think like a local, with the risk of letting their standards be eroded by local customs. If you are too friendly with your local managers, if you socialise too much, then they may take advantage of this to probe your weaknesses, and then block you. It could also undermine your authority. Keeping them at arm's length, on the other hand, may prevent them from detecting any weakness but, then again, might stop you from being able to achieve anything.

So as a *farang*, a *mat salleh*, a *gweillo*, a *bulleh* or any other brand of foreigner, you must choose. Do you try to learn the language and respect the local customs? Do you accept all the invitations to attend weddings and funerals – and as the big boss and father figure in a hierarchical society this will be expected of you – or do you rigidly maintain your status as an outsider? Do you limit yourself to a beer on staff days and a chat to the reps, so nobody will be able to feel they have a handle on you or get too close? It's a personal decision. The strategy you adopt will depend on how you view your role, as a would-be insider or an unrepentant foreigner. Experience has shown, however, that it is no good pretending to be local. It is more important to be open and honest, 'then they will say that at least he is consistent'.

Moreover, remember that in some parts of the region, like it or not, you are a paternal figure expected to participate in the key events of your employees' lives. And as the boss, you will have to get used to people crouching in front of you to ensure that they are never taller than you, or running ahead to open doors. It can be very insidious. One expatriate manager returned to the UK after three years in Thailand and was so used to doors opening like magic before him that on his first day back at head-quarters, he walked into a plate glass door.

Strategies for Change

So what strategies for change have been found to work well in this environment? One veteran advised that the best method of attack was through a combination of expertise and getting key appointments in place as soon as possible. 'You have to come in with the numbers ready and blow them away, and then recruit in people who owe nothing to the old organisation, and are unhampered by owing favours.'

The Need for Patience

However, this does not mean a rush to make wholesale changes as fast as possible but, instead, spending the first few months trying to understand the organisation; who exercises influence and who is connected to whom. The language problem may make it difficult, but experience should help you to see who exercises influence, who is connected to whom, where the bells, buttons and levers are and where the proper processes and systems are missing. Then, when you are ready, begin with a non-contentious issue where you can justifiably bring in outside agencies to help make changes, so avoiding accusations of partiality or unfairness.

One such area is the introduction of job descriptions. While in Asia, 'everyone is a manager of some sort (including the tea lady) according to their business cards', full job descriptions of their responsibilities and accountabilities are neither common nor welcome. Inviting an independent and respected firm such as the Hay organisation to devise and implement such descriptions can be the ideal way to gain a measure of control, without arousing strong resistance.

Along with this goes the recruitment of key staff through head-hunting agencies, making sure to recruit and settle new staff in before taking people out. The bait of working in a multinational company which offers wider career opportunities is a powerful one in attracting high-calibre managers. They will be the basis of a team that is loyal to you alone and form the bedrock of the new culture. One key appointment here is a secretary who is discreet and loyal, and whom you can trust absolutely.

An alternative tactic is to establish your own network of loyal managers from the cadre already working in the company. This is a slower method, but can be equally effective. One experienced expatriate found that his weekly badminton sessions eventually resulted in a strong team spirit being built around him. 'It took about six months before anyone dared to beat me but then, hearing me swear at missing a point and showering and changing afterwards changed their attitude towards me, and through these sessions strong bonds of loyalty were forged.' This group became his own network, his personal *guanxi* through which he was able to get messages across and glean valuable gossip. Offered other jobs, a couple of managers even refused to leave out of loyalty.

Once you have a team in place that you can trust, you can afford to turn your back while you deal with other parts of the organisation. Generally, the three most frequent flashpoints will be human resource issues, finance and communications.

The Human Resource Labyrinth

The human resource function, covering issues such as working hours, bonuses, recruitment and promotion, can be quite undeveloped in most Asian companies. This is because, since people are promoted purely on the basis of relationships with senior managers, there is little need for a recognised organisational structure in terms of evaluation and the terms and conditions that go with it.

This especially applies to the issue of salaries. A look at the salary system will probably reveal a labyrinth, in which the lower grades are underpaid and the top managers overpaid, thanks to their big bonuses. They also benefit from a variety of fringe benefits – parking subsidies, lucky draws, football competitions, parties, gold necklaces and so on. Even where systems exist, they do not necessarily work in the accepted way. In one Indonesian company, for example, tables were published showing what people could expect to earn for each grade. In practice no two people in the same grade ever earned the same amount; everyone knew that inequality existed, but everyone accepted it.

A key change, therefore, and one that multinational headquarters are increasingly demanding, is the implementation of a Western-style appraisal system. Unfortunately, the idea of a salary increment based on appraisal, and without an automatic cost of living rise, is completely alien to Asian managers. Previously, as they will point out to you: 'We have always got 10–20% or even 30%, even those who have not performed well.' So how do you even begin to introduce the concept of assessment and reward according to a performance matrix?

Introducing an appraisal system

In fact, it is usually achieved after months or even years of patient negotiation. One expatriate first offered his managers the chance of being assessed according to a performance matrix, in which the top line represented the percentage of budget achieved, ranging from 80–120% and the other side the percentage of market share. A manager who maintained market share and achieved his budget got a one-month bonus. To get more, managers had to improve on both axes. However, the managers considered this far too difficult and rejected it. When the expatriate refused to give in, a compromise was finally reached whereby all the managers just settled for a thirteenth month's pay.

To roll out a clearly defined performance appraisal system that can form the basis of performance rewards can take months. One expatriate working for a Swiss multinational was under pressure from his head office to initiate such a system to conform with their global best practice.[2] He found it almost impossible, first, because the culture made it difficult to give negative feedback. His managers did not expect a frank discussion of their performance, but to be told how well they had done. He found himself giving a monologue at each evaluation meeting, and any attempt to provoke discussion was met with a polite, brief and non-controversial reply. Setting their own objectives was out of the question.

Even more controversial was the concept of a performance rating. The head office used a standard A–E rating in which, according to a normal distribution, an A grade would apply only to the top 3–4% of outstanding managers, and not necessarily the most senior. A C grade, into which 60–70% of managers usually fell, implied a good overall standard with all requirements fulfilled. The Western manager noted that his predecessors had clearly decided not to rock the boat by giving everyone an A grade, although there was some attempt at differentiation by giving an A+ or A−. This situation, he discovered, was a product of the country's school marking system, where a B grade meant 'could try harder' and C meant disgrace. Psychologically, only an A grade was acceptable.

His attempts to award a C grade brought nothing but trouble. Hurt managers threatened to resign, and every attempt to explain the system foundered on total incomprehension. The first year, the Western manager gave up and created an 'Asian exception', but the second year, having aired the problem at a regional conference and discovered others in the same boat, he introduced an adaptation that he first discussed with his staff. The A–E grades were replaced with more qualitative descriptors; C became a good performance, B very good and A exceptional. The D and E grades were replaced respectively by 'satisfactory' and 'unsatisfactory'. Having been devised by the managers themselves, the new approach was deemed acceptable and they felt more committed to make it work.

Finance

There is unanimous agreement that a key move is to take control of the finance function, either by putting an expatriate finance director in place or by taking responsibility for signatory authority and visibility. This means insisting on having sole authority for signing any cheque or note involving money going out of the company, including credit notes, discounts or goods given free of charge and all cheques over a certain threshold. One manager recalled how amazed he had been at the number of times that tyres had to be replaced on company vehicles. After he insisted on signing every bill for tyre replacements, he did not see a single one during the next 12 months. Many other credit notes also disappeared.

From this, he concluded: 'You can manage these things politically if you let them know you have rumbled them in a particular area – but you leave the back door open for them. They know they must not do it again and this is OK. The thing not to do is to paint them into a corner ... But you need to keep control.' Eventually, the solution will probably lie in IT systems, in particular systems to interlink customer forecasts with orders and manufacturing.

Communications

Spreading the word about what you are trying to do and improving communications is one of the most difficult problems to crack because 'Information is power and so they keep it to themselves'.

To succeed, you must find a way to get round this obstacle and reach directly the younger managers, who may be more receptive to new ideas. But, given the hierarchical nature of local society, bypassing the senior management to do this will be a major challenge. Leave your door open – but will anyone walk through it? After all, you will only be here a few years, and they have seen others come and go. Their seniors will still be here, bossing them around when you are back in your home base. So how to convince your junior managers that, this time, things will be different? One way is to hold regular meetings with as wide a group of managers as possible in order to tell them what you are doing and why, and what behaviours you expect from them, in the hope that they will then pass the message down the levels of the organisation.

The Effects of Change

Predictably, the net effect of any move you make will be that morale plummets. For example, once they realise that you mean to reduce numbers, a stream of managers may come to see you and say something like 'What you are doing is right. We know it should have been done a long while ago but we don't like change, and when it happens it is upsetting for us.' How do you answer them? Insist on firing someone and they will probably reply, 'OK, this person has got to go, but let's give them until the year end, give them time to get used to it.' Incidentally, they will use the same technique with any price increase that you try to implement. They will tell the dealers in advance that the price increase will be in three months' time, 'so they can get used to the idea' – or, in reality, so that they can buy up the stock.

You will then have to decide who does the firing. Will it be the heads of departments, who have worked with that person for years and will feel extremely uncomfortable about doing it? Or you, as the hatchet man from the West? The consequences of you doing it may be twofold. Your managers will lose face if they do not do it (which may be a way of convincing them to act) and it could rebound negatively on the image of the company locally. So if you do start to reduce numbers, make sure that you also maintain the reputation of your firm as a fair international company, which people should be proud to work for and which can attract high-quality people.

One expatriate, reflecting on the consequences of firing people, noted that 'Morale is always lower at the point of uncertainty. Once things become clear, morale recovers remarkably quickly.' In his experience, 'They didn't think they would get over the loss of their buddies, but three weeks out of the organisation and they were almost forgotten.'

Another, however, believed that, sometimes, firing people for the sake of reducing numbers could do more harm than good. In his experience, making junior staff redundant saved very little money, since they were paid so little, and any benefits were far outweighed by the resentment caused, since they would invariably turn out to be someone's friend or relation. Also, they performed all sorts of tasks and ran errands that more senior people would feel was beneath their dignity. Sometimes, perhaps, the most positive action could be to allow things to remain as they are.

Leadership

Finally, think about how you yourself can set an example by your personal behaviour. Remember, any attempt to change an entrenched system is frustrating. It is not easy; no matter what personal energy you have, you can't do everything yourself. You can only lead by setting an example. And although you can dictate strategy, you cannot implement it. At the end of the day, it is the people in the organisation that have to do the work.

Remember also that only so many ideas can be introduced at any one time. Therefore you must prioritise what you want to change. It may help to try and analyse the root causes of the situation. The problem may be not so much resistance, but ignorance. They have been doing things the same way for years and cannot imagine another way. Moreover, change is not only difficult in an Asian firm; the weight of inertia is just as solid in the West.

Once you have your list of priorities, think how to control the key points and make sure that the message is continually reinforced to keep the momentum going. You have to find a way to counteract the tendency for people to think that this will go away, it is not really happening and they should just keep a low profile for however long it takes.

How to Measure Change

Given that you are only going to be in place for a finite time, then from the beginning you should think about your successor. How far in the change process do you aim to be when you hand over? This in turn means you have to think of a way to find out whether or not you are having an effect. How do you measure change? How long do you need to make sure that things really are different, so that your successor can act more as a maintenance manager, with the task of fine-tuning the organisation?

According to psychologists, people themselves do not change. What changes are their behaviour patterns. Take away the pressure for this behavioural change, and they will revert to the old preferred ways. So it is important to keep the pressure on and drive through change to the extent where they cannot revert. This means that you have to have everything in place, the right terms and conditions. For example, systems such as swipe cards to check the hours people keep and logging telephone calls are effective tools in making people conform and keeping a check on them.

However, although you can bully people and force them to change outwardly, you won't get the inward commitment necessary to make it last any longer than your term of office, or the next business crisis. It is far better to set in motion that most powerful force for change, peer pressure. Experience has demonstrated that the best method is to convince a significant percentage of managers that this is the way forward, for once some managers buy into the new culture, others will follow. If the new working patterns result in greater profits and an enhanced reputation for the company they work for, nobody will want to leave, attracting good people will be relatively easy and they will automatically conform to the status quo.

After that, hopefully, momentum should take over. Once the ball is rolling then keep it rolling, so that the momentum becomes irresistible. And then, as soon as your people catch up with one new idea, move on to the next target. It is important to innovate and always keep one step ahead. This is classic business school theory, but, as with many things, it is a lot easier said than done.

Managing change is not something everyone can do and, often, it is too easy for expatriates to give up. You have got to have the confidence to drive it through, without leaving too much blood on the walls. But remember, given the fate of some who have tried to introduce changes in Asia such as restructuring or downsizing, that blood may well be yours!

Managing change in Asia

- Have patience – don't make managers lose face by your actions

- Begin with non-contentious issues and bring in neutral external agencies where possible

- Build your own team

- Try to involve local managers in devising and introducing new systems

- Prioritise and control key points

- Constantly reinforce key messages

- Communicate as widely as possible

- Think long term.

Notes

1 Taken from 'Blowing in the Wind', case study written by Charlotte Butler and Professor Henri-Claude de Bettignies, 1994 INSEAD-EAC.
2 Taken from 'The Evaluation', case study written by Charlotte Butler and Professor Henri-Claude de Bettignies, 1996 INSEAD-EAC.

Strategy 14

Intellectual Property Abuse: Contain the Risks

The Problems you will Face

A visit to Beijing's Bar Street, the city's famous nightlife area, demonstrates clearly what copyright enforcement officials are up against. Pirated CDs and DVDs are widely available in the area but not from shops or even from street stalls. Instead, passers-by are invited to step inside bars where hawkers carry bags full of pirated music and movies. It's discrete and the vendors are highly mobile. Walk along The Bund in Shanghai and the problem is the same, only this time, every vendor seems to sell not pirated movies but fake Rolex watches.

Pirated music and movies are a massive problem across Asia. Another big offender has been Malaysia. Hundreds of copies of British popstar

Robbie Williams' latest album were selling in Malaysia less than a week after its 2001 release in London. The only problem was that it hadn't yet been released in Asia. Malaysia's copyright pirates had been at it again. Well resourced and highly technically proficient, they are among the best in the world when it comes to illegally replicating CDs, VCDs and DVDs, whether for films, music or software. Stalls in Kuala Lumpur's Chinatown night market routinely displayed copies of the week's US Billboard Top Ten, and the films – all illegal copies on VCD priced at only US$1.50 each – were available for purchase.

Films were sometimes available in Malaysia before they had even been released – anywhere. Preview screenings might be held in the US and someone might go along with a concealed digital camera and film the movie as it was screened. The recording was then e-mailed to Malaysia and replicated over and over for sale the next day. Sometimes the Malaysian versions even showed people's heads popping up as they head out to the toilets or to buy popcorn during the illegally filmed screening!

But then in 2003, things changed. Suddenly, the supply of pirated movies and music dried up in Malaysia's night markets. At last, enforcement officials were serious about enforcing their own laws. But the enforcement was selective. Louis Vuitton and Gucci handbag rip-offs still abound in Kuala Lumpur's Chinatown as do fake designer perfumes, sunglasses, T-shirts and wallets.

One little-realised driver of the demand for pirated movies in countries like Malaysia, is government censorship. Scenes that feature intimacy or bad language, and subjects that touch on religious matters in a way deemed to be socially detrimental are doctored or cut before being aired or formally distributed in Malaysia. Watching pirated movies is one way to circumvent this. The movie *Babe* for example was banned outright in Malaysia. But many Malaysians have seen it because pirated versions of it were sold freely in the country's night markets. Movies like *Kill Bill*, with heavy language and violence, similarly are censored and occasionally banned. What this means is that the film industry's claims that viewers of pirated movies are watching an inferior product are wrong. Often, the pirated version is the complete product and so, in this regard, is superior.

But intellectual property rights abuse is not restricted to manufactured and audio-visual goods. Services too are targeted. Around 1997 a 'Dome' coffee shop first opened in Jakarta's upmarket Pasa Raya shopping complex. The concept, the name and the interior all looked like a Dome coffee shop, the Australian-based chain which now has dozens of outlets in Singapore, Malaysia, the Middle East and Australia. But the first official Dome coffee shop did not open in Jakarta until 2000, at least three years after the first 'Dome' appeared. In the meantime, Dome's management found that there was little it could do about the copycat Dome.

Patents, copyrights and trademarks are all at risk in Asia. Patents are legal, scientific documents that disclose the technology associated with an invention and award exclusive rights over a period of time to the inventor or registrar of the invention in order to exploit the technology or license others to exploit it.[1] They are granted to the first to invent in the United States and to the first to file for the patent in much of the rest of the world, subject to tests of utility, non-obviousness and novelty. Patents expire after a specified period and they confer monopoly rights on the holders for that period. Copyrights are similar but apply in respect of certain creative endeavours such as film making, music and writing.

Trademarks differ in that they endure indefinitely, subject to recurrent registration. They offer the developers of brand names, logos and geographic indications protection against infringements by others.

Violations of intellectual property rights are not unique to Asia. Counterfeit Calvin Klein underwear can be bought in many street markets in London. Nigerian migrants selling fake designer handbags beset Europe from Italy to France. Full intellectual property rights have not always been recognised even in the United States. Alexander Hamilton, the first treasury secretary of the United States, established a copyright system for authors but only if they were American. The intended consequence was that foreign authors – largely British authors – could have their works copied endlessly in the United States without them receiving any royalty payments whatsoever.

What makes Asia unique today is perhaps the degree to which intellectual property rights are disregarded generally. The idea that intangibles such as ideas and designs should be paid for is a very new concept in Asia, particularly in China. 'Why should I pay for something if I can get it for free?' is a common question and one that is difficult to answer in the Asian cultural context. Traditional Asian entrepreneurship is about trading – which means low margins and high volumes. Voluntarily lining up to make payments that will go to a faceless creator somewhere and that will chip away at margins that might already be wafer thin simply beggars belief among the old school. Paying for services comes unnaturally but to pay for something as intangible as an idea is beyond comprehension. So in Asia, intellectual property violation comes from a mixture of wilful intent and simple bewilderment at the laws. Legislators have trouble getting compliance to laws anywhere if those laws are seen to be ill-founded and illegitimate. So the size of the challenge is clear, given the cultural context and Asia's variable legal systems.

Estimated levels of software piracy are higher in Asia than anywhere. Vietnam was the worst offender in 2000 in terms of pirated software in use as a proportion of the total. An estimated 97% of all software in use was believed to be pirated. The figure for China was 94%, in Indonesia 89%, in Pakistan 83% and in Thailand 79%. Even in rule-bound Singapore, half of all software in use was believed to be pirated, placing Singapore considerably above the estimated world average of 37%. The figure for Japan was 37%, right on the estimated world average. But given the size of Japan's economy, this means that, in dollar terms, the loss to software manufacturers from software piracy in Asia is highest in Japan – about US$1.7 billion annually, according to industry estimates.[2] Figures such as these suggest not only that laws for the protection of software are practically unenforceable but that there is a general consensus that breaking them is quite acceptable.

Microsoft did win a rare victory in 2001 in a Jakarta court when a local computer vendor, who had installed pirated versions of Windows and other software, was ordered to pay US$4.4 million in compensation and take out newspaper advertisements apologising to the company. The company had argued that Indonesians were 'too poor' to pay Microsoft's full retail price. No doubt it was a pyrrhic victory for Microsoft, as enforcing such decisions is another battle.

Books too are copied mercilessly around Asia. High-margin trade and technical books are routinely copied in Korea and Taiwan to the point that the copies sometimes look better than the originals. Even governments are not immune. In 1995, Australia's embassy in Hanoi found that photocopies of the *Vietnam Country Economic Brief*, a summary of Vietnam's economy produced by the Australian Department of Foreign Affairs and Trade and supposed to be available only to Australian businesses, were being sold on street corners in Hanoi to anyone prepared to pay. Similarly, pirated versions of the Chinese government's own anti-corruption propaganda film *Life and Death Choice* was widely available around China throughout 2000.

Manufacturers sometimes circumvent copyright laws, rather than breaking them outright by slightly modifying existing brands. And it is not only American and European brand names that are targeted for such mimicry. Executives from Hitachi of Japan once travelled to Jakarta to find that their local competition included electronic goods branded 'Hitachin' and 'Mitachi'. There's the Crocodile brand of polo shirts sold across Asia with a crocodile logo embroidered over the left breast, which look suspiciously like Lacoste polo shirts from France. A book called *Malaysian Eclipse* was published by several Malaysian academics in 2001. Not only was the name remarkably similar to the book, *Asian*

Eclipse, published two years earlier by one of the authors of *Big in Asia*, but so too was its cover, which featured a darkened visage of the world on a black background with yellow and white writing. Mimicry as opposed to outright copying makes the application of intellectual property laws just that little bit more difficult.

Industrialised countries account for about 97% of patents worldwide. Around half of all royalty payments made in the world for patents are channelled to patent holders in the United States. It is therefore not surprising that there is a huge domestic lobby in the United States urging protection for intellectual property rights. Japanese manufacturers of course are a big target for intellectual property rights abuses in Asia. The Japanese Patents Office is an important source of funding for the APEC-sponsored Asia-Pacific Industrial Property Centre which trains delegates from APEC (Asia-Pacific Economic Co-operation) member countries on intellectual property protection. But as Asia outside Japan develops its own brands, the problem of counterfeiting and other intellectual property rights abuses will be felt more there too and slowly lobbies in Asia will arise that will themselves demand better protection. In China, perhaps 40% of all tobacco products that are sold are counterfeit, but the crime hurts not so much Western brands as the makers of China's most popular local brand, Hongtashan (Red Pagoda) cigarettes.

What is TRIPS?

Western countries and particularly the United States have invested huge resources into pressuring other countries to better protect intellectual property. The means for doing this now is TRIPS, the Agreement on Trade-Related Aspects of Intellectual Property Rights. It is administered by the World Trade Organization (WTO) and was an outcome of the Uruguay Round of trade negotiations concluded in 1994, the same round that led to the WTO being established. Developed countries were required to comply with TRIPS by 1996, developing countries by the beginning of 2000, and those with least developed status by 2005.

Under TRIPS, all countries must commit themselves to a uniform set of intellectual property protection rules or face retribution from other countries and most particularly from the United States and the European Union for non-cooperation and non-compliance. Retribution is largely in the form of trade sanctions.

WTO member countries must establish judicial channels to protect intellectual property rights and enforce effective deterrent penalties against violators. TRIPS also creates a harmonised global system under which inventors are granted patents for a minimum of 20 years. The logic of establishing property rights in this area is clear but the 20-year figure is arbitrary, other than it was the period in use in the United States, the prime mover of TRIPS.

Regimes for intellectual property protection were enormously diverse across Asia 10 or 20 years ago due to differing histories and legal systems, but international pressure for better laws has seen a flurry of legal reform in the area so that intellectual property protection laws across Asia are now more consistent than ever before. Many are now signatories to TRIPS. This means that now more than ever a uniform approach can be taken by companies to protect their patents, trademarks and copyrights in Asia.

Which Countries are the Worst Offenders?

What are the most typical abuses of intellectual property in Asia? And in which countries? The following list has been developed from information supplied by the Office of the US Trade Representative.

China
Intellectual property protection laws commenced in 1982 with the passing of the Trademark Law. Other similar laws have been passed since. In combination they are sufficient to protect intellectual property. Also, there is genuine concern at the top levels in China for greater intellectual property protection and China's courts have issued some significant decisions in the area. But the problem is enforcement, which varies across China's regions and is hampered by a lack of transparency in procedures, poor coordination between police and government agencies, penalties that are too low and the all too rare filing of criminal actions.

Trademark counterfeiting and the large-scale manufacture of fake goods from designer sunglasses to shampoos to pharmaceuticals is widespread, as is the unauthorised production and sale of copyrighted products. Foreign books are commonly pirated. Pirated movies have become so common that it has become almost impossible to sell legitimate versions in many parts of China. The film *Titanic* did sell 300,000 legitimate copies in China, although it is estimated that another 20–25 million pirated copies were also sold.

China is also an important manufacturer of clothing and footwear for leading US and European fashion houses, but factories licensed to make the goods sometimes overproduce and secretly sell the overruns in the same markets in which the licensed goods themselves are sold. In this case the goods are not counterfeit, making detection even more difficult.

China is a major exporter of pirated goods, particularly to Hong Kong but also to lesser markets in the region such as Myanmar. Smugglers use large, custom-made, fully submersible containers which they pack with pirated goods. These are then dragged by ships along the bottom of Hong Kong harbour to avoid detection. The containers are landed at night, emptied and usually dumped where they are landed.

India

Copyright legislation is a good standard in India but inadequately enforced and so piracy of films, music, software, books and video games is rampant. India's patent system is not compliant with its TRIPS' obligations. Patents are difficult to obtain because of a large backlog of applications (30,000 patent applications were pending in mid-2001), too few patent examiners and opposition procedures to the granting of patents (usually launched by competitors) are overly generous. All this can conspire to delay patent registration until the patent period has actually expired. The term for patent protection for pharmaceutical processes is seven years, compared with the 20 years demanded by TRIPS. Patent protection is not available for pharmaceuticals and agricultural chemical products. Fake goods abound – it is said that more Johnny Walker Black Label whisky is sold in India each year than is ever produced in Scotland.

Indonesia

Copyrighted and trademarked goods are pirated across Indonesia with more vigour than perhaps anywhere else. Everything from blue jeans to television sets to cigarettes is pirated, and done so with such brazenness that it would appear that, from manufacturers to distributors to retailers, some of the operators in the chain do not even realise that laws are being broken.

Industry estimates that piracy levels for music and business software are 87%, 90% for all forms of motion pictures sold and 99% for games software.[3] These are among the highest figures in the world.

Indonesia had not passed TRIPS-consistent copyright, trademark and patent laws by the beginning of 2002.

Korea
There is widespread piracy of trade and educational books in Korea. Intellectual property laws are not fully TRIPS consistent, and some are so vaguely worded as to make it difficult to determine if they are TRIPS consistent. The quality of pirated goods is sometimes superior to the originals.

Macau
Convictions for intellectual property infringements have been few and when they do happen the penalties levied have been light. Many of the counterfeit goods sold in Macau come from China.

Malaysia
Copyright infringements in Malaysia are substantial, particularly with regard to films, music and software. Although a crackdown in 2003 appeared to be effective, it remains to be seen if the crackdown will continue. Trademark violations in respect of clothing, footwear, watches and perfumes remain common. Numerous raids have been launched by police and copying equipment confiscated but there have been few prosecutions. The growing intensity of raids in recent years is pushing some of the piracy industry offshore, particularly to neighbouring Indonesia. Not only have pirate VCDs been available widely in Malaysia but films are frequently screened without authorisation in public, such as on long-distance public buses. To add insult to injury, the versions screened are themselves usually pirated. Malaysia is also a regional centre for credit card cloning and fraud – not because its residents are any more devious than those elsewhere in the region but once again because of the degree of technical sophistication in that country.

Pakistan
All manner of goods are pirated in Pakistan from books to CDs and these flood the domestic market and are exported to neighbouring countries such as Afghanistan and India. Court proceedings are delayed and non-deterrent fines hamper the effectiveness of intellectual property protection.

Philippines
Copyright enforcement is weak and piracy of textbooks and other trade books is rampant in the Philippines. The production of pirated films has increased in recent years. Judicial procedures for intellectual property violations, like judicial procedures generally, are slow to the point of being glacial, and cases can drag on for years.

Taiwan

Taiwan is one of the largest pirated optical media producers in the world and production capacity is thought to outstrip local demand, suggesting that Taiwan is an important exporter of pirated films. Enforcement is sporadic, prosecutions rare and legislation patchy. Taiwan's manufacturing sector largely comprises tens of thousands of small, dynamic, family-owned and managed companies, which makes monitoring and enforcement difficult.

Thailand

Intellectual property violations, although common, are not as great as might be expected in Thailand. Trademark abuses are common as are pirated films and software. Legislation is relatively good and has improved considerably in recent years but as usual it is enforcement that is the problem. Pirated goods are visible on the streets in important commercial centres such as Bangkok and Hat Yai but in lesser quantities than in Kuala Lumpur, Jakarta and Guangzhou. Foreign business representatives enjoy a good working relationship with Thai intellectual property enforcement agencies, although the degree to which property rights are enforced varies with whichever government minister is in charge of anti-piracy policy. Frequent ministerial reshuffles have meant frequent changes in policy emphasis.

Pantip Plaza is the most notorious location in Bangkok for obtaining pirated VCDs, DVDs and CDs. Buyers choose from empty CD jackets from any of the Plaza's dozens of fixed shops. A runner returns ten minutes later from a hidden location bearing the ordered goods.

Vietnam

Both protective laws and enforcement are weak in Vietnam when it comes to intellectual property rights. Trademark abuse is rampant and the country abounds with pirated goods of all types.

What to Do?

Violations against intellectual property rights can be combatted in the following ways:

- Effective laws must be in place and they must contain sufficient deterrent provisions.
- The laws must be enforced – enforcing agencies must be well resourced.
- Courts must be prepared to impose deterrent sentencing.

- There must be the political will to protect intellectual property rights.
- Police and judicial corruption needs to be minimal.
- The system of protecting intellectual property rights must also have legitimacy. Patents and copyright protection that can be portrayed as 'unfair', such as the registering of patents for Asian food crops such as strains of jasmine rice, have elicited government protests from Thailand. They serve to undermine the whole intellectual property rights system and legitimise violations.

But what can companies do to protect themselves against intellectual property rights violations? The London-based British American Tobacco (BAT) now says that its real competitor in the world marketplace is not America's Philip Morris but counterfeit cigarettes and other tobacco products. It estimates that around 30% of all tobacco products sold in the world today are counterfeit. And what is BAT doing to combat this onslaught and protect its many trademarks? It is urging governments to enforce penalties against counterfeiters and passing on information about counterfeiters to the relevant agencies. Beyond that, it is at a loss as to what to do. Most other multinationals are in the same position.

The powerlessness of even big companies effectively to combat intellectual property infringements was summed up by a 'Leaders' Meeting' of senior officers of some of the world's biggest companies in February 2002 in New York. Present were the CEOs, chairmen or similar of BAT, Gillette, GSK, Henkel, Nestlé, Pentland, P&G, Richemont, SC Johnson and Unilever. Johnson & Johnson, Microsoft, AOL Time Warner, Diageo and Compaq sent observers. The group met again in London a few months later. To date, little has come from the meetings apart from general agreement that no one has yet come up with an adequate solution to the problem of intellectual property theft. One of the resolutions of the initial meeting was that those present needed to 'embrace the interests of brand-owning companies from developing countries' to help build coalitions against intellectual property theft in those countries. A decision to establish a task force to look at the problem served to highlight just how impotent companies are when it comes to this problem.

The intangible nature of intellectual property rights makes violations difficult to combat especially in countries where legal systems – both the laws and their enforcement – is poor. This calls for a multi-pronged approach. Companies should also devise a plan to combat intellectual property violations of their products from the time that they set up in Asia. What avenues for redress are there?

Legal

Legal remedies are an obvious measure, particularly in Singapore, Hong Kong, Japan and Malaysia. But in many parts of Asia, while seeking legal recourse should still be attempted if for no other reason than to signal a determination to assert intellectual property rights, little real benefit might eventuate. Also, legal action can drag on for years, especially in the Philippines, India and Pakistan. Interim orders to cease and desist may not be given or enforced. So, while the legal processes are worked through, the trademark, copyright or patent violations might continue unabated. Nonetheless, laws in this area have improved greatly in Asia with the advent of the WTO and TRIPS, and violators have been brought before the courts in many countries.

Lobbying

US companies can complain to the local US chamber of commerce, which will make representations on their behalf to the host government and the relevant intellectual property enforcement agency. Representations can also be made by companies directly to politicians and the relevant local commerce ministry. Written and oral briefings can also be made to the commercial section of the relevant embassy or high commission, if the aggrieved company is foreign. Such companies should also enlist government support at home to have serious intellectual property breaches brought via TRIPS mechanisms to the WTO, if combative measures prove ineffective locally.

Help the Agencies and Pay for Investigators

Perhaps the biggest problem in the area of intellectual property rights enforcement in Asia is that those agencies charged with enforcement are not unwilling to act but are underresourced. When provided with evidence of violations and information on where and when violators can be apprehended, they will act. Accordingly, some larger American and European companies have banded together to hire local investigators to assemble the necessary information. Production facilities have been identified and evidence collected. The authorities are then tipped off and representatives of the US and European companies have accompanied them on their raids to ensure that the desired arrests are made and the replicating equipment is confiscated. It is an expensive business, but it has led to police raids in China, Thailand, Malaysia and the Philippines.

Reduce the Incentive Gap

A new release music CD that goes on sale at London's Tower Records in Piccadilly Circus for £16.49 (US$23.42) sells for the equivalent of RM8 (US$2.10) in the night markets of Kuala Lumpur (the prices of pirated CDs and VCDs at Kuala Lumpur's street markets are surprisingly uniform). A similar legal copy in Malaysia sells for around RM46 (US$12.11).

One way to reduce intellectual property violations is to reduce the incentive for it. Prices for legitimate products could be reduced so that the difference between the price of legitimate and pirated copies is reduced. Such action should reduce but will not eliminate the incentive for counterfeiting. International record companies tried this in Malaysia in 2001. It was accompanied by a police crackdown on vendors selling pirated CDs and the taking effect of the Optical Disc Act 2000 which allowed for greater penalties, including jail terms, for producers and exporters of pirated films. Two things happened. The number of street vendors selling pirated CDs and VCDs fell noticeably, and the price of a pirated CD fell from RM10 (US$2.60) to RM8 (US$2.10). The pirates dropped their prices to maintain their competitiveness. Producing pirated CDs in Malaysia was no longer as profitable as it had been.

Another incentive gap relates to time. For example, films released in January in North America might not be officially released in China and elsewhere in Asia until the following September, yet the media hype for the US release spills over to Asia where consumers might well purchase pirated versions simply to see what all the fuss is about overseas. Timing the release of new products in Asia with releases elsewhere is one obvious measure to help make the pirated products less attractive.

One final consideration is that the quality of pirated goods may be superior to the licensed product. This means that if consumers are to stick with buying the licensed good, not only must they pay more but also buy an inferior product. This is asking a lot of consumers. Pirated textbooks in Korea, for example, are sometimes printed on better quality paper than the originals (which can lead potential buyers to believe that it is the legitimate copies that are pirated), or Malaysian pirates will add maybe six bonus tracks to a new release CD from the artist's previous recordings which are not present on the original new release.

Staff

Commercial in-confidence information is often lost in Asia, as elsewhere, via companies' own employees. Disgruntled staff are a prime cause of sensitive information leaking from a company. But so too are lowly paid staff who may be susceptible to monetary overtures from competitors to leak confidential information. Here are some things to consider:

- Where are the loyalties of the local staff – to the company, the state, or friends and relatives who work with competitors?
- How would local staff react to offers of bribes to copy documents and pass them on? (Keep in mind that many companies which undertake due diligence work in countries such as China actually source information about companies by bribing their staff to hand over copies of documents.)
- Have non-disclosure agreements been signed with local joint venture partners?
- Is it possible to limit the circulation of proprietary information to local employees on a need-to-know basis?
- Local vendors and subcontractors can be another problem. Have due diligence checks been carried out on them? Do they also work for or supply competitors? Have they signed confidentiality agreements?
- Should data be encrypted when it is transmitted between factories and between factories and the country head office?
- What procedures are in place for staff terminations to ensure that data security is not compromised?
- Is it worth having offices, executive residences and boardrooms swept regularly for bugging devices? Most Western embassies in Asia have at least one room that is routinely swept and isolated from local staff and cleaning contractors to render it 'safe' for confidential discussions. Is it worth establishing a similar 'safe room' on the company's premises?

Technical Solutions

Some manufacturers have taken to adding technically difficult design features to their products such as holograms and watermarks. These are useful in some circumstances but might be ineffective when consumers are indifferent to the problems of pirated and legitimate goods – consumers after all, often know that they are buying counterfeit goods. Hitachi of Japan has created what it calls flexible mu-chips – small microchips which can be embedded in items such as clothing labels to help with tracking and anti-counterfeiting measures. But again, innovations such as these are ineffectual in the context of a poorly enforced legal environment.

■ Some things to consider before setting up in Asia:

- Do you have industrial processes or products that are at risk of intellectual property violations?

- If your industrial processes are at risk, might it be better to manufacture elsewhere – in environments where there are more guarantees for intellectual property safety?

- Are there technical processes that can be used to make your products more difficult to copy?

- How are your competitors dealing with violations of their intellectual property?

- What legal protection is offered in the countries of your choice and are they TRIPS consistent?

- What judicial protection is there and can judicial decisions be enforced?

- What is the most relevant intellectual property protection agency for your particular products? Are its officers amenable to cooperation? Are they aware of the nature of the potential violations of your particular intellectual property rights?

Notes

1   These definitions follow those used by Cheah – see Note 2.
2   Cheah, H.B., 'Monopoly rights and wrongs: Two forms of intellectual property rights violations in Asia' in Kidd, J.B. and Richter, F.J. (eds), *Corruption in Asia*, World Scientific Press, Singapore, 2002.
3   Office of the United States Trade Representative, 'USTR Special 301 Report', 2001: and *Asian Wall Street Journal*, 'Asian-Pacific region takes lead in purchases of pirated software', 23 May, 2001.

Selling Consulting Services in Asia

Why Don't Services Sell Well in Asia?

Services do not sell well in Asia, and when they do, rarely are the fees comparable to what can be achieved elsewhere. Corporate Asia under-appreciates the value of services as a business input. Management consulting, information technology, employee training, marketing, public relations, legal advice and research and development are all underacquired by most Asian firms. Instead, there is a bias to tangibles – goods – as inputs. The reasons are twofold.

Partly it is a matter of cultural bias and partly it is to do with countries' levels of economic advancement. As a country's economy matures, the proportion of national output attributable to services grows. Rich countries have a high component of services in their GDP figures, while poor countries do not. Services are not capital intensive but people intensive, so it is difficult to get much productivity growth from the services sector. This is one of the reasons why economic growth rates of rich countries slow down the richer they get.

The low appreciation for services is apparent among Asian consumers too. A survey by managing consultants McKinsey & Co. conducted in ten Asian countries in 2000, concluded that, while 75% of consumers in the United States are willing to pay for financial advice, in Asia the figure is less than a quarter.

All too often, when consultants and other outside professionals are used, they are brought in as window-dressing to impress bankers or stock analysts; to lend an air of modernity when in fact family members are still very much in control. Sometimes, consultants must accept that they have done their job simply by being engaged.

The Cultural Bias

Traders at heart

Many of Asia's entrepreneurs are ethnic Chinese. Like refugee and migrant minorities elsewhere, they are conservative and survive and prosper through trade. Trade is about buying and selling physical goods. It is not about services. Thus the most important group of entrepreneurs in Asia has little direct experience with the professional services sector, either as customers or providers.

Physical items are valued in corporate Asia, while intangibles are not. The Western manager might commission a consulting firm to review production processes and then marvel at the recommendations in the consultant's 100-page final report. The US$250,000 cost might even seem like a bargain to him. The ethnic Chinese founder/entrepreneur on the other hand is more likely to hold up the report and wonder how a 'book' could possibly cost so much. As with payments for licensing and copyright, there is a mindset in Asia that militates against paying for ideas and other intangibles. Those of the old school simply cannot see the value in such things. If they spend money, they want something to show for it. And if it doesn't work or they decide they don't like it, they can cut their losses and sell it. Services, on the other hand, cannot be sold on once they are acquired. Once the money is spent, it is gone.

Loyalty vs. Productivity

As we have seen, the typical Asian firm, especially in Hong Kong and Southeast Asia, is family controlled and family members are trusted most. Outside professionals usually find that they are trusted far less than, say, in the West. When loyalty is valued above all else, the concept of hiring consultants whose loyalty is at best only temporary and never really guaranteed is something of an anathema. If a professional manager in Asia leaves his company to work for another, it is seen as treacherous. Yet consultants work for one company after another, so what standing can they have in such a cultural setting? At best they can expect to be regarded with suspicion.

Employees reach each rung on the corporate ladder in the typical Asian firm after having passed tests of loyalty. Productivity is often a distant second consideration. Consultants who breeze in and out of a firm in this setting stand little chance of being trusted, valued, taken seriously, or even having the necessary information for their work disclosed to them so that they can make sensible recommendations, let alone implement them. Sometimes consultants are invited in but then not given the access, information or freedom they need to do their work. Consultants need to learn about Asia but Asian companies also need to learn how to make use of consultants.

Getting used to Low Fees

The cultural bias across Asia against services is reflected in the fees that can be achieved. Typically, they are way below those for comparable work performed in, say, the United States or even Australia. This is not just a Southeast Asian problem. Even in Japan, the fees that can be achieved are substantially lower. Where the auditing fee charged to a major Japanese corporate might be US$600,000, the fee for a similarly sized company in the United States might be around US$5 million.

The Asian dot-com boom saw huge numbers of locally owned service sector firms spring up. Usually they were owned and run by young Asian entrepreneurs trained in the United States and other Western countries. Educated about the value of services, they took the philosophy back home, set up their new businesses and hoped for the best. Anecdotally, few have done well and when they have, they have not done so on the backs of local firms but by selling services to the local offices of Western firms or Western firms in the West. But the low-cost and high-grade skills of these small firms together with the speed of communications afforded by the Internet mean that tasks can now be divided up and parcelled off to wherever good-value expertise resides.

A case in point is *Asian Eclipse*, a book previously published by one of the authors. Professional editors in Australia and Singapore edited it. A small firm of art designers based in the Philippines designed the cover. A small firm of Indians based in Mumbai did the index. Lawyers in Hong Kong did the legal work. The actual publishing and marketing was done in Singapore as was the typesetting. Cost is the reason for such divisions of labour. In Asia, competition between service providers can be fierce. The potential market for their services is enormous, but the actual market is small.

So, if professional services in Asia are yet to be rewarded to the degree that they are elsewhere, which subsectors yield the highest returns? A survey published in August 2000 by international IT specialists Gartner Dataquest[1] concluded that of the consulting, education and training, development and integration, IT management, transaction processing and business process outsourcing subsectors in the Asia-Pacific region, consulting was the segment that had the highest proportion of providers that earned gross margins of 41% or higher. It also had the second lowest proportion in the low-margin range of 0–10%. Margins in the business process outsourcing segment were not as high as expected, which Gartner concluded was due to the immaturity of the segment in the Asia-Pacific region and the fact that many providers are still in the investment phase. But that is the problem for services generally in Asia. The market is still only in its infancy.

Five reasons why Asian firms don't like consultants

1. They are not trusted.

2. They are likely to have worked and will work again for competitors.

3. They charge a lot for apparently little.

4. They lack legitimacy.

5. They undermine the management's 'face' and authority.

Management Consulting in Asia

The problems faced by management consultants in Asia are many. Management in Asia is via networks and relationships. Operational control is personalised rather than through systems. Asian managers typically like to rule through personal diktat and not with the aid of a transparent set of written rules. Nor are they good delegators, instead they tend to be auto-cratic. New management systems mean replacing personalised rule with something else, but it is personalised rule that is so ingrained in the Asian workplace. Asian entrepreneurs often see anything else as their loss of power, face and prestige. This is the cultural context in which management consultants in Asia must work.

Management consultants redesign companies' structures to enhance productivity. But most Asian firms are designed around job ladders based on loyalty rather than productivity. So there is a mismatch of aims that needs to be resolved before management consultants begin work.

Asia's entrepreneurs also tend to operate very closely to their markets. Many personally know their customers and sellers. They observe keenly and gather in all the information they need from their observations; they do not rely on outsiders to tell them what is going on. Their knowledge base is both highly detailed and built up over many years. Thus, when a management consultant comes along offering a management model that can be introduced to the firm in a matter of months, Asia's entrepreneurs might well react with scepticism. Each feels that their own market is unique and complex, and major changes cannot be sensibly proposed unless that same intimate market knowledge is first acquired. Consultants, especially management consultants who work with theories and models that are broadly applicable to whole classes of firms, simply lack legiti-macy in the eyes of many Asian entrepreneurs.

Finally, the sort of services offered by management consultants are simply not wanted by many Asian entrepreneurs and their firms, no matter how much they would appear to be needed from the outside. Large, diver-sified conglomerates with dozens of subsidiaries which look as if they have overreached themselves might well be structured that way to match large, complex Asian families – to ensure that each family member has a job. Structures which lack transparency might be that way so that taxation can be avoided and assets, costs and capital can be moved from one unit to another with ease. If Asia's entrepreneurs see virtues in tangled corporate structures – and from their point of view there might well be clear virtues – then management consultants who advise on how to enhance transparency when many clients have rational reasons for not wanting it face a hard sell.

Consumer and Industrial Market Research

Western companies tend to set up in a new country after first commissioning market research to demonstrate a market gap and the potential profits should they fill it. But Asian companies (apart from the Japanese, who are extraordinarily thorough in their market entry research) are more likely to invest in new markets simply on the basis of local connections. For example, a Thai businessman might choose to trade in Singapore because his son has moved there and he can act as the local agent. This is a cheap and efficient way of expanding to a new market but it is also rather limiting – entry to new markets is restricted not by demand but by the number of one's relatives. But while it works there is little reason to change.

Companies which specialise in consumer and industrial market research in Asia have found that most of their clients are the local units of Western multinationals. Asian firms are very reticent to commission outside market entry research and typically only do so if their bankers demand it, and then it becomes a piece of documentation to show outsiders and will be quickly forgotten internally.

Even consumer market research is still of most interest to Western multinationals in Asia, largely because they are most interested in brands and trademarks. Home-grown brands are emerging in Asia but they are still relatively minor compared with branded fast-moving consumer goods owned by Western giants such as Unilever and Procter & Gamble. Trial and error remains the preferred mode of market entry by Asian firms.

The way in which such market research proceeds in Asia differs from the West. Typically, in mature markets such as the United States, the United Kingdom and Australia, desk research comprises 80% or more of the work that might need to be undertaken. But in Asia, desk research typically comprises as little as 15%. The reason for the difference is because companies are required to file and to disclose publicly much more information in mature economies than is generally the case in Asia. Also, companies in mature markets have more of a culture of disclosure and transparency and are less likely to hold back information when it is requested.

Media Management and Media Training

Professional media trainers have their work cut out for them in Asia. There ought to be a huge demand for their services, but the actual demand is small, as Asian entrepreneurs are notoriously media shy. They see their companies as theirs and theirs alone and, even if they are big employers and have outside shareholders, rarely do they feel the need or obligation to explain their intentions to the public. The media is not seen as a means for getting their message across – as something to be used to their advantage. Instead, it is seen as something to be avoided at all costs. Western entrepreneurs typically spend a lot of time trying to get themselves media exposure, whereas Asian entrepreneurs probably spend as much time trying to avoid it.

Similarly, company directors could use training on how to handle themselves at shareholder meetings, but, Asia-wide, directors are notorious for not bothering to show up at annual general meetings.

Media outlets in Asia have enormous trouble securing interviews with locals, particularly if the outlet is television, and more so if it is not live and therefore subject to editing. Local entrepreneurs are enormously distrustful of the media. They dislike the lack of control they have if they agree to be interviewed. This is one of the reasons why stock analysts are quoted ad nauseam in the Asian business media rather than representatives from companies themselves, and also why, on Asian business television, a disproportionate number of the people interviewed tend to be Western expatriates rather than local entrepreneurs. When local businesspeople do agree to be interviewed, they typically demand to be given a list of all the interview questions beforehand, whereas Western expatriates and businesspeople almost never ask for this. Not surprisingly, researchers and assistant producers prefer to have Westerners on their shows because it means less work for them. The interview also has more spontaneity.

Regional business television such as Singapore-based CNBC Asia which has sought to be more 'Asian' has found its efforts largely rebuffed. The local audience might want to see more locals on television but few locals want to appear. The Hong Kong-based *Far Eastern Economic Review* has a spot for a guest columnist for its weekly 'Fifth Column' and it too has trouble finding Asian faces to fill the spot.

The main Asian markets for media training are Hong King and Singapore, the two centres for regional media. But, many Asian entrepreneurs largely see this as one service that they don't need to spend money on, even if it actually occurred to them. Most have no intention to appear in the media. Furthermore, very few Asian companies empower middle or even top-level staff to appear in the media to speak on their company's behalf. There are some exceptions – professional companies such as Singapore Airlines and DBS Bank have used professional media trainers – but the number is small. It is still very much a case of 'it's the tall bamboo that catches the wind'; the best profile is no profile.

The Blame Game – An Asian Spin on Blaming the Consultant

Consultants and after-hours office cleaners share an important attribute. They both offer convenient, face-saving targets for blame. Management can blame consultants for its own inadequacies, and after-hours office cleaners can be blamed for anything that goes missing. It is the same the world over.

Blaming consultants for mistakes is one of the reasons why they are engaged, be it in the United States or Asia. But a nasty cycle of blame can evolve in Asia if it is mixed with nationalism, as in 'the *American* consultants flew in, told us they could fix everything but instead knew nothing about local ways (read: Asian culture, Asian values) and have messed up.'

Consultants face difficulties defending themselves publicly because of client confidentiality agreements. They might like to cite their client's chronic mismanagement, for example, and list a whole litany of errors and malpractice but are prevented from so doing.

Some Ideas on Selling Consulting Services in Asia

What Sells?

Many Western consultants come to Asia, see a vast, barely tapped market with obvious and huge needs and expect to make a lot of money. Inevitably, they are disappointed. Doing well in any type of consulting in Asia almost inevitably means accepting far lower margins and fees than those for comparable work undertaken in, say, the United States, Western Europe or Australia. And very often, the main clients in Asia are not Asian firms but the local offices of Western multinationals.

The fastest growing market for consultants in Asia is China where restructuring and streamlining management is becoming big business. McKinsey & Co[2] claim that their practice in China is growing by 20–30% a year, after having first set up there in 1994. Early on, its clients were multinationals but now almost 80% of its current clients in China are domestic companies. But then China's large companies are state rather than family owned and not run as they are in much of the rest of Asia. So the cultural context and management ethos differs in China compared with elsewhere.

So what sort of services are in demand in the rest of Asia? Try marketing. Ethnic Chinese traders dominate the regional economy outside Japan and Korea. Trading is about buying and selling, and marketing is about selling more. So, logically, marketing should be one of the first services that many Asian firms are likely to reach out for, and so it is. Most medium and large Asian firms which have something to sell now have a marketing department.

Traditionally, Asian entrepreneurs outside Japan and Korea have been poor at developing brands. Branding requires money spent on intangibles such as brand development, consumer research and advertising, hence the past reticence. But, increasingly, truly Asian brands are being developed and they are becoming known beyond their domestic markets. Examples are Haier, the white goods brand from China; Shangri-La Hotels, Pacific Coffee and Giordano clothes of Hong Kong; the British India Company, Padini clothing, Selangor Pewter and Proton cars of Malaysia; Acer computers of Taiwan; and Tiger Beer, Raffles Hotels, Tiger Balm, and Creative Technologies of Singapore. Thailand's carbonated, high-caffeine drink Krating Daeng or Red Bull is now the number one non-alcoholic beverage in London's club scene and in 2001 entered the ranks of the top ten best-selling carbonated drinks in the United States.

Public relations companies too are slowly gaining a foothold, particularly in the wake of Asia's economic crisis. So many large Asian firms were hit hard by the crisis, had problems servicing their debts and bond-holders and were caught up in the general milieu of corporate Asia's 'dark' side that some engaged public relations consultants to try to bolster their image. The Indonesian conglomerate Gajah Tunggal Group hired the PR firm Ogilvey in 2001 to help improve its image, for example. It did so on the advice of its bankers.

Managing Clients' Expectations

One problem with consulting in Asia today is that the number of blue-chip companies which are comfortable with consultants and understand the role of a consultant is so small that many consultants are forced to accept clients who lack the necessary sophistication to understand and implement the advice they have been given. This leads to disappointment and misunderstanding, with the consultants inevitably being blamed.

Western consultants and local clients may differ widely on what the advice from the consultants is supposed to accomplish. One of the key things consultants must do if they are to be Big in Asia is not just win new clients but also manage those clients' expectations. Sometimes getting Asian firms to use consultants is an enormous battle and when they finally decide to do so they expect that the process will lead to their recovery and prosperity. They might expect an immediate jump in revenue or profits and feel cheated when it does not happen. Management consultants cannot turn around all companies. Some have problems that are too deep-seated.

In Asia, it is extremely important for consultants to specify clearly and precisely what they will and will not do for their clients. This needs to be in writing and clients need to be talked through it and reminded of it as work progresses.

Things to Keep in Mind when Consulting in Asia

The *need for* consultants and their services in Asia is great. The *desire for* them is not. In this way, they are a bit like dentists – it is only through education that people visit dentists and almost never because of the pleasure of the experience. How can consultants go about tackling the Asia market? Here are some ideas:

- Many consultants and other service providers should establish a foothold in Asia first by chasing business from local offices of multinational firms and then later attracting work from local companies. This is the pattern followed by most new entrants in Asia, whether by design or default.

- Consultants who want to target a local Asian firm for business should first see if it employs any Western expatriates in influential positions. If so, they can be used as an entry point to the firm. Western expatriates (almost by definition) understand the importance of services as business inputs. They will understand their company's deficiencies and its needs. If the expatriates are trusted within the company, they can prove effective agents for change. Slowly, they can raise problems with management and then suggest the services of a consultant as a possible remedy. They can arrange for meetings and demonstrations for the management. Many big consulting assignments with local firms in Asia have been won because expatriates working in those firms convinced management of the virtues of seeking outside help.

- Local clients will tend to want to bargain hard on fees, be demanding on what physical deliverables they get, take a long time to decide whether they want to engage the consultant and, in the meantime, spend a lot of time calling for additional meetings, further details and fee reworkings. Winning business in Asia from local firms can be very costly and then the rewards in terms of fees can be comparatively low.

- It is sensible in countries where legal systems are poor to require 40–50% of the agreed fee upfront and not to commence work until that first payment has been received. No or few exceptions should be made to this rule.

- Many Asian entrepreneurs are suspicious of slick marketing brochures, big names and high fees. The tried and tested method of gaining business knowledge in Asia – chitchat and gossip for want of better terms – will be an important way in which consultants will acquire new clients. Many will succeed or fail on the basis of word of mouth.

- Asian entrepreneurs tend to be very protective of their internal corporate information, even if this concern is not vocalised. Consultants must be prepared to sign strict confidentiality agreements. If such agreements are not presented, they can be offered to potential clients to give them a greater feeling of security.

- Trust and loyalty are important so confidence building is important. Consultants might need to be prepared to, or offer to, break up what would normally be one large project for a Western firm into four smaller modules, with progress (and payment) for each one being contingent upon client satisfaction with the previous one.

- Consultants need to work closely with staff and management and appear non-threatening, part of the team and observant of internal, informal structures of loyalty and respect. If this is not done, the clients' staff are likely to try quietly to undermine the consultant. Repeat business will certainly be unlikely.

- Asian clients are likely to want more oral briefings than Western clients. They are less receptive to research reports that must be read, compared with briefings which their staff and management can attend. Briefings tend to beget demands for further briefings. The client might even take the opportunity to use them as staff training sessions. Briefings also lead to questions and requests for more work to be undertaken, often with the expectation that the existing contract and fee cover the additional work. Consultants need to have clients agree beforehand the precise point at which the consulting work is to be considered completed by both parties and the final fee is to be paid.

'Act global, think local' applies even to management consultants. Names such as McKinsey & Co. and Boston Consulting Group mean less in Asia than they do in the West. It will be their staff – the personalities – that count most when it comes to winning projects. As always, personal connections are everything. It is important that some measure of trust can be established; that local consulting staff are sympathetic to local firms and conditions. Said a local consultant based in Pakistan interviewed by the authors:

> The challenge is to drop the functional business templates and vocabulary and work with the ethos of the client. Socially, this may mean sharing the same regional language rather than business school English, being equally comfortable eating from plastic plates while seated on the floor as one is with full china and cutlery with corporate regalia in a multinational's dining room and genuinely sharing the personal experience of the client … It's hard work to develop such a working relationship but believe me, the payoffs for the business as well as for the consultant are great. If management consultants are prepared to use their emotional intelligence first, only then can their business competence and IQ get them and their clients anywhere. Establishing this trust and loyalty may take time and may initially seem fuzzy but I feel that it can be an extremely important driver of changing the way many businesses and their owners in Asia function.

A bonanza in consulting in Asia is not just around the corner. There is an enormous gap between what ought to be done and actual demand for management consulting and the like. The obstacles to closing that gap are largely cultural, and culture takes a long time to evolve. Consulting in Asia is still in its infancy. There will be solid business in the sector for those willing to lay the foundations now. But, in the meantime, consultants will need to learn more about Asia, and their clients will need to learn more about how to be a client.

Notes

1   Gartner Dataquest Research Brief 'Professional Services Gross Margins in Asia/Pacific', 21 August, 2000.
2   *Wall Street Journal*, 'McKinsey and Chinese client spar over quality of services', 13 June, 2001.

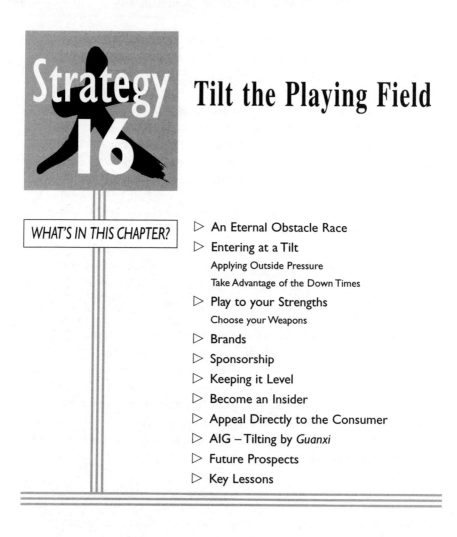

Tilt the Playing Field

An Eternal Obstacle Race

Few Asian markets are level playing fields, and, if they were, few local companies would be able to compete successfully with competitors from outside. During the past 30 years, the ethnic Chinese conglomerates in Southeast Asia, the *chaebol* in South Korea, the state-owned enterprises in China and the *keiretsu* companies in Japan operated behind protective barriers which foreign firms found almost impossible to breach. Those hardy or fool-hardy firms that did succeed in entering markets in the region then found themselves up against every kind of obstacle from government monopolies, preferential tariffs, provincial and local interests, bureaucracy, local rules and controls, not to mention barriers linked with differing ethical standards.

Thus for most Western firms, the Asian experience became more of an unending game of snakes and ladders. Just as they had avoided one snake and had their foot on the ladder, another obstacle appeared to block their way – often aimed specifically to stop any foreign competitor who did seem to be succeeding despite the odds. However, since the economic crisis in 1997, there has been a loosening of the protective reins, allowing a swathe of new foreign entrants to set up and compete in the region. Some have built up strong positions in several markets and managed to tilt the playing field a little further their way. How they did it and what lessons there are for companies attempting to emulate them are the focus of this chapter.

Entering at a Tilt

Applying Outside Pressure

Some Western firms have utilised international organisations to help them break into heavily protected industries. The WTO and the IMF have both played a major role in levelling playing fields in the region. The IMF has pushed Southeast Asian governments into liberalising, albeit reluctantly and slowly, sectors such as banking and generally opening up previously closed markets, such as media, power and telecommunications. China's long-awaited entry into the WTO raised high expectations among foreign investors of the benefits – easier access to markets through cuts in import tariff rates, action on problems connected with IP and so on – they would reap from this move. Some of these expectations have since proved a little ambitious yet despite China's snail-like progress on many trade issues (see Chapter 20), the recent successes (relative to earlier attempts to operate there) of multinationals in China is proof that WTO membership has indeed delivered a slightly more even playing field.

One of the best examples of the successful use of outside pressure in recent years was the use of the US Trade Representative (USTR) by the tobacco companies to prise open the potentially highly lucrative markets of Asia-Pacific. According to WHO (World Health Organization) figures, in 2000 Asia had the second highest annual per capita growth rate in tobacco consumption, thanks to 50–80% consumption levels among men in China, Cambodia, Vietnam, the Philippines and South Korea (where one in three of its 46 million population smokes an average of one packet a day).[1] Markets such as Japan, Taiwan, South Korea and Thailand were potentially highly attractive markets, given their prosperity and a combined population of heavy smokers that is larger than the US.

However, they remained closed to foreign manufacturers, protected by the high tariffs and punitive excise taxes imposed on imported cigarettes.

Not until the 1980s were these markets opened with assistance from the Office of the USTR. The US began to impose retaliatory tariffs on countries discriminating against US goods, using Section 301 of the 1974 Revision of US Trade Act. The first to cave in were Japan and Taiwan in 1987. Subsequently, imported brands grew from 1% to 20% in less than two years in Taiwan.

South Korea, traditionally a nationalistic and xenophobic market, was less easy – citizens caught smoking American cigarettes were subject to the equivalent of a $1,000 fine. After prolonged negotiations, protests against the US invaders and a boycott, taxes and tariffs were finally lowered to enable foreign brands to compete there. BAT, which set up the first foreign-owned cigarette company there in 2001, announced that during the next decade it planned to spend over $1 billion on expansion in Korea.

The toughest nut to crack turned out to be Thailand, whose government had banned the import of foreign cigarettes. In 1989, the USTR announced it would initiate Section 301 proceedings against Thailand unless it opened its market to US cigarettes and removed its advertising ban. The response was strong opposition locally and loud protests against this 'tobacco imperialism'.

Linking up with the anti-smoking lobby in Washington, Thailand took its case to the US, where it found vocal support. Under pressure, the USTR referred the case to the GATT (General Agreement on Tariffs and Trade), which ruled in 1990 that Thailand had to admit foreign cigarette brands but could restrict marketing techniques in the light of public health considerations, provided the rules applied equally to foreign and domestic brands. The entry of foreign firms into the market resulted in a rise in the number of imported packs of cigarettes from 12 million in 1991 to 85 million by 1997 – a fourfold increase. Whatever the virtues of smoking, it was a victory for the levelling of the field.

Take Advantage of the Down Times

The 1990s saw an invasion en masse of Western hyperstores into the food retail markets of the region. In Thailand, Indonesia, Malaysia and later China, foreign retailers moved quickly to take advantage of the 1997 economic crisis to buy up assets sold off by indebted Asian firms.

New foreign entrants, for example, swamped Thailand. The UK food retailer, Tesco, the French hypermarket chain, Carrefour and Ahold of the Netherlands all entered the country within the same short period. In 1998, Tesco went into partnership with the CP group to operate the Lotus chain of supermarkets, eventually buying 93% of Ek-Chai Distribution System, which operates the Tesco-Lotus stores in Thailand. Its success can be gauged by the fact that in 2001 it had 27 stores but planned to have over 40 stores within the next two years. In South Korea, Tesco joined up with Samsung and by 2001 ran seven stores, and had one fully owned store in Taiwan. It also planned to open in Malaysia and was researching the feasibility of opening up in Japan and China.

Carrefour, which had been an early entrant in Taiwan in the early 1990s and China in 1995, seized the opportunity of the downturn to open its first hypermarket in Indonesia in October 1998, five months after President Soeharto resigned and despite frequent street riots and other political unrest. It also expanded its presence in China and went into Hong Kong. Makro entered a joint venture with local partners in Metro Manila in 1996, and evolved into a distribution giant, the fourth biggest retailer there, albeit in a sector with a host of small players.

Having successfully entered, the next task was to fortify their positions so that they would not be easily dislodged when the tide turned. The ways in which they did this should provide some heartening reminders that Western firms do possess some powerful strengths when it comes to competing, even on uneven playing fields.

Play to your Strengths

Marketing in the world's mature economies – the saturated markets of Western Europe and the United States where companies scramble not for new markets but market share – has been honed to a fine art. Techniques have become sophisticated and complex and are light years ahead of the Asian approach, which amounts to little more than selling. Most Asian companies rely on their cost and speed advantages, and so have not developed strong marketing skills. Therefore, although in Asia foreign firms may be competing with similar products and targeting the same customer groups, their superior marketing approach can give them an enormous competitive edge when it comes to winning customers. Going one stage further and leveraging this know-how and technical superiority to the full, Western firms can revolutionise the market so that even when an attempt is made to tilt the field back in favour of local players, it is too late.

The truth of this has been demonstrated by the success of the Western hypermarkets. Few would have predicted that Thai consumers would desert their traditional wet markets which catered to their preference for fresh food, or their conveniently local 'Mom and Pop' stores. But competitive pricing, a better range of goods and pleasant shopping conditions won the day. Hypermarkets have proved to be a success. Thai consumers voted with their feet.

Choose your Weapons

Good service and competitive prices are two elements that foreign firms can use to tilt the balance in their favour. Service, in particular, is often underestimated by Western firms. Customer service is still embryonic in much of Asia and thus one area in which new entrants can readily out-compete existing players. Simply by doing the basic things right, Western firms can transform the shopping experience of customers in China used to the eternal cry of '*méi you*' (No, I don't have it) usually accompanied by a 'couldn't care less' shrug. Foreign firms put more emphasis on the avail-ability of goods, consistent quality, money-back guarantees if customers are not satisfied, complaints procedures that really work and a general respon-siveness to customer needs – elementary to Western retailers and consumers, but a surprise when you are used to a less welcoming shopping experience. Air conditioning, for example, was a winner in Western hyper-market stores, where shoppers were happy to find bikes, furniture and food all under one roof and be able to browse in comfort. Comments such as 'the prices seemed lower, the aisles roomier and the staff a lot more friendly', or 'They have the best selection of products here, and they sell at good prices so I don't even bother going to the traditional market any more' show how easily firms can take for granted factors that Asian shoppers find irre-sistible, and how simple tilting can be.[2]

Price is an important weapon when it comes to tilting the balance. Their previous experience in low-margin, high-volume operations gave Western retailers a big advantage over local firms; goods sold in Tesco-Lotus stores in Thailand were on average 10% cheaper than in local stores. Western firms also have an armoury of special offers, price promotions and loss leaders used at home in the frequent price wars that have shaken out the European and US markets. Western firms also have deeper pockets than most local players, many of whom face strict credit terms. And since they are in it for the long term and know the difficulties, Western firms are prepared, although not happy, to sustain losses for a time in order to build a long-term position.

Another great strength of Western firms is their superior IT systems. Supply chain management as an information-sharing exercise is a technique widely used by European and US firms such as P&G, Nestlé and Unilever, but its cost makes it an expensive luxury for Asian firms. Systems such as these allowed the Western retailers to monitor inventory levels, turnovers, margins and the profitability of different product categories. In particular this delivers great savings in cost and efficiencies in the supply chain, which can respond more quickly to consumer demand and forecast future needs. The system also leads to better inventory control and lower inventory overall. Consumers are guaranteed that products will be available on the shelves when and where they want them, another reason for remaining loyal.

Tesco, which has been at the forefront of technological innovation, played this card very well, using the combined strength of its superior supply chain management and greater purchasing power to revolutionise the food retail industry in Thailand. Tesco-Lotus installed Integrated Software Solutions' (ISS) NT Controller, a new point-of-sale back-office system. Being totally web-based, this system can open or close stores from any location. It provides better service to customers by improving the processing time in the back office and at checkout lanes.[3]

The company also built up an excellent distribution network and developed close relations with the suppliers from whom it sourced cheap local produce. It was always ready to experiment with new products, always ready to innovate. Above all, it tried to understand its new set of customers and translate that understanding into new products and marketing ideas.

The Western food retailers brought a whole new approach to the Thai food retail industry, and since nothing succeeds like success, once word got around that these companies were doing well, they began to attract the best and brightest of young local managers who wanted to work for them and learn the new techniques.

Brands

Brands can be another potent weapon. Asians have long been among the world's most conspicuous consumers: pre-crisis, Thailand was the second largest market for Mercedes-Benz cars. However, no Asian company has yet matched the allure of brands such as Cartier, the LVMH stable, Gucci and Prada. In Japan, where most have their Asian flagship stores, these brands continued to sell well despite the economic crisis. Post-recession, sales of luxury goods held up particularly in Japan. Consumers switched to buying their luxury goods at home rather than going abroad to buy the same goods.

Not every firm can have the branding of a Cartier, so it is worth building up your brand on other factors such as reliability, taste, value for money. In the past the most mundane product – such as Scottish biscuits or canned drinks – could bear a higher price, given the cachet of a Western brand name. Although this compulsion is less strong, it can still be a deciding purchasing factor. Carrefour charges premium prices for its French wines. Scottish brands of whisky and French brandy have long made great profits in markets that do not always have a tradition for drinking spirits, merely buying the brand as a status symbol. Once established, brand extensions are a way of keeping sales churning, as football clubs have learned only too well – change the strip and sit back as the customers roll in.

Sponsorship

Sponsorship has been one means used by Western companies for putting their brand names in the public eye. When it first entered Asia, Cartier had an edge through sponsoring major cultural promotions. In Hong Kong, for example, it used highly prized concerts and ballet performances to get across the message of Cartier as an exclusive product, available only to the elite.

Another group that found sponsorship a useful way to communicate was the tobacco companies. Following the prohibition of cigarette advertising on TV and radio, sponsorship, first of major sporting events and later of the arts and social foundations, became a major tool in promoting their brands. In Asia, where advertising regulations, tax conditions and other factors proved unfavourable, sponsorship became crucial in the long-term image building of a brand, providing national media publicity, access to influential people and promoting a positive image. Therefore the US companies built their brands largely through sponsorship; a Marlboro Soccer League, a Marlboro Music Hour, a Kent Billiards contest and a Salem tennis tournament. Cross-border media such as the Internet and satellite TV opened up further opportunities. For example, Star TV, which by 2000 had 300 million viewers in Asia, aired 1,237 hours of tobacco-sponsored commercials in a one-year period.

Keeping it Level

Using your marketing strengths and skills may help to build your position but playing fields in Asia rarely remain level for long. Once Western firms become successful, new obstacles are likely to appear. The nationalist card is one that is often played, regardless of the interests of consumers. Foreign retail companies, welcomed as saviours of local firms initially, later found themselves under attack precisely because they were too successful. Under pressure from local retailers, the government planned new zoning laws and restrictions on opening hours, measures specifically aimed at stopping their further progress.

In another case, the Chinese authorities accused Carrefour, the most successful foreign retailer in China, of breaking central government regulations. In fact, in order to enter China in 1995, Carrefour had cleverly tilted the field by circumventing the State Economic and Trade Commission (SETC), from whom it should have obtained approval to open up stores. Instead, it had made individual joint venture agreements with local partners and authorities. This had proved a fast track for Carrefour, so that by the time the central authorities caught up with it at the end of 2000, it was well entrenched in the market, with 27 stores and 16,000 employees, and planned to open 10 more stores in the next year.

There was wide expectation that Carrefour would be heavily punished for its temerity. Either it would be forced to close down its stores or sell its stakes to its local partners but, in the event, it got off very lightly. The secret is that the bigger the local employer you become, the more reluctant the central government will be to upset provincial authorities by adding to their unemployment statistics. In fact, Carrefour had created its own *guanxi*, one that proved a powerful talisman.

It was also lucky in its timing, as with entry into the WTO imminent, China was keen to polish its image. Consequently, after the usual round of lengthy negotiations, Carrefour was merely required to suspend the opening of its ten new stores for six months, although Beijing did deliver a sideswipe by giving permission for the US retailer Wal-Mart to open five supermarkets in Beijing as a reward for playing by the rules.

Carrefour was lucky, but not every firm can rely on the WTO to save it from attack. However, there are some moves that Western companies can take to protect themselves from unfair recriminations and keep the playing field tilted in their favour.

Become an Insider

One way in which foreign firms can counter the argument that they are taking away the livelihoods of local traders is to become insiders themselves, by showing that they are benefiting the local economy with additional employment, technological expertise and exports.

Steps that might arouse local antagonism should be avoided. Don't get a reputation as a cost cutter or for laying off staff, instead respect local customs and be known as a good employer. For example, if existing dealers get rewards or have bonus systems, then work with it, rather than try to cut them out as soon as you take over. Invest in training schemes and make your company one that ambitious workers will want to join.

Again, Tesco proved itself a master at this.[4] It set up its head office in Bangkok, from where it supported logistics, IT, operational policy and the financial management of all its supercentres in the region. It also exported local food products for sale in its UK branches. In the first six months of 1999, these had a value of over Bt700 million. It also helps to source products for export to the EU, and to negotiate with EU officials if products are barred from the Thai market. The company works with Thai farmers to introduce new technology to increase crop yields and work on the distribution supply chain for fresh and processed foods. It has also set up a distribution centre responsible for Bt1 billion in annual exports of locally raised chicken from CP to the UK and the EU. And its stores employ 3,000 people. In short, Tesco has been busy spreading the message that it is a good citizen, bringing new technology, new markets and creating employment. The January 2004 outbreak of avian flu affecting Thailand and other parts of SE Asia and China, and the subsequent import bans by Thailand's two largest markets, Japan and the EU, will be a good test of this image and the strength of Tesco's relationships with its local partners. It also underlines how companies operating in Asia must be prepared to deal with the unexpected at any time.

Taking your social responsibilities seriously is another worthwhile strategy; support local charities, fund educational scholarships, contribute to the worthy causes that get publicity. Tesco, for example, has donated Bt36 million to Thai charities since 1998. Each of its supercentres operates a collection box, from which it makes donations to selected community projects. The company also renovated a ten-storey building for use as a training centre for underprivileged children. When planning new stores, it is very careful to meet local community officials and discuss their concerns. As it underlines, its developments bring improvements to the local infrastructure such as improved road, water, electricity and waste systems as well as bus stops, street lighting, green spaces and public seating. Who wouldn't want a Tesco-Lotus store near them?

Appeal Directly to the Consumer

Your greatest allies in any war of words with local competitors or governments are your employees and consumers. No government will risk upsetting millions of shoppers and Tesco, the French groups Carrefour and Big C (run by Casino), together account for over 30% of the nation's grocery sales, which makes for a lot of clout. In such cases, although government might slow your progress down, it won't be able to stop you. At the end of 2001, a Tesco-Lotus branch in Bangkok was the target of a rocket-launched grenade attack, the fourth such incident in a year. To counter this and attacks in the media, the company launched a massive PR campaign. In one newspaper advertisement, a store manager described how he was able to return from Bangkok to his home province, thanks to a job with Tesco-Lotus. All change creates winners and losers, and it's important to ensure that it is not only the noise from the losers that is heard.

AIG – Tilting by *Guanxi*[5]

In 1992, the American International Group (AIG) re-entered China. The company was taking advantage of Deng Xiaoping's opening of some cities to foreign insurance companies. One of the largest insurance companies worldwide, AIG had actually been founded in Shanghai in 1921 and had sold insurance there from the 1920s until its expulsion from the country following the Communist takeover in 1949. Since then, AIG had waited for the day it could return to its roots.

In the meantime, it had built up a strong presence in Asia-Pacific. By 1975, it was the biggest foreign insurer in Hong Kong, Japan, Taiwan and Southeast Asia, and the only one with worldwide sales and support facilities. In 1987, it entered the South Korean market. However, its main target was always China.

As early as 1975, AIG's CEO, Harold Greenberg, began visiting China to begin the process of building up relations. In 1980, AIG opened a representative office and, to show its commitment, set up a joint venture with the People's Insurance Company of China (PICC). AIG began investing in Shanghai which led to Greenberg forging a strong relationship with the city's then mayor, Zhu Rongji. Greenberg was also a founding member and chairman of the International Business Council, which played an important role in establishing Shanghai as a leading financial centre. At the same time, Greenberg continued to keep up links with Beijing, lobbying successfully for China in the US so that the Clinton administration severed the links between its human rights record and renewal of most favoured nation (MFN) status.

In 1992, AIG was awarded the first licence to sell insurance in China since 1949. By then, Zhu Rongji was the country's vice prime minister. In recognition, Greenberg traced ten bronze windows that had disappeared from the Emperor's summer palace in Beijing at the turn of century. Greenberg bought them and donated them to China. 'No foreign corporation has ever returned missing relics to us. They only took things away', observed a Chinese official at the ceremony to mark their return.

Its long history and strong government links continued to give AIG a privileged position in China, the only foreign insurer allowed to offer life and non-life insurance. It was also the only company with wholly owned life insurance subsidiaries; every other foreign company had to be part of a joint venture.

In 1993, Greenberg was elected chairman of the US-China Business Council and, two years later, was appointed senior economic advisor to the Beijing city government. The next year, AIG began operating in

Guangzhou (Canton). Such was Greenberg's *guanxi* that the WTO negotiations were actually held up while he got an agreement that AIG could
maintain its privileged position in China. At one point, his insistence on
AIG maintaining the right to set up wholly owned branches even threatened to derail the talks. In the end a compromise was reached; AIG would
be allowed to open two more wholly owned subsidiaries and would then
have to enter 50/50 joint ventures like everyone else.

With such a start, success was virtually guaranteed, although profits
remained 'relatively small'. In pursuit of greater returns, AIG announced in
October 2003 that it was taking a 9.9% stake in PICC, China's largest property insurer. This move would enable AIG to expand by marketing accident
and health insurance through PICC's 4300 branch offices. In January 2004,
it announced plans to launch a credit card in China in order to be able to tap
into the higher margin personal finance sector. The slogan chanted by the
AIG salesforce in China left no doubt as to the company's ambition; 'Grow
together, increase value together and create a new world for American International Insurance in 2004'. In Shanghai, AIG owned the Shanghai Centre,
and visiting executives could stay in the Hank Greenberg Suite at the Ritz-
Carlton. His *guanxi* remained strong: as one foreign rival remarked, 'Every
time he comes to Shanghai, he leaves with something new'.[6]

Two of AIG's competitors, one Japanese and the other German, pulled
out of the market, citing restrictive rules and the lack of likely profits in
the short term in a market dominated by AIG. In a way it was the ultimate
irony that Greenberg achieved this strong position by tilting the playing
field his way, at the expense of his fellow foreign insurers.

Future Prospects

Competition in Asia will undoubtedly become keener as protection is slowly
removed in the markets of the region. In this battle, Western firms should
clearly have an edge, since they have, after all, been accustomed to playing
in cut-throat markets for the last two decades, and possess both the techniques and the weapons. Asian firms, accustomed to having the playing field
tilted for them, have not yet developed these powers. In this less protected
environment, Western firms have a better chance of becoming Big in Asia.

However, do not expect miracles overnight. The WTO might have
opened the gate a little for Western companies but certain sectors – telecoms, finance, media and oil exploration – are still heavily protected, and
the legal maze is not likely to get significantly easier to navigate in the
near future. State-owned companies may be disappearing, but you can still
expect resistance from entrenched interests. There are still some uneven

playing fields you just cannot tilt – for now. Even the all-conquering Carrefour eventually pulled out of Hong Kong, having failed to make any inroads on this preserve of two old Asia players in the local supermarket business, Jardine Matheson and Li Ka-Shing.

A few other straws in the wind show that, perhaps deep down, things have not changed so much after all. In 2002, the Bank of Central Asia, Indonesia's largest private retail bank, was finally sold after two years, not to the Standard Chartered consortium that had bid heavily for it but to Farindo Investments – which included the Hartono brothers, owners of Indonesia's largest cigarette manufacturer but with no apparent experience of running a bank. In South Korea, LG Telecom and its foreign partners won the auction for a 3G licence for mobile services in Korea. Speaking in June 2001, the country's information minister spoke of 'the need for an unlevel playing field and asymmetrical regulation'.[7]

Key Lessons

- *Play to your strengths:* Use the many weapons in your competitive armoury to fortify your position – build brands, innovate, change consumer tastes, change their habits. Customers will vote with their feet. Once you have captured them, leverage your IT systems to collect information on these tastes and preferences and build a database to monitor consumer tastes and spot unfulfilled needs. In fact, take a normal marketing approach.

- *Be a good citizen:* Show you are benefiting the local economy, not taking away livelihoods.

But remember, no firm can afford to rest on its laurels. Tilting is a never-ending process, so never relax your vigilance. The most dangerous time is when you think you have finally levelled out the playing field. That's when you will hit another obstacle.

Notes

1 Inter Press Service, 'Health-Asia : Activists worry as more women puff away' by Marwaan Macan-Markar, Bangkok 16 August, 2001.
2 *Asiaweek*, 'Forget Politics. Go Shopping', 1–18 June, 2001, pp34–5.
3 *Business Wire*, 'Asian Supercenter Completes Rollout of ISS Technology', 18 September, 2000.
4 'Tesco Lotus in Thailand', briefing paper, Tesco, April 2001.
5 Taken from 'Back to the Roots: AIG Returns to China', case study by Guido Meyerhans and Professor Qiwen Lu, 1998 INSEAD-EAC.
6 *Financial Times*, 'AIG reaps benefits of early arrival', 26 June, 2003 p18.
7 *EIU Business Asia*, 'Auction or stitch-up?', 11 June, 2001.

Think Global, Act Local – But How Far?

Going 'Glocal'?

Most Western companies marketing their products in Asia have long recognised the need to adapt their products to local conditions and tastes. Some adaptations are straightforward and for obvious reasons. McDonald's, for example, does not sell burgers made from beef in India. The skin pigmentation and hair composition of Asian people differ from those of, say, European descent and, consequently, the formulae for personal products, cosmetics, shampoos and skin creams need to be changed. Different cultural habits are another reason for product adjustment. When L'Oréal decided to launch its cosmetics products in Indonesia, it had to take into account the customs of the mainly Muslim female population. For example, while the market for nail varnish was small for religious reasons, customers were heavy users of powder on their bodies and faces to protect their skin from the sun. Also, tampons do not sell well in Islamic countries but sanitary towels do.

By contrast, the need for some other adaptations has been less immediately obvious. The first cars marketed in Asia by European auto manufacturers were not adapted to the humidity and heat of Asia, and so rusted quickly. However, it took some time for Western manufacturers to appreciate the implications of this and adjust their product specification to make their cars saleable.

Until recently, adaptation in Asia concentrated on this type of adjustment to match local customs and tastes – an approach characterised by the famous phrase 'think global, act local'. Even those who once believed that they possessed truly global products were eventually forced by poor sales in secondary markets to admit that perhaps the global village was yet to arrive, and that adaptation to local tastes was unavoidable. Coca-Cola, one of the greatest exponents of the global brand, was eventually forced to tinker with the formula of its most cherished product, the original Coca-Cola, and give it a sweeter taste. The company also had to adjust the product lines it sold in the region; about a quarter of the products it sells in Asia are not found elsewhere in the world – including oolong tea, bottled waters and a range of soft drinks.

Of course, adaptation did not stop at the product or product range, it also meant making adjustments to the rest of the marketing mix; price, promotion and place (distribution), all of which might need to be tuned to local purses, customs and market structures. In particular, distribution can be a difficult hurdle for Western companies in Asia. There is little point in having well-adapted products that are beautifully packaged if you cannot get them to the customers.

This vital part of the marketing mix often calls for a new approach since, in Asia, distribution networks may be tightly controlled, interwoven (as in Japan) and difficult to crack. Some firms try to build their own distribution networks, although this can be expensive in terms of time and financial resources. Others, such as the Western food retail giants, wait until they have grown to a critical mass and then use their size to bargain successfully with local distributors and suppliers.

Direct selling methods have worked well in countries such as India, where disparate rural markets make for poor and costly distribution systems. Here, the US-based Avon, Amway and Tupperware and the Swedish company, Oriflame, recruited an army of housewives working from home on a commission basis. Such was their success that Unilever copied the concept in parts of the country where it operated. Clearly it was best suited to the local environment and, in addition, research showed that customers felt more comfortable buying relatively high-priced cosmetics when they could discuss and try the products first.

However, apart from the more obvious situations such as those described earlier, when and how far foreign companies should adapt their products and marketing strategies to Asian markets remains an open question. Price has been the most important of the four marketing 'Ps' in the region but, as markets become increasingly fragmented, it is anticipated that promotion and the way the product is positioned may move further up the list. This will have important implications for the way firms promote and package their products in Asia. In packaging and marketing, for example, should companies translate the ideograms conceptually or phonetically to avoid losing the intrinsic concept of their offering? (The now defunct Australian airline Ansett once launched a campaign built around its new fleet of passenger jets that it claimed were especially spacious inside. 'The space-ships are coming' was the campaign slogan. The literal Chinese translation of this in Hong Kong was 'Empty every day' – a slogan guaranteed to kill sales rather than generate them.) In Asia, brand management is still a fledg-ling subject but, in the near future, finer segmentation will require the use of more sophisticated marketing techniques, especially as more local brands emerge and compete more strongly.

Both markets and consumers are changing rapidly, and the right answer for 'today' can only come out of a combination of thorough market research and experience. Many Western firms finally settle on a mix of global and adapted brands, while dividing the region between Japan and the rest of Asia. For them, the important thing is to convey the message which it wishes consumers to associate with their offerings; good value, luxury or reliability. The French group L'Oréal has global and adapted brands but, for both, the message remains the same; the emphasis is on quality and performance in every market it serves.

In the future, globalisation may result in less need for a fully adapted local approach, but rather a halfway house between the two, an approach that has been christened 'glocal'. This will certainly be welcome in terms of cutting costs, but how will it go down in Asia? Are the markets there still so very different to the extent that intense adaptation is necessary, or are Asian consumers, increasingly exposed to Western products and adver-tising, more like their European and North American counterparts in their tastes and habits? Or are they growing more like each other, making a pan-Asian positioning possible? The next sections look at the experiences of some of the most successful companies in the region, to see how far they have been willing to go to satisfy their customers – the people who can make them Big in Asia.

Adaptation

Those Who Do

Retailing is a very localised concept, where companies need to be sensitive to local tastes and habits. Consequently, Western firms in the fast-moving consumer goods (FMCG) sector have been at the forefront of adaptation. For them, the necessity for some adjustment in order to operate successfully in the food retail or personal products sectors is not in dispute. Rather, their dilemma is the degree of difference in the Asian markets that should be considered when formulating their strategies. Are these differences of substance or context? Is Asia, or at least parts of it, so different that it merits a completely different approach, or are there sufficient similarities to allow for some coordination?

One set of reasons for acting locally that has remained constant in Asia is the existence of what are known as 'structural inhibitors'. These include factors such as the low purchasing power of households in many parts of the region, the lack of storage space in most homes and the small number of private vehicle owners. Taken together, these factors mean that consumers want low prices, they shop regularly (perhaps every other day), buy products in small sizes rather than in bulk and visit their local shops rather than a big store situated on the edge of town.

These habits obviously had particular implications for the foreign hypermarkets when they moved into Southeast Asia. Those that did not take these factors into account made some expensive false starts, such as opening poorly sited stores in areas not served by public transport. Sometimes the errors can seem astonishingly basic, particularly with hindsight. The US-based Wal-Mart realised rather too late that trying to sell clothes to the Chinese in US sizes was a mistake.

Generally, the most successful Western companies in the FMCG sector have taken their basic business model and adapted it to take account of local tastes when entering the region, while retaining key home strengths, either because they appealed to Asian consumers or they gave them a competitive advantage over local rivals. One of the best operators to have used this formula in the food retail sector is the French hypermarket group, Carrefour. Known in its home markets for offering low prices and value for money – a positioning ideal for Asia – it also possessed strong IT capabilities that put it way ahead of the domestic competition in Asia.

Carrefour, which was the first hypermarket to move into the region, undertook a careful study of local conditions before opening its first store in Taiwan in 1989.[1] As a result, it adapted the Carrefour concept to take into account the particularities of the local environment. This meant adapting both the physical layout of the stores and the products it offered to suit local tastes, besides managing its relationship with suppliers very differently. However, onto these changes Carrefour grafted its home competitive strengths; one-stop shopping, free parking and low prices. The result was the successful launch of a store in Taiwan which was the first of many; ten years later it had 18 stores in the country, and had expanded successfully elsewhere in the region.

By the time Carrefour opened up in Indonesia in 1998 (despite the economic crisis), it had 44 stores operating in the region and an 'Asian recipe' ready to roll. In Indonesia, Carrefour focused on sites in central business areas and shopping malls – which were also much cheaper to rent in the aftermath of the crisis. The stores stocked more Indonesian than French goods, fresh prawns and leafy vegetables at low prices which customers could afford. In Malaysia, where more widespread car owner-ship allowed people to shop in bulk two or three times a month, Carrefour's hypermarkets completely changed the habits of consumers, offering them shelves stocked not just with all their favourite local noodles and herbs, but French wines and Carrefour brands exactly like those sold in France.

As this example illustrates, the tradition of local adaptation is fairly well entrenched in the retailing sector. However, even players in newer industry sectors, such as telecoms, have discovered that it pays to research local tastes and adapt your product accordingly. The Finnish company Nokia gained a commanding lead over its rivals in the Indonesian mobile handset market by adopting a classic segmentation strategy towards the developing market. It segmented the market into four types, premium, business, fashion and entry-level users, and then introduced a range of handsets to match the tastes of each segment. To sell these offerings, Nokia built its own distribution network with four major handset distributors and an accessories firm. While Nokia provided the branding for the mobiles, the locals provided the tactical promotion.[2]

But a word of warning; going local does not automatically guarantee success. Carrefour, perhaps surprisingly, failed in Japan due to overadapt-ation. Its strategy of being local meant that there was no incentive for consumers to shop at Carrefour rather than a Japanese supermarket.

So they didn't. Therefore, it had to go into reverse and emphasise its French heritage.

Boots, another UK retailer, first entered Thailand very successfully. A spokesman for the company noted:

> Clean shops and good service have gone down a treat, but we did have to make some adjustments. Customers were uncomfortable that the shops were so quiet — so we had to install banks of video screens broadcasting pop music and videos.[3]

Boots' key ranges underwent some adaptation, for example in Thailand, it found a high demand for tights because of air conditioning.

However, in Japan, it was less successful despite its attempts to be local. There, registration rules meant that Boots often had to reformulate its offerings and the majority of its products were repackaged with Japanese text. Yet the Boots' brands, even the specially developed Boots No. 7 Face Whitening range, failed to gain a foothold in the market and, at the end of 2001, the company withdrew.

Unilever

> Successful brands can only grow out of a deep understanding of Asian consumer attitudes and behaviours. Transferring Western mixes is by no means a certain recipe for success. (a Unilever manager)

Undoubtedly, the grandfather of local adaptation is the Anglo-Dutch consumer giant, Unilever.[4] Many of its portfolio of 400 brands – known throughout the world – began as local brands which were acquired by Unilever and turned into international brands. The famous Pond's range, for example, was originally a US brand, bought and adapted by Unilever and a bestseller in China. It is a skill that the company has honed to perfection.

Unilever's heritage of strong local autonomy meant that the degree to which products were adapted to suit local markets was the decision of Unilever country managers throughout its global empire. In Asia, its hair products ranges – shampoos and conditioners – were designed and crafted for each market in the region and tested to the liking of, say, Indonesians and Thais before going on sale.

In Southeast Asia, where markets had a high proportion of poor, rural customers, Unilever sold its hair care products in small quantities, one-shot sachets which consumers could buy two or three times a week, rather than the big bottles of shampoo sold in the West. This was backed up by a highly efficient sales and logistics system, since the company was producing millions of these sachets, often selling three a week to the same consumer. Where necessary, the company built up a distribution system from scratch, training local salesmen who travelled by whatever form of transport was best suited to the local terrain – tricycle, boat or motorcycle – in order to reach retailers in remote areas of the country. This is a consideration that has broader application across Asia. Roads, particularly in rural areas, are poor or often too narrow to allow for conventional delivery trucks.

In these markets, Unilever rolled out its product range according to a well-tried and tested pattern which the company had identified as most appropriate for developing markets. It began with the cheapest products, and then slowly introduced more expensive ranges to develop consumer tastes, increase market share and forge brand loyalty. In India, it reinforced its presence by also providing a local film show for villages which would never otherwise have had such entertainment. Unilever's strategy might be described as the 'Jesuit' approach to local markets – get the customers while they are poor and grow with them, and they will be yours for life. It was also a long-term approach, since it can take 10–15 years to get a return. Consequently it is only a strategy for companies with strong financial resources and shareholders prepared to wait for a return.

The Unilever strategy proved highly successful in India and Southeast Asia and, more recently, Vietnam. There, Unilever put all its experience to work to steal a march on its rivals to build a strong position in soaps, detergents and personal products (especially hair), virtually gaining a 100% share of the markets in the poor rural parts of the country. In these areas, where consumers typically bought just enough for their daily needs, Unilever expanded aggressively via its one-shot shampoos, toothpaste and detergent packets that could be found in every village.

Its sales managers visited remote retailers in the country regularly – often by boat in the Mekong Delta area – to push them to expand and offer the full range of Unilever products, from soaps and shampoos to tea and skin-whitening products. From time to time, Unilever would flood the local market with a new product at a slightly higher price, to push consumers up the value chain. Retailers were offered incentives such as refrigerators to display Unilever brands, while a big advertising campaign reinforced the brand identity.

However, although Unilever remained the strongest exponent of local adaptation, in the early 1990s it concluded that its emphasis on strong local autonomy meant that its products were often adapted unnecessarily, leading to losses in economies of scale. Increasingly, given the trend towards large scale economies, rapid innovation and flexible response times, such an approach was proving a handicap. Therefore, Unilever opted for a more regional or 'glocal' approach, whereby it would take a Southeast Asian idea and adapt it marginally for Thailand, the Philippines, Malaysia and so on. Instead of expensive and time-consuming total adaptation, the basic product would merely be fine-tuned.

One of its biggest successes using this approach was in its Wall's ice cream business.[5] Unilever was quick to identify the huge potential that existed for a regional ice cream created specifically for Asians, whose tastes differed markedly from the rest of the world. When its red bean ice cream failed to make any impression due to poor marketing and inadequate research into the choice of ingredients, the company's Bangkok innovation centre (one of 11 set up by Unilever in Asia) was asked to completely redesign the product, its packaging and promotion.

Asian Delight was launched first in Malaysia in 1994. It used Thai and English on its packaging in Thailand, and English only in Malaysia, Singapore and Indonesia. It was targeted at the segment located between products which Unilever sold worldwide, such as its Magnum range, and local brands acquired by other multinationals. The basis of the recipe was coconut ice cream, mixed with a variety of fruits and vegetables traditionally used in sweets throughout the region. It was a runaway success. By 1998, varieties of Asian Delight were being sold in supermarkets, and available on sticks, in cups and pint containers. In Thailand, a television advert showed Asian women teasing each other into doing a native dance in order to get a taste of Asian Delight. In 2000, Wall's dominated the market with 41%, followed by Nestlé with just 15%.

When the Asian economic crisis hit the region, Unilever was well able to adjust its strategy to suit the lower spending power of its Southeast Asian customers. Using its wealth of experience, it focused on the 5 Cs – the consumer, the customer, costs, cash and communications – and introduced less expensive product lines. Its competitors adopted similar strategies. For example, Nestlé's Thai subsidiary sold its powdered coffee and coffee-mate products in economic refill bags rather than tins and glass jars. Interestingly, L'Oréal, which went ahead with the launch of a new cosmetics range in Indonesia despite the crisis, found that sales of its make-up products stood up well. Customers might select cheaper products, but only 3% of its customers stopped buying make-up entirely.

Media and Advertising

The cultural diversity and strong national pride that characterises many countries in the region means that anything other than a local positioning is difficult to sustain in the media industry. A big story on Thailand, for example, does not pull in readers in Malaysia or the Philippines. The experience of the weekly *Asiaweek*, which tried to position itself as a pan-Asian journal, appears to confirm this view. *Asiaweek*, which became part of the US Time Warner media empire, tried to straddle the diversity of the region by aiming at Asia's emerging middle class – English speakers interested in Asian affairs. Unfortunately, the journal found itself caught in a no man's land between global players, such as *Time* and *Newsweek*, and local competitors. In the end it folded, defeated by the struggle to find the right audience among so many local ones.[6]

Advertising is another area where it still pays to be local. As the head of Leo Burnett Worldwide observed: 'The key to making money in the Asian advertising business is to recognise that it is not one region but many.'[7] The evidence supports his contention that those who understand, and have some insight into, the various markets in Asia are more likely to succeed than those who 'arbitrarily globalise or generalise Asian Pacific'. Take the flagship brand of the US-based tobacco group Philip Morris, Marlboro, incarnated in the world famous image of 'Marlboro Man', the free-ranging cowboy roving Marlboro country. It was the most successful and longest running campaign in history – until it got to Asia. There, the image of a hired hand was not one locals aspired to and so when the brand was launched in Hong Kong, Marlboro Man became a boss.

In some countries, censorship and cultural norms shape what can and cannot be shown in television advertisements. In China, Western advertising companies discovered the hard way that using sexily-dressed women to advertise products was not acceptable. L'Oréal tried using the Chinese film star Gong Li, now famous in the West, to sell its products in China, but the glamorous image did not prove as attractive as the company anticipated, suggesting that Western notions of beauty differ from those of average Chinese viewers. In Beijing, local scenes and historical characters as a background to television advertisements were long the preferred choice of local viewers. However, foreign advertisers have noted that tastes are changing and that more creative ads for rice cookers, sports shoes and even hamburgers are succeeding. In October 2003, McDonald's announced that its next global ad would come from a Chinese firm, although this level of sophistication is as yet limited to urban audiences. Otherwise, advertisers must continue to respect certain no-go areas, for example 'We can't undermine the position of authority figures, primarily teachers and parents, in Chinese society'.[8]

Adverts must be further tuned to take account of the differences between north and south China. Food adverts, for example, emphasise different ingredients according to regional tastes; in Sichuan, where the locals like spicy food, the type of noodle advertised is chosen accordingly. In Xinjiang, which has a largely Muslim population, pork noodles are not advertised. Only a few established brands, such as Unilever's Lux and Pond's cold cream, use the same advertisements throughout China.

However, Unilever itself roused the anger of women's groups in Malaysia following the running of an advert to illustrate the efficacy of its Pond's skin-lightening moisturiser.[9] The implication that the girl in the advertisement was more attractive after using it caused great offence, since it seemed to send the message that only fair people were beautiful. This again raised old prejudices, since historically a fair skin was associated with wealth and status and a dark skin with those who worked out of doors. The modern version of this is that 'white' means 'Western'. Even the most experienced can get it wrong.

Adaptation

And Those Who Don't

Western producers of luxury and designer goods have had a field day in Asia in the last few years. Although volatile economic conditions in Europe and North America have an effect on sales in Asia, and most notably in Japan, demand has remained fairly constant. Japanese shoppers buy about 40% of the world's high-quality leather goods, and account for more than half the sales of luxury goods groups such as Gucci and Louis Vuitton. Christian Dior alone opened seven stores in Japan between 2000–01. And then there is the purchasing of luxury goods outside Asia by Asians. The long queue that forms daily outside the Louis Vuitton concession within the Galeries Lafayette department store in Paris almost exclusively comprises visiting Japanese. All this reflects the Asian perception of Western luxury brands as status symbols. Buying them to keep up appearances is the main motivating factor in their purchase.

These are companies for whom brand adaptation clearly makes no sense. The chairman of the Vendôme Group, which houses brands such as Chloé, Jaeger, Cartier and Karl Lagerfeld, noted that 'We represent tradition. We don't want to dilute that tradition by over-adaptation to the Asian market', while the chief executive of Cartier has said that 'Culturally, Asia is not a luxury market. It is only a consumer market. Luxury was born in Europe. Here it is just a status symbol.'[10] These companies' struggle in

Asia is not with adaptation but with counterfeiting, the need to protect the value of their brands from being diluted by fakes.

Other brands that trade on the cachet of being expensive Western products include Scotch whisky, BMW cars and French cognac Hennessy XO. For some of its premium perfume and cosmetics products, L'Oréal has insisted on keeping its positioning as international brands, while making some cultural adaptation in its advertisements. Thus, Christy Turlington, the then top US model, was replaced by a famous Asian model for certain cosmetic products. However, in the advertisements to promote L'Oréal's Maybelline range, the tag 'Maybe she's born with it/Maybe it's Maybelline' was kept in English or, if translated, kept the same meaning and rhyme.

Local Branding

One way that companies may achieve an edge in advertising is to change the name of their product for something with local meaning. This can have more impact than keeping a Western brand name that is meaningless to locals. In China, names with clear and positive meanings such as 'good health' or 'good fortune' seem to be better appreciated by consumers. For example, the Chinese name for Coca-Cola is pronounced *Ke-ko-ke-le* and means 'palatable and enjoyable to your mouth'. BMW (*Bao-ma*) means 'treasured horse' and Pepsi-Cola (*Bai-shi-ke-le*) means 'hundreds of enjoyable things'.[11]

Another potentially advantageous move can be to localise your website by adding foreign language versions. By communicating with customers in their own language, you can both inform them about you and ask them questions to gather important information on their likes and dislikes.

Finally, be on the lookout for brands that can be reverse-engineered from Asia into Western markets. One famous example is the French magazine *Elle*'s range of bags, T-shirts and shoes. This range began life in Japan in the 1980s as special gift items to be given away to new *Elle* subscribers.[12] However, they became so sought after that the company began to produce the range of products, at first just for the Japanese market where it became the fourth largest foreign brand and, after 1991, for the rest of the region and later, the West. Another is Red Bull, the caffeinated soft drink which originated as Krating Daeng in Thailand. This drink, used in Thailand by truck drivers to keep themselves awake, is now used by London nightclubbers for the same purpose, making a billionaire of the Austrian entrepreneur who thought to take the drink global.

Brands: Understand the Message

Although Asian consumers are very familiar with the notion of the brand as image – hence the obsession with luxury designer goods – this does not yet extend to a widespread understanding of the message behind the brand (or brand identity) that companies wish to convey. This can mislead foreign firms, especially if sales of their products are strong, into believing that their Asian consumers are susceptible to the same message as in the West. The realisation that they are not can mean a rethink of their strategy for promoting their product in Asia.

The South African diamond group, De Beers, for example, has been successful in promoting diamond rings as a 'gift of love', since the custom of the diamond engagement ring is culturally embedded in all its Western markets.[13] It entered the Japanese market with the same 'symbol of love' message, and its first cinema advertisement showed a Hollywood rather than a typically Japanese romantic scene. Despite this, the concept of a diamond engagement ring was readily accepted, partly because its value was associated with status by Japanese families, and also because it fitted in with the traditional engagement ceremony or *yuino*. By the late 1980s, Japan had become the second largest market in the world for diamond jewellery.

However, by 1996 engagement ring purchases had plunged to 64% from a peak of 76%. This was partly due to the effect of several years of economic recession but, more importantly, it reflected a trend among the younger generation away from the formal traditions of the *yuino* with which De Beers had successfully associated ring-buying. De Beers discovered that, in fact, the 'gift of love' message had not really been accepted in Japan; the motivation for buying a ring had not been emotional, but rather a desire to conform socially.

It further concluded, as it researched other markets in the region, that there was no such person as an 'Asian consumer'. The company had first thought of opting for a 'glocal' pan-regional positioning but, in fact, in the face of the different historical and cultural influences that drove jewellery sales, this proved impossible to sustain. In countries such as Korea, Taiwan and Hong Kong, the insecurity of life meant that jewellery was viewed as a store of wealth. Love and romance were not so freely discussed – there was not even an equivalent word for 'romance' in the Chinese, Thai, Malay or Korean languages. In Southeast Asia, some women 'did not feel dressed' unless they were wearing jewellery.

Through its research, De Beers eventually uncovered a whole new segment of diamond purchasers in Asia that it had never targeted before;

women who bought jewellery for themselves, just for the joy of wearing it. Instead of waiting for tomorrow and the 'happy day', when their true love would present them with a diamond ring, they were quite prepared to buy diamonds for themselves today. The Western 'gift of love' message actually risked alienating this powerful segment. In the face of this, De Beers decided to create a special 'women's desire' advertising campaign to appeal specifically to the Asian self-purchase market. By 1997, this segment accounted for up to 60% of the company's total sales in every Asian country except Korea. It existed nowhere else in the world.

China, as usual, was a special case. De Beers entered China as early as 1986 and developed relations with government officials, working on diamond certification standards (to deal with counterfeiting). It targeted 14 of China's wealthier cities with the greatest potential for sales growth, based on its finding that the diamond acquisition threshold was a monthly income of Rmb2,000 (US$250) and above.

Again De Beers sought to use the wedding ring as the sales vehicle. Unfortunately, 'love' in the Chinese context proved a difficult concept to pin down, since attitudes to marriage were highly materialistic. A survey of the 'X' generation (18–28 year olds) commissioned by De Beers and a consortium of Western firms, showed that this generation used wealth as the key criterion for judging success. Marriage was a partnership towards achieving future success, and husbands were chosen on the basis of their financial status and prospects. Consequently, positioning diamond rings in the context of the romantic wedding day image made little sense.

After a great deal of research, one of the final advertisements chosen by De Beers followed the life and times of a young Chinese couple. The advert began with the husband giving his wife a wedding ring. The next frames followed through the subsequent years of happy marriage, so associating the diamond with a future together. The positioning was expressed as 'The symbol of our enduring commitment, to build a future of harmony, brightness, success and marriage'. And so the diamond ring in China has come to symbolise not so much love as a successful joint venture. That's some adaptation.

Key Lessons

■ Remember the importance of research: never enter a market without undertaking thorough market research into local spending habits, purchasing power, customs and so on.

■ Don't automatically jettison your home business model; think how you can combine your own well-tested strengths to give you a competitive advantage in Asian markets.

■ Adaptation does not end with the product or the product range; set it in the context of the whole marketing strategy – the price, how it will be packaged and how it will be promoted and distributed.

■ Try out your products first in chosen points of sale. Try to collect customer feedback and use it to make final adjustments.

■ Use IT to gather information about the market that can feed into developing new follow-up products.

■ There is no such thing as an Asian market. There is not even a singular Chinese market. The degree of adaptation will depend on your product and where in Asia you hope to sell it.

Notes

1 Taken from 'Carrefour in Asia' (A) and (B), case studies by Pierre Courbon and Professor Philippe Lasserre, 1994 INSEAD-EAC.

2 *EIU Business Asia*, 'Lifestyle in a phone', 29 May, 2000.

3 'Tesco braves the dangers of taking brands abroad', by Claire Murphy, *Marketing*, 22 April, 1999.

4 Taken from 'Unilever in Asia', case study by Charlotte Butler and Professor Philippe Lasserre, 1994 INSEAD-EAC.

5 Taken from 'Wall's Ice Cream in Thailand', case study by Deborah Clyde-Smith and Professor Peter Williamson, 1998 INSEAD-EAC.

6 Taken from '*Asiaweek*: Positioning a Regional Magazine', case study by Jocelyn Probert and Hellmut Schutte, 1999 INSEAD-EAC.

7 *Wall Street Journal Europe*, 'Interview with Leo Burnett', by Jennifer Saranow, 29 November, 2001.

8 *Wall Street Journal Europe*, 'China proves unexpectedly rich in Ad talent', 23 October, 2003, pA9.

9 *Wall Street Journal Europe*, 'Unilever Ads Are called Racist', by Chris Prystay, 30 April, 2002.

10 *Asian Wall Street Journal*, 5 October, 1994 and 7 May, 1992.

11 *Journal of Asia-Pacific Business*, 'Naming Products in China : Local or Foreign Branding', by Zhan G. Li and L. William Murray, vol (3) 2001, pp53–70.

12 *Far Eastern Economic Review*, 'Elle is for Label, in Asia', by Suh-kyung Yoon, 28 February, 2002.

13 Taken from 'De Beers: Diamonds are for Asia', case study by Jocelyn Probert and Professor Hellmut Schutte, 1999 INSEAD-EAC.

Strategy 18

Caveat Emptor: Beware the Banks of Asia

Financing in Asia

You have spotted a window of opportunity, you have done your research, devised a business plan and now you need some financing. Most large companies will have an existing global arrangement with a bank or group of banks, but smaller investors may not. One possibility then is a local bank in Asia, but very few Asian banks are involved in banking alone and most are still controlled by a majority shareholder. This makes them very different from banks in the United States, Australia and Europe. It also makes them potentially quite dangerous. Table 18.1 gives a brief view of the main local banks in Asia.

Table 18.1 Local banks in Asia (the top three in selected Asian countries, ranked by assets)

China	Industrial & Commercial Bank of China Bank of China China Construction Bank
India	State Bank of India Bank of India Bank of Baroda
Japan	Bank of Tokyo-Mitsubishi Mizuho Financial Mitsui-Sumitomo
Taiwan	Bank of Taiwan Taiwan Cooperative Bank Land Bank of Taiwan
South Korea	Kookmin Bank Hanvit Bank H&CB
Thailand	Bangkok Bank Krung Thai Bank Thai Farmers Bank
Hong Kong	HSBC Hang Seng Bank Bank of East Asia
Malaysia	Malayan Banking (Maybank) Bumiputera-Commerce Bank RHB Bank
Singapore	United Overseas Bank DBS Overseas-Chinese Banking Corporation
Philippines	Metropolitan Bank & Trust Equitable PCI Bank Bank of Philippine Islands
Sri Lanka	Bank of Ceylon People's Bank Hatton National Bank

Asia's 1997–98 economic crisis hit the region's banks hard and they have not all recovered at the same rate. Banking in Asia today is perhaps healthiest in Singapore, Hong Kong and Malaysia. Malaysian banks suffered much in the crisis but made a quick recovery. Non-performing loans were cut out of the system quickly and efficiently by Danaharta, the vehicle established by the Malaysian Government for the purpose. Overseeing Malaysia's banking sector is Bank Negara, Malaysia's central bank, which, although not above making mistakes, is now widely regarded as highly professional and free of corruption. Malaysia's moves quickly to restore confidence in its banking system in the wake of the crisis won wide praise. Lim Say Boon of Crosby Corporate Advisory said at the time:

> [Malaysia] has followed the textbook prescriptions – setting up a bad debt agency, a bank recapitalisation agency, and a corporate restructuring committee. Run by thorough professionals, the processes have been transparent and unrelenting.[1]

Banking problems appear almost intractable in China. Some progress has been made, but the state-owned banks are moribund with bad debt. The China Banking Regulatory Commission admitted in 2003 that 24.1% of the loans at the Big Four are non-performing. But analysts thought the true figure to be at least 40%. And that is after the government bailed out the Big Four in 1998 with a capital infusion of US$33 billion and removed another US$169 billion in bad loans the following year.

Part of the problem is that most of the bad debtors are other state-owned companies, and they and their owners, usually local authorities, combine and simply refuse to pay back their loans. They also make for a strong coalition against effective reform. In any event, loans are often handed out to this or that sector as a matter of government policy, rather than from any tenets of sound banking practice. The reality is that China's formal banking system has become another arm of the central government's welfare delivery programme.

There are around 20 local banks in South Korea. Laws prevent Korea's conglomerates – the *chaebol* – from owning more than 8% of the equity in any given bank, so banks are relatively independent of the non-banking business groups in the country in terms of equity. But the past practice has been for the Korean Government to direct the bank's lending. This meant that lending decisions were not based on due diligence and credit assessments but on government orders. There was US$130 billion worth of bad debt on the books of South Korea's banks by mid-2000. There has long been a culture in Korea that private corporate interests are subverted to national goals, which has caused banks and other Korean companies to invest in sectors for reasons other than the expectation of maximising returns.

The Japanese banking system is also beset by problem loans, largely because banks tend to reschedule loans endlessly and ease their conditions rather than declare them in default. In this way, loans worth hundreds of billions of dollars which are inadequately serviced and in technical default have been hidden. One problem in cleaning up bad debt in Japan's banking system is that banks have been reluctant to admit to them.

Banks, like so much else in Asia, may not be all they seem – some-times literally. Central Jakarta is full of banks with obscure names but they're housed in office blocks with modern, reflective glass windows. Prominent signage announces their existence, the foyers might be marbled and the staff have their corporate uniforms. But look again. Many of these banks with their shining, mirrored, high-rise offices are a fiction. The 'windows' are in fact cladding on billboards several storeys high to make customers feel as though they are banking with a solid bank. The actual building is often little more than a converted bungalow or a shop-house.

Many banks like this aren't really interested in lending to outsiders anyway. Their owners have set them up to accept deposits from the public. These are then lent to the owners' other interests. The benefit to the owners is that they then pay deposit rates of interest on large loans that they would otherwise have to pay far higher interest on. Nor do they need to go through due diligence and loan approvals processes – which they may not pass. They simply lend the money to themselves, regardless of their creditworthiness. Beyond some point, the practice is illegal and highly imprudent.

The Sins of Asia's Banks

The ownership structures and behaviour of Asia's banks differ from the way banks tend to operate in the more mature markets of the West. This can mean some traps for the unwary. What can happen in Asia, and why?

Beware Spiders at the Centre of the Web

Asia's big banks are moving away from majority family ownership but that does not mean that their founding families no longer control them. Bangkok Bank, which prior to Asia's economic crisis was Southeast Asia's largest private bank (Singapore's DBS Bank now has that honour), is controlled by the founding Sophonpanich family even though it owns only around 15% of the bank's stock and not much more in the way of guaranteed support from other shareholders. The family retains control because other shareholders are so dispersed and own such small parcels of shares. Similarly, Wee Cho Yaw and his family control Singapore's United Overseas Bank and do so even though they now own little more than 10% of its stock.

One problem with a single entity such as a family controlling a bank is that rarely does it want to give up that control. That can mean that it will be loath to hold a new share issue to help to recapitalise the bank if one is needed. A new share issue might see the family's equity diluted, pushing it closer to losing its control.

The most likely local bank that a foreign firm might borrow from in Southeast Asia is a Singaporean bank. Singapore is the regional supplier of financial services to Southeast Asia. It is to Indonesia what Hong Kong is to Guangdong, for example. Its banks are well managed, accessible, professional and, most importantly, have the cash. Contracts and other loan documents can also be drawn up under Singapore law, which is important. However, Singapore's banks are not without some problems – problems shared with banks elsewhere in the region but less likely to be encountered in Western economies.

Consider for example, Singapore's United Overseas Bank (UOB). It is controlled by its founder Wee Cho Yaw. Wee is a banker but he is more than that and therein lies a potential danger. He also controls United Overseas Land and many other companies which are outside banking. He is the chairman and part owner of United Industrial Corporation. This company manufactures household detergents, is involved in printing and packaging, running shipping and travel agencies and trading in computers. In turn it controls Singapore Land, an important commercial real estate owner in Singapore. Wee is in the hotel business as well, with controlling stakes in Singapore's Plaza Parkroyal, New Park Centra and Grand Plaza Parkroyal Hotels. Some of Wee's interests are privately held, others are not. It all leads to many potential conflicts of interest.

Henny Sender wrote about this in an article in *Institutional Investor* back in 1991:[2]

> As the principal family asset of Singapore's Wee Cho Yaw, United Overseas Bank is subject to an inherent conflict of interest – the Wee family's temptation to use UOB to build their personal wealth rather than that of their shareholders. This concern arises at least partially from the fact that there is a string of private investment companies that compete with the public investment companies in which UOB has a stake. Stories are told of the bank's foreclosing on choice properties (Gold Hill Square in Singapore being the *most* recent example) at the first hint of difficulties – only to have ownership pass to UOB's property arm.

UOB's control over Singapore and its banking system was strengthened in 2001 when it acquired its rival Overseas Union Bank (OUB). OUB had been controlled by its founder Lien Ying Chow and his family. They are now shareholders in UOB. They too have vast real estate interests. 'Buildings are my hobby', Lien said in 1992, which must have been cold comfort to borrowers with desirable real estate mortgaged to OUB.

Overseas-Chinese Banking Corporation (OCBC) Bank is Singapore's second largest private bank. In 1999 it disclosed for the first time that it had a massive landbank of some 187 properties and pieces of land around Singapore, of which only about a quarter was actually used for banking purposes. It turned out that OCBC Bank was probably Singapore's biggest holder of land among Singapore's non-property companies. It also owned stakes in many listed companies, including 8.3% of soft drinks bottler Fraser & Neave. OCBC said that it would sell off its non-financial assets, but in 2001 announced that the sell-off would be delayed and then staggered. OCBC's revelations showed that it too was not just a bank but a web of potential conflicts of interest. Its declaration that it intended at some point to sell its non-core assets seemed to be an admission of that.

Finally, Singapore's DBS Bank, the city-state's largest, is controlled by Temasek Holdings, an investment arm of the Singapore Government. Temasek also has large stakes in Southeast Asia's biggest property company Capitaland, Singapore Airlines, ST Engineering and Chartered Semiconductor Engineering. Possibly the same conflict-of-interest arguments made above could be made in respect of DBS Bank.

Yet corporate and banking supervision is better in Singapore than anywhere in Asia. But then who could feel comfortable mortgaging real estate to a bank that is also a significant player in the local real estate market?

Beware Chinese Whispers and Chinese Walls

Borrowing from a bank involves giving information to it that companies give to few others. Their financials, their business plans and other commercial in-confidence information are handed over. How safe that information is in Asia, even if it's with a bank, often depends on who the bank is and who are its business partners.

An ideal banking system is one in which banks are not compromised in their lending decisions by their other business activities or the other business interests of their principal shareholders. But the number of banks in Asia like that are in the minority.

If a bank belongs to a group of companies that all have a common controlling shareholder, there are board meetings at the group level and the companies all routinely trade with and help one another, would it be so surprising in Asia, where in many countries the legal system is patchy, for the bank to tip off its sister companies as to what its clients are up to? If you were the founder of the group, from the old school and a strong believer in winning at all costs, you might even expect your bank to do that.

One reason why so many business families in Asia have owned a bank of their own is simply that they didn't trust anyone but themselves when it came to borrowing money. Take Indonesia for example. It is a 'low trust' society. Laws are weak and often the only protection available is that which you provide yourself. It is one reason why almost every one of Indonesia's top 200 conglomerates founded a bank. Few of them dared to borrow from anyone else. It left Indonesia with a banking system populated by more than 200 banks. The system was said to be over-banked but under-branched. The Government did close down 67 banks in the wake of the region-wide economic crisis of 1997–98 and took over 13 others. But the industry remains absurdly fractured with many small banks that do not generate sufficient economies of scale.

Of Relatives and Related Parties

Banks work because they pool risks. This is fundamental to banking. Loans are given to a range of borrowers, and the more the loan portfolio is spread across as many borrowers as possible, the less likelihood there is that the default of one or several borrowers will destabilise the bank. And then there is Asia.

Most banks in Singapore and Hong Kong are thought to be prudent lenders. Banks in Malaysia are less prudent but not dangerously so. Elsewhere, banking is a mess. Banks in Korea, Japan, Thailand and Indonesia have tended to lend far too much to too few and very often to borrowers linked to the owners of the bank. Their behaviour endangers the funds of their depositors and their other borrowers.

Banks in Indonesia were permitted to lend 20% of their total capital to any single non-affiliated party and no more than 10% of their capital to related parties. These restrictions were comprehensively ignored. The banking supervisory unit of Indonesia's central bank was either incompetent in administering these provisions, corrupt or both. In the Asian economic crisis, some banks were found to have lent more than 60% of their total loan portfolios to companies which were all related to each other and in turn often related to the owners of the banks.

'Circular' loans are often used to get around rules designed to restrict lending to affiliates. Bank owners might organise back-to-back loans to each other's non-banking subsidiaries. The owner of Bank Y might organise for Bank X to lend US$50 million to his property business and, in return, Bank Y lends US$50 million to Bank X.

What Protection the Central Bank?

Asia's central banks have faced difficulties in carving out a role that is both independent and accountable. Independence is fine if bank officials conduct themselves in a professional manner. But less accountability can spell corruption, nepotism and other ills. Indonesia passed a new central bank law in 2001 which guaranteed its central bank more autonomy. It was meant to prevent government interference in the bank's monetary policy decisions but instead was misused to protect criminal activity in the bank.

This is not a particularly Asian phenomenon. All countries face difficulties in managing their central banks but none so keenly than developing countries. A study in 2001[3] found that at the Peruvian Central Bank of Reserve, almost half the employees were related to other employees at the bank. Among the 1,300 staff were 77 brothers, 52 married couples, 52 uncles and aunts and their nephews or nieces, 54 brothers-in-law and sisters-in-law, 40 cousins and 7 fathers and sons.[5] The recent past records of some central banks in Asia are similarly less than honourable.

In early 1998, almost 100 senior staff at Japan's central bank, the Bank of Japan, were disciplined for accepting lavish entertainment from banks and other financial institutions. One official was arrested for providing sensitive information to private banks in return for entertainment. The bank's then governor and his deputy both took responsibility and resigned.

In late 2000, five of the seven directors of Indonesia's central bank attempted to resign. They claimed that the bank's 'loss of legitimacy' made it difficult for them to continue in their posts. A dispute between the government and the IMF over changes to the central bank law made it impossible to appoint replacements and so the directors remained in their posts.

There are some highly professional central reserves around Asia. The Monetary Authority of Singapore, the Hong Kong Monetary Authority and Malaysia's Bank Negara immediately come to mind. The rest, such as Thailand's, have some work to do.

Avoiding Corporate Suicide

Banks have grown stronger in Asia since the 1997–98 economic crisis. There have been banking mergers particularly in Singapore and Malaysia. Banks there are now bigger and better capitalised than perhaps they have ever been. Progress has been slower elsewhere and so a few precautions are advisable when dealing with them.

If depositing in Asia's banks, split the funds between several banks and preferably in a range of currencies. The last Asian economic crisis saw many banks close and their depositors' funds frozen. Also, in the midst of the Asian economic crisis, many banks simply ran out of foreign exchange and were unable to buy any. Transfers of even relatively small amounts of US dollars between banks even within Indonesia took days to be completed, and international transfers which previously had occurred overnight took weeks, with the funds simply unaccounted for during the intermediate period. Diversifying your holdings of deposits makes sense in Asia, particularly in those countries with weaker banking systems.

For borrowers wanting to borrow from an Asian bank, some new options have appeared since the economic crisis. Foreign banks and Singaporean banks have acquired strategic stakes in some banks in Hong Kong, Thailand, the Philippines and Indonesia. This should see these banks become more professional and able to draw on the capital of their new and well-capitalised shareholders. Some of the banks acquired were seized by their respective governments during the economic crisis to save them from collapse. Singapore's DBS Bank acquired a 60% stake in Manila's Bank of Southeast Asia in 1998, for example. It bought 71% of Hong Kong's Dao Heng Bank Group in 2001. The UK's Standard Chartered bought Thailand's Nakornthon Bank in 1999. It is now known as Standard Char-

Strategy checklist

If you wish to borrow from a local bank in Asia, here are some points to consider when choosing a bank:

1. Does the bank have a controlling shareholder? If so, research the controller's other interests. Do they compete with yours? Are there

any obvious incentives for the bank to foreclose on your loan and seize your collateral that are suggested by these other interests?

2. Get hold of the bank's annual report if one is available and learn about its directors and their other corporate interests. Look at the related-party transactions, if any. They will provide an indication as to what sorts of company are related to the bank.

3. What guarantees does the bank offer about the security of your information? Where is the information sent, how is it stored, who is authorised to see it and who can access it? Are loan approvals made at the branch level or centralised with a commercial loans unit?

4. Does the bank itself have a property arm?

5. Does the bank have a reputation for foreclosing too early? Does its controlling shareholder have a reputation for buying up the assets that have been foreclosed on? Are there local rules to prevent this and how well are they enforced?

6. Is the bank prudent or likely to be a significant lender to related parties?

7. Does a broad cross-section of local companies choose to borrow from the bank?

8. Is there a banking ombudsman or equivalent to whom improper banking practices can be reported?

tered Nakornthon Bank. Singapore's UOB bought 75% of Thailand's Radanasin Bank in 1999. It is now known as UOB Radanasin Bank.

One final thing to remember when dealing with banks in Asia, whether you are a big or small customer, is that practically all aspects of their activities can be negotiated upon. Published rates and fees need not be fixed. Consider negotiating on not just the interest rates on loans but also on deposits, particularly term deposits. Negotiate on exchange rates for foreign exchange conversions, as well as all fees and charges.

Notes

1   Lim, S.B., 'Real change in Asia', Rethinking Asia column, *Far Eastern Economic Review*, 22 June, 1999.
2   Sender, H., 'Inside the overseas Chinese network', *Institutional Investor*, August 1991.
3   *International Herald Tribune*, 'A family affair at bank', 9 May, 2001.

Strategy 19

Avoid Blood Loss as a Minority Shareholder

Majorities, Minorities and Families

Question: What's the best way to avoid losing out as a minority shareholder in Asia?

Answer: Don't be one.

That's what the California Public Employees' Retirement System (CalPERS), one of the largest pension funds in the world and the largest public fund in the United States with US$151 billion under management, decided in February 2002. It announced that it would pull out of Indonesia, Malaysia, the Philippines and Thailand because those countries did not meet its new standards on 'political stability, labour standards, and transparency, including a free press and good accounting'.[1] (The Philippines was later reinstated). The more likely reason, however, was that it was simply tired of being ripped off.

Western companies tend to list on the stock market so that they can raise funds to expand. But the situation is often quite different in Asia. Listings all too frequently are little more than exit strategies, as founding families seek to off-load assets that no longer perform well and that they no longer want. 'What is profitable is mine, but what is not is yours' is the guiding principle of many a majority shareholder in Asia. The result is that Asia's stock markets are not so much home to Asia's great companies but often home to companies that nobody really wants.

Families control most listed companies outside Japan and China. And typically these families list not their holding company but just one or two of its subsidiaries. That means that most listed companies are not stand-alone entities but parts of webs of mostly privately held companies. So not only are Asia's stock markets full of second-rate companies but the companies are parts of wider groups with all the potential conflicts of interest which that might entail.

Ratings agencies have a hard time in Asia assessing credit ratings for the business groups of Japan, Korea, Indonesia and elsewhere. Should companies be assessed as stand-alone entities or is it the group as a whole that should be rated? But some groups are more integrated than others. And when the group comprises a mixture of privately owned and publicly listed companies with cross-shareholdings, cross-borrowings, loan guarantees and plenty of related-party transactions, the ratings process becomes very complex – and more imprecise. How to rate a member of a *chaebol* in Korea, when loan and other guarantees are given but not often declared? Many Asian companies traditionally have borrowed only locally and on a secured basis, but now many borrow internationally, usually by issuing securities. These borrowings are subordinated debt, which introduces more complications for outside investors trying to get a window on the risks of investing in Asia.

The risks for investors who wish to buy stakes in unlisted firms can be more perilous. The general rule of thumb is do not buy into an unlisted firm in which you cannot take the major stake and control the board of directors and management. Even then, it must be asked why the company is up for sale. Good companies are rarely sold in Asia, particularly to outsiders; if they are sold, it is to insiders. Any company in Asia that comes onto the open market can be assumed to be in trouble. In that case, it might be best to consider buying the company's assets rather than the company. Buying the legal structure as well as the assets can mean inheriting huge but undeclared tax liabilities and other hidden contingencies. It might also mean inheriting large numbers of employees that you may not want and local labour laws might make it difficult and costly to shed. Buy the assets alone and then hopefully they will come free of the legal, tax and labour problems that the previous owners have accumulated, which presumably are part of the reason why they are selling out.

Sin, sin, sin and not much repentance
The 12 major sins against minority shareholders in Asia

Sin 1   Ownership is spread too thinly

Sin 2   Listing as a form of dumping

Sin 3   Too many rights issues

Sin 4   Unfair related-party transactions

Sin 5   Refusal to return excess funds

Sin 6   Bizarre morphing

Sin 7   Too many AGMs held on the same day

Sin 8   Stock price manipulation

Sin 9   Insider trading

Sin 10   Poor disclosure

Sin 11   Boards are often too small or too big

Sin 12   'Independent' directors not so independent

The 12 Biggest Sins Committed against Asia's Minority Shareholders

Sin 1

Ownership is spread too thinly – the vast majority of Asia's listed companies have less than 30% of their equity traded publicly (compared with the United States where most companies have at least 95% of their stock traded freely). Most stock exchanges in the region have rules on the minimum number of shareholders a company must have to be and remain listed. This can be manipulated with the use of lots of nominees, each taking out small numbers of shares especially among small capitalised stocks that are of little interest to most investors.

Sin 2

Listing as a form of dumping – Asia's truly profitable companies generally are not those that are listed. If they are very profitable, they usually remain in private hands. Often companies are listed when their owners want to get rid of them. (Significantly, China has decided that one remedy for moribund, poorly capitalised state-owned enterprises is partly to list them.) Similarly, listed companies that become highly profitable are quickly delisted and made private.

Sin 3

Too many rights issues – a rights issue is an invitation only to existing shareholders to acquire additional shares in the company. The benefit of a rights issue to the company is that it is an easy way to raise money; such issues impose on it few additional statutory obligations. The benefit to the controlling shareholder is that its control of the company is not lost or weakened if it takes up its quota of new shares. Minority shareholders, however, find that they must either buy the new shares or their minority stakes are made even smaller and so too their returns. In Asia the complaint has been that companies raise too much cash too frequently from their shareholders and are not sufficiently focused on returns. Minority shareholders might find that no dividends are paid, instead it is they who are always handing over cash to the company rather than the other way round.

A practice that is more insidious than too many rights issues is when there are too many share placings. These are shares issued by the company and then 'placed' with certain parties – normally associates of the controlling shareholder. Minority shareholders are not given the option of taking up any of the shares so placed. Again, the effect is to dilute their equity and their returns.

Sin 4

Unfair related-party transactions – related-party transactions among listed and unlisted companies are rife across Asia and many are not on the commercial basis that they should be. This has the effect of moving inventory, costs, revenues and profits around groups of companies, usually to the detriment of minority shareholders.

Controlling families in Asia habitually sell assets which they no longer want to their listed companies. These might be old plant and equipment or even entire companies, which end up as subsidiaries of the listed company. There is nothing wrong with the practice if the sale price is fair. But often it isn't and the controlling family has the incentive to ensure that it is not. Transactions such as these are used by controlling shareholders to strip listed companies – and thus their minority shareholders – of their capital and their profits.

Receivables – which are contracted payments for goods and services for which cash is yet to be received – are something to watch for in a company's accounts, particularly if they appear high and especially if they are to related companies. Receivables are a common way for companies to boost profits and revenues but without cash actually having to change hands. Profits might grow year after year but if receivables are growing at the same rate then the company might actually have no more funds flowing through than in the initial year.

Another way in which listed companies can be milked by a controlling shareholder is when a private company owned by the shareholder provides services to the listed company. These might be for 'management' and general consulting. Such vague services are hard to quantify, which makes it difficult to determine whether the payments are fair or not.

One final aspect of unfair related-party transactions is when the books of companies do not all close on the same day. Some companies, including banks in Indonesia, for example, end their financial year at the end of the calendar year but others end theirs on 30 June. This means that there is a six-month window of opportunity during which funds can be transacted between banks and non-banks within the one group to boost the revenues and profits of each artificially. One guide to fictitious profits is when companies announce large profits but then don't declare a dividend.

Minority shareholders do have rights. Related-party acquisitions and sell-offs usually must be voted upon by the minorities in most stock exchanges in the region, but related-party transactions involving goods and services often do not. However, votes are not always as they should be. Shareholders who pose as independent of the controlling shareholder but are in reality nominees and will vote for whatever the controlling shareholder proposes are common at AGMs and EGMs around Asia.

Sin 5

Refusal to return excess funds – listed Asian companies tend to do anything with surplus funds other than return them to shareholders. The safest thing for shareholders would be to get their cash back. Instead they find that the management wants to sit on it and wait for the next big acquisition, lend it to related parties or use it to play the stock market themselves. Rarely is excess cash returned to shareholders.

Sin 6

Bizarre morphing – it is not uncommon for a listed company suddenly to change its core business or have another added to it which has little to do with the first. This comes about largely because many listed Asian firms are controlled by a single majority shareholder and many of these have other businesses that can be sold into the company.

Perhaps an investor wants to invest only in cement stocks and so buys shares in an Asian cement producer. However, the controlling shareholder might happen to own a textiles factory which he no longer really wants so sells it to the cement company. Minority shareholders who wanted to invest in cement now find that they are also investors in textiles; the synergies between the two are not exactly obvious.

Sin 7

Too many AGMs held on the same day – AGMs frequently clash in Asia, sometimes excessively so. This is common in Japan and also in Singapore, although to a lesser degree. Most listed companies in Singapore have a 31 December financial year end. The Singapore Stock Exchange requires listed companies to hold their AGMs within six months of their financial year end, so in the last week or so of June, many companies rush to hold their AGMs. Individual shareholders who hold stock in more than one of these companies can find it difficult getting to all the meetings, as some inevitably clash. Not all AGMs are held in city hotels, some are held at distant factory sites and industrial parks, further hampering ordinary share-holders' access to them.

The situation has been far worse in Japan. Out of 1,864 listed Japanese companies that closed their books at the end of March 1996, 1,766 or 94.2% of them held their AGM on just one day, 27 June of that year. Investors with a well-diversified portfolio stood little chance of attending more than a few of the AGMs of companies in which they held stock. Not surprisingly, the average Japanese AGM is very brief. The average duration of all those held on that one day in June was just 26 minutes.[2] The tradition in Japan has been that directors enter and leave an AGM accompanied by the applause of shareholders, hearing little or nothing from them in between.

The docility of local minority investors in Asia means that company managers rarely face direct criticism. Local investors prefer simply to sell out. Typically, Asian minority investors do not use 'voice'; they just use 'exit'. Things are changing in the wake of the Asian economic crisis but only in so far that there are now some examples of local minority share-holder activism when before there was none. There is still a long way to go.

Sin 8

Stock price manipulation – the prices of small capitalised stocks are routinely manipulated all over Asia, from Malaysia to Indonesia to Hong Kong. Stocks which have thin markets tend to be highly volatile. They may not trade at all one day and then rise the next day by 30%, fall the following by 20% and then barely trade for the next two days, a not uncommon week for a small cap stock on an Asian bourse.

Not surprisingly, they are prone to price manipulation by buying syndicates. Stocks can 'ramped', whereby companies trade in their own shares to force the price up and then sell out at a profit. They might be 'pooled', whereby investors collude to buy and sell shares rapidly in a company to each other, so that turnover increases, the stock looks 'hot', thereby attracting other investors, which forces the price up and then the members of the pool sell out at a profit. Stocks might be 'cornered' too. Cornering is relatively easy in Asia's stock markets because in most firms so little equity is publicly traded. It involves a syndicate quietly acquiring a large proportion of the publicly traded shares and then contracting with brokers to buy even more shares at a later date and at a given price, knowing that the order is unlikely to be filled because they already have most of the available shares. When the contract falls due, brokers have little choice but to pay an exorbitant price for the shares to fulfil the contracts, usually from the syndicate itself via nominees.

Sin 9

Insider trading – insider trading is rife in Asia. Company announcements are frequently preceded by movements in the share price suggesting that those with inside knowledge are trading on that basis. Trading by public auditors in the stock in the companies which they audit is not uncommon in Asia.

Singapore Hong Kong Properties Investment announced on 27 March, 1999 that it was in discussions with another company about its possible takeover by that company. Astute followers of the Hong Kong Stock Exchange might have noticed that something was in the wind. SHKPI's shares had rocketed up by 97% in the three days before the announcement was made.[3]

But generally, stock market and other corporate misdemeanors rarely lead to successful prosecutions. Even in Hong Kong, despite millions of dollars having been spent on investigations and the preparation of cases, there have been few convictions. Prosecutors face heavy burdens of proof and cases can be so complex that about the only thing which can guarantee a conviction is an open confession.

Sin 10

Poor disclosure – listed Asian firms tend to be remarkably poor at disclosing information. It is as if their controlling shareholders refuse to accept that, once listed, the companies are no longer totally theirs. Minority shareholders are expected to hand over their cash but then are denied the right to have a full explanation about what happens to it. Annual reports might be glossy and full of fine photographs but not much else. Stock exchange filings can provide more information but are often provided late. Sometimes requests for further information from minority shareholders are simply ignored.

Sin 11

Boards are often too small or too big – being appointed to a board is often seen in Asia as an honour. It is not viewed as an obligation charged with fiduciary duty but as a reward, a title to be collected and displayed. This is especially so in Japan where boards with more than 20 directors have been the norm and some have had as many as 60. The Nissan Motor

Company cut its board from 37 to 10 after France's Renault acquired a 37% stake. But Nissan remains an exception to the rule. Being elevated to the board is seen as a sinecure for retired executives in Japan, the local equivalent of the gold watch retirement gift.

The small, family-run listed companies of Hong Kong have the opposite problem. Many have boards that are too small. Hung Fung Group Holdings listed on the main board of the Hong Kong Stock Exchange in 1998 with a board of just three executive directors. Two of the three were married to each other. One of the two 'independent' non-executive directors was a consultant to one of the co-sponsors of Hung Fung's IPO.[4]

Almost all Asia's stock exchanges now require listed companies to have an audit committee. Few imposed this requirement prior to Asia's economic crisis. It has been a move in the right direction, although many companies in Asia, particularly those that have a relatively thin professional class, have found it difficult to find enough directors sufficiently knowledgeable about auditing processes and willing to accept the additional personal liability that being on an audit committee involves. Consequently, most companies now have an audit committee but they may not be as diligent or as skilled as needed.

Sin 12

'Independent' directors who are not really independent or just plain lazy – about 40% of listed companies in Japan now have one or more directors who have been recruited from outside the firm – but that means that about 60% do not. Elsewhere, listed companies continue to indulge in all sorts of questionable actions to benefit their majority shareholders, begging the question of where are the independent directors?

The Hong Kong Stock Exchange now requires that all listed companies appoint two independent non-executive directors, which sounds fine in principle but has been a flop in practice. Most listed Hong Kong companies are controlled by a single shareholder. Independent non-executive directors are appointed by the board of directors and then re-elected by the shareholders at the next annual general meeting. But with the majority shareholder typically controlling the board and most of the votes at the AGM, only independent non-executive directors who are 'friendly' to the majority shareholder tend to get appointed. Independent non-executive directors must comprise a majority of the audit committees, but with these directors being sanctioned by the majority shareholder, the audit committees lack the independence that they should have.

Look first, buy later
Some things to consider before buying
into a listed company in Asia

1. Prudent and cautious investors in Asia would do well to buy stock only in those companies that either have no controlling shareholder, are not part of a wider group, or both. Do your research on companies in which you might invest. Are they part of a group of companies?

2. Who controls the company? Is there a single majority or controlling shareholder? Assessing a stock in Asia involves more than just looking at the company's 'fundamentals'. The appropriate way to value a company must also include consideration of who is the majority shareholder and what else they own.

3. What is the company's policy on transactions with related parties and does it engage in them?

4. Does the company pay fees in relation to management services, intellectual property, secretarial or other administrative services to any private companies and if so, what are the relationships between those companies and the controlling shareholder?

5. Does the company have any inter-company loans? Are they high and have they been increasing year on year? Are they on a fully commercial basis?

6. Do the company's accounts contain a lot of receivables and how has this changed in the last three or more years? Have the receivables arisen from transactions with related companies?

7. Is the market for the company's stock deep and wide? Does it trade each day? Is there a good spread of shareholders? Are there any Western institutional shareholders who are likely to give voice to minority shareholder concerns?

8. Does the company have a substantial core business or is the company an amalgam of assets with few complementarities pushed together for the convenience of the majority shareholder?

9. Is the board of directors an optimal working size, say about seven directors? What are their qualifications? Do at least some of the directors have recognised accounting or legal qualifications?

10. Are there independent non-executive directors? How independent are they? How are they elected and by whom? How many other boards do they serve on? Do they have the time to exercise sufficient vigilance over the company? Is there an active and well-qualified audit committee?

11. What is the company's record on rights issues and share placings?

12. Does the company have an investor relations officer or office and is the company responsive to requests for information?

13. Is the company related to other listed companies with differing financial year ends?

14. Asset-backed securities are still a comparative rarity in Asia, but they do offer more transparency and less risk to investors. They differ from conventionally collateralised loans or bonds in that the assets to be securitised are separated out from the other assets of the issuer and are normally held by a special holding vehicle. The Wisma Atria shopping mall on Singapore's Orchard Road, for example, was used to back the issue of S$451 million in bonds by the mall's owner in mid-2002. Are asset-backed securities available as an alternative investment option?

Finally, minority shareholders can consider taking class action suits against majority shareholders or companies themselves. But the expense of this in those Asian countries where legal systems operate inadequately often prevents this course of action. Elsewhere, legal systems are too abysmal or may not recognise class actions. Shareholder lawsuits have become more common in Japan. They were once taboo but minority shareholders have been emboldened by a decision by the Osaka District Court in September 2000 in a case brought by shareholders against 11 former and current directors of Daiwa Bank to pay the bank US$775 million in compensation for having insufficient safeguards to protect against unauthorised bond trading in the United States.

Notes

1   *Asian Wall Street Journal*, 'Big US pension fund says it will leave markets', 22 February, 2002.
2   Backman, M., *Asian Eclipse: Exposing the Dark Side of Business in Asia*, Wiley & Sons, 1999, 2001.
3   Webb, D., 'Singapore Hong Kong Properties', Webb-site.com, 7 July, 1999.
4   Webb, D., 'Money for nothing', Webb-site.com, 8 August, 2001.

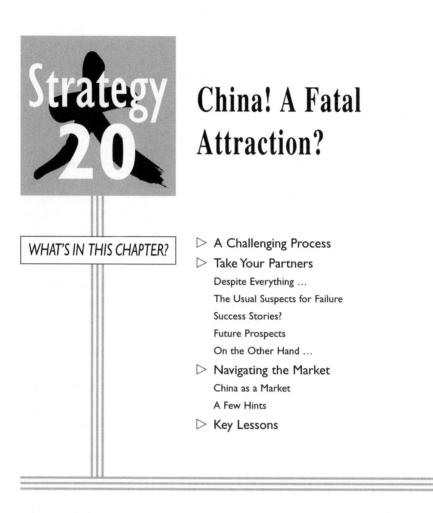

Strategy 20

China! A Fatal Attraction?

A Challenging Process

Entering the Chinese market as a foreign company is generally described as a 'challenging process', a phrase most businesspeople (whether Asian or Western) with any experience of China would regard as a massive understatement. The first Western companies entered China as early as 1979 when Deng Xiaoping announced the famous 'Open Door' policy, and these brave pioneers were followed by successive waves of optimistic investors. Mesmerised by the sheer size of the market and the increasing wealth of China's urban middle class, they all made major commitments in anticipation of reaping massive gains. Unfortunately, as the full extent of the obstacle course between themselves and any profits became clear, their expectations gave way to cruel disillusionment. For many, the first blow to their hopes was delivered by their local partner.

Take Your Partners

For the pioneers into China, just setting up the legally required joint venture was frequently an epic struggle. Most found themselves taking part in protracted negotiations amidst a maze of heavy bureaucracy, in which vague laws and regulations (themselves subject to arbitrary change) were unevenly applied. Complicated approval procedures, usually involving several different levels of authority at central, regional and local stages virtually guaranteed long delays, as Western firms navigated the minefield of political infighting and struggled to deal with officials more often than not steeped in a culture characterised by corrupt business practices. Managing this pre-partnership dimension was a hurdle at which foreign firms frequently stumbled.

Once set up, running the operation in partnership with local Chinese managers was equally tough, given the strictly limited opportunities for foreign firms to exercise any influence. Controls on hiring, firing and recruitment protected an inflated and, by Western standards, uncommitted and unproductive workforce, but left employers with high labour costs. To add to their frustration, Western managers found themselves forced to seek further permissions to sell in markets which were undeveloped, never as large as the optimistic forecasts on which entry had been based, and where the lack of infrastructure made building distribution and marketing capabilities a nightmare. There was also the piracy problem: any product that could be copied would be, in the shortest possible time.

As if all this was not enough to contend with, after the first few years, foreign investors frequently had to bear the financial burden alone, as the Chinese contribution tailed off, sometimes to less than 10%. Many also discovered an unbridgeable gulf between their aims – to build a market for their goods – and those of their local partners who, guided by the current five-year government plan, had little motivation to expand or increase productivity.

Too late, Western firms found that they had grossly underestimated the difficulty of entering this most frustrating of business environments. As they struggled to turn around the state-owned enterprises which they were forced to work with and tried in vain to find good local managers, they were hit by keen competition from local players who benefited from the favours of local officials. Some hardy survivors stayed in and gritted their teeth for the long haul (the average time for turning a profit was ten years) but the majority of Western investors eventually withdrew to count the cost. The French car maker PSA Peugeot Citroen, for example, entered China early in 1985 with a 22% stake in a joint venture to produce the Peugeot 505. The story was downhill all the way as losses piled up until finally, 12 years later, it sold its stake to the Japanese automotive group, Honda.

To add insult to injury, the collapse of their joint ventures left foreign companies with little hope of recovering any of their investment, since the bankruptcy laws put them well down the queue for compensation, behind the claims of employees and the tax authorities. And although joint venture rules became more flexible after 1994, those on management control remained weak, making it still the biggest potential point of conflict. Many of the other obstacles – non-existent markets, workforces which are not as productive and hardworking as is commonly believed, poor infrastructure, broken contracts and no profits – all remained in place. A 1998 survey conducted by AT Kearney found that of 229 joint ventures, only 38% were covering their costs.[1]

Following further changes in investment rules after 1998, there was a move away from joint ventures and half the new investment was directed into setting up wholly owned companies. Many took the opportunity to convert their joint ventures into wholly foreign owned enterprises (WFOEs). The US firm Kimberley-Clark, for example, which had set up seven joint ventures between 1994–97, bought them all out and turned them into WFOEs. However, both these and the FIEs (foreign invested enterprises) were still tightly controlled. Any corporate restructuring or change in business subject needed permission from the all-powerful Ministry of Foreign Trade and Economic Cooperation (MOFTEC) and other authorities. The rules remained opaque and liable to sudden change, a habit many observers doubted would be broken, even following China's entry into the WTO in December 2001 after 15 years' negotiation.

Despite Everything ...

The dismal history of failure by Western firms by no means diminished the rush of foreign investors eager to join up with Chinese partners. During the 1990s, China attracted around US$350 billion of FDI, with joint ventures the preferred method of entry.[2] In 2002, China overtook the US to become the biggest recipient of FDI with $52.74 billion and, taking 25% of the M&A market (excluding Japan), with 766 deals valued at $25.1 billion.[3] Although

2003 saw a slower rate of increase due to SARS and structural factors such as emerging power shortages, the final figure of $53.5 billion was still another record for Chinese FDI.

The US has been especially faithful to the Chinese dream. US firms have entered partnerships with Chinese companies in every sector open to it, from machinery, automotive, computer, communications, energy, infrastructure and finance, to insurance, oil and petrochemicals. And this despite the fact that the combination – or perhaps clash – of American 'can do' entrepreneurialism with the well-documented shortcomings of local managers and the SOE (state-owned enterprise) workforce, set in the context of the bureaucratic political maze, was hardly the most promising recipe for success.

Meanwhile, their European and Japanese counterparts proved just as eager to gain a foothold in markets that, by 2003, were being hailed as some of the fastest growing in the world. The auto industry, for example, saw a positively lemming-like rush of foreign manufacturers entering or boosting their investment in a market that saw sales growth of almost 90% in the first eight months of 2003. With demand exceeeding supply and margins estimated at double elsewhere in the world, all the major manufacturers invested heavily to ramp up production. Volkswagen, producer of the top two best-selling cars in China during the first nine months of 2003, announced it was spending €6 billion ($6.75 billion) to expand capacity over the next five years. Its success in the market meant that this expansion that would be paid from its current business in the country. Ford, a recent entrant, increased its investment by over a billion dollars, while GM planned to invest $108 million to take control of its fourth car plant in China. Nissan and Toyota committed $1 billion and $1.2 billion respectively and DaimlerChrysler announced that it would begin assembling its Mercedes models. Even Peugeot, undeterred by its previous experience, announced substantial investment in its venture with its second partner, Dongfeng Motor Corp, despite the two having earlier been close to 'divorce'. As with other Western companies, hope had yet again triumphed over experience. Of course, they were all well aware that, in the long term, their actions would inevitably lead the market to crash under the twin weights of overcapacity, and a killing price war led by local competitors. But in the meantime – let the spree continue.

Companies in other industries too – hotels, ice cream, fast food, telecoms, semiconductors, heavy machinery and equipment (to build the roads and hotels) and so on – were by then seeing China as their saviour in a world of saturated markets. In 2003, GE, Accor, Coca-Cola, KFC, Kodak, Siemens, Groupe Danone, P&G, Unilever, Otis and Amway were all expanding fast and, more importantly, said to be doing well. Nokia, Cap Gemini and Motorola were among those moving their regional headquarters to Shanghai or Beijing to be nearer the action.

So China remains an irresistible magnet; the market everyone wants to get into, the one that Western companies believe can make them Big in Asia. But any route will involve a relationship with a Chinese partner, something that few foreign firms have managed successfully in the past – what are the odds for any greater success in the future?

The Usual Suspects for Failure

Not surprisingly, how to do business in China has become one of the hottest topics for business writers and an overcrowded field in academic research. Much has been written about the pitfalls and how to avoid them. How to negotiate in China is a well-ploughed field, and any company not sufficiently clued up on the importance of preparation and post-negotiation periods, and the tactics used by Chinese negotiating teams to pressurise would-be investors (changing the personnel or location, or imposing false deadlines), would be wiser to hold back until it has obtained and digested the information.

Similarly, companies should be aware of the different values which Chinese negotiators might have when assessing the potential benefits of your investment. For example, given the central government's high anxiety about unemployment and the threat of civil disorder, especially in rural areas, it would be wiser to emphasise how your involvement will help to create jobs, increase skills through training, and of course, transfer technology. The more usual Western emphasis on partnerships as vehicles for delivering cuts in costs or manpower would clearly be a mistake.

When assessing the projected profitability of any venture, the need for thorough market research by the investor, rather than relying on figures supplied by the local partner, should by now also be obvious. Equally, the importance of concentrating not just on production issues, but on how the products are going to reach their markets (distribution is one of the top three difficulties faced by foreign firms) has been well researched and recorded.

All this information is easily available and so is not repeated here. Instead, and in the spirit of optimism that characterises all foreign investment in China, what follows focuses on some successful partnerships, and recent changes that may help future foreign investors have a happier experience there.

Success Stories?

Partnerships with one of the few excellent Chinese companies where both sides have something to offer have, by and large, prospered. Amstrad, for example, entered the mobile phone market via a joint venture with the successful, formerly state-owned, consumer electronics group Haier and Hong Kong CCT Telecom. Haier has a proven marketing and manufacturing record and is one of the most lauded of Chinese companies. Hence, this particular joint venture, Haier CCT, was one of only a handful of companies granted the necessary licence to manufacture and distribute phones in China. Similarly, the next well-known Chinese success story, the leading computer maker, Legend Holdings, appeared a safe bet for America Online, which entered a 49–51% $200 million joint venture in 2001. Legend wanted to expand and diversify, AOL wanted to get into the market ahead of the pack.

As always in Asia, those with a long history in the country have had the most successful partnerships. Volkswagen (VW), the German auto manufacturer, Alcatel, the French telecoms company, and Unilever, the Anglo-Dutch consumer products manufacturer, have all had a long and relatively profitable presence in China. Those companies that have stayed in the market are beginning to reap the benefits as their affiliates develop knowledge and capabilities that can be transferred back to the parent company. Technology transfer is no longer a one-way street, and the R&D capability in China is evolving rapidly. Alcatel, for example, which entered China in 1984 and established a dominant position early on, hopes that by 2004 it will have 80% of its R&D based in Shanghai.

However, it should also be noted that these companies bear many scars from their experience. Over the years VW, for example, learned to cope with inefficient distribution systems, pirated parts and the problems of achieving economies of scale which make it difficult to justify the costs of building a plant. Analysts finally hailed it as a great success but, in June 2002, relations were 'disturbed' by the revelation that its partner, Shanghai Automotive Industry (SAIC), had been using VW's original parts in a best-selling car made by a rival company which was 20% owned by SAIC. Similarly, a sudden cloud fell over the prospects of those allied with Brilliance China Automotive Holdings, listed on the NY and HK exchanges and long regarded as the most reliable and trustworthy guide for any foreign auto manufacturer. In 2002 Brilliance had licensing arrangements and alliances with Toyota, joint ventures with BMW and GM, and a strategic alliance with US MG Rover. Unfortunately, in June of that year, the company found itself immersed in scandal following allegations of asset-stripping, and the flight of the Brilliance Chairman to the US to avoid arrest on charges of fraud. The price of joint venture success in China is eternal vigilance. You never know when you might get an unpleasant surprise.

Future Prospects

For those firms which cannot resist the Chinese challenge, there are signs that, in the future, conditions for foreign entrants will not be so firmly stacked against them. Changes in the attitudes of local workers and managers, observers believe, seem to indicate brighter prospects for the success of joint ventures.

SOEs, for example, had long had a poor press as joint venture partners. Unfortunately, until now, these have usually been the only type of partner available to foreign firms. Generally characterised as badly managed, corrupt and inefficient, many are also accused of falsifying their financial statements with the help of accountants, underwriters and local government officials. Some are being investigated by the Chinese Securities Regulatory Commission, although even then few go bankrupt. SOE managers are also famous for some of the scams they have pulled on their joint venture partners; one US firm discovered that, over a long period, one of its managers had been transferring equipment from the pipe threading shop to his father. Over the next year, the father sold US$150,000 worth of pipes back to the company.

The lack of a strong work ethic, sufficient commitment and discipline among SOE workers is equally well known, as are the obstacles to imposing any control or introducing notions of performance orientation. Having worked for years to set targets, these companies lack any formal planning processes for sales, resource management and project management, since the long-term survival of the firm has never been their problem.

To turn them around and make them profitable is a considerable task, especially since few foreign firms were prepared to act as ruthlessly as Haier. Assembly-line workers who failed to meet Haier standards were required to stand on a pair of yellow feet painted at the end of each production line to confess their failings to their colleagues and promise to do better.[4]

However, since the end of the 1990s, when the state sector began cutting jobs, attitudes among SOE workers have begun to change, and many see foreign investors as the only way of saving their companies and jobs. At the same time, another set of potential partners is emerging, as China reorganises its industries to conform with WTO membership, splitting up large former state monopolies to create new companies.

These companies are being run by a new generation of managers with a different approach to business. These younger managers (below the age of 40) are the 'little emperors' born after the introduction of the single-child policy. Frequently described as more entrepreneurial and better educated than their predecessors, they are said to be more attuned to foreign ways and easier to deal with. But they are gaining a reputation for greater venality than previous generations.

Finally, it is also becoming easier for companies which entered China before the laws changed to restructure their agreements and take control, either by grouping their joint ventures together under a Chinese holding company, acquiring the partner or increasing their equity share. By doing this, they can alter the balance of management control so as to introduce new systems and reduce headcount. In 2002 Alcatel raised its 31% share in its joint venture firm, Shanghai Bell, to take a majority holding. Its ten joint ventures will be merged into a new company, ASB, which will have full access to Alcatel's patents and technology.

On the Other Hand ...

On the other hand, foreign firms will continue to be dogged by the same old problems of repatriating their profits, piracy, counterfeiting, and administrative delays at every bureaucratic level. Many firms pinned their hopes of a fairer playing field and a more predictable business environment on China's entry into the WTO at the end of 2001. However, two years later there are question marks over China's commitment to implementing the promises it made. As the chief executive of Volkswagen commented in August 2003, 'WTO is spelt very differently in Chinese'.[5] Commentators point, for example, to the two year delay in allowing the operation of foreign auto financing companies, finally announced in October 2003. Then there is the two year wait Royal Dutch/Shell has had for government approval for its joint venture with Sinopic to run 500 petrol stations. In September 2003, the project was said to be 'bogged down indefinitely'. True, a few high profile trials for 'commercial crimes' have taken place *'pour encourager les autres'* – especially among those who appeared on the 2002 Forbes list of China's richest 100 tycoons. But corruption and piracy are still endemic and any redress in local courts difficult if not impossible.

In June 2003, Japan's Matsushita became the latest in a long line of foreign firms to warn its partner, in this case Haier, against patent infringement. Even more disturbingly, five months later a Beijing court summarily dismissed Toyota's lawsuit for alleged copyright violations, indicating that it did not recognise Toyota's logo as 'a distinctive brand in China' that required protection.[6] Government interference also remains an ever present danger, since, although there is official recognition that the government should change its style and be 'a good football referee or a good investor or manager of the court, but not a player or boss of the team', it is not a lesson that has yet been taken to heart.[7] In February 2003, fears of the dominance of foreign retailers such as Carrefour, Makro and Wal-Mart led the State Economic and Trade Commission to announce new rules to curb the expansion of these stores.

Realistically, foreign companies can only expect the competition to get tougher and the markets even more difficult to call, since Chinese companies that were medium sized a decade ago have learned fast and today consider themselves the equal of any foreign multinational. However, many of them are also keen to spread beyond the domestic market and go global, following in the footsteps of Haier and Legend. This ambition may give an opening for foreign companies that can offer export opportunities to enter more equal partnerships with their Chinese partners. In November 2003, the Chinese electronics firm, TCL, and the French firm, Thomson announced a merger of their television and DVD-player manufacturing activities. Thomson would be responsible for the European and North American markets while TCL (albeit with the major 67% share of the venture) would be in charge of Asian sales. For Thomson, the deal was a solution to its loss-making television and DVD operations, while for TCL it represented a chance to fulfil its aim of becoming an international player in this market. However, when it comes to operating on their home ground, the strategy of local companies will remain as it always has been – cooperate with foreign partners for their technology; learn from them how to gain market share; improve distribution and service – then leave them defeated at their own game. So how to survive in these perilous markets?

Navigating the Market

The China markets have long presented a riddle to foreign firms. In theory, they present a target of over a billion consumers, and this prospect has long set dollar bells ringing in boardrooms the world over. But in practice, few foreign firms have been able to boast of the high returns they have made, and many have retired after suffering years of loss. For no country has suffered more hyperbole about market size than China, and nowhere has the gap between potential and actual returns been greater, as foreign companies entered to find the gloss was just that, and market forecasts were designed merely to please. Repeating the mantra that 'China is a 'must', they focused on the huge potential, the low labour costs and the supposedly high rates of return. Unfortunately, what too many failed to notice was that of the 1.3 billion Chinese, only 400 million were the urban consumers of their dreams and far fewer had any significant spending power. The rest lived in poor rural areas, often at subsistence level, without the means or desire to buy expensive Western goods. So for a long time, Western firms found the bottomless markets of their dreams singularly elusive.

Of course, their calculations were not all based on a myth. Since 1979, the Chinese economy has been expanding steadily, growing at an average annual rate of 9.6%. In the first quarter of 2003 the economy grew by over 9%, the fastest expansion in six years, and one barely dented by the SARS outbreak. But one of the first rules about China is never trust government statistics, since, as the country's chief statistician acknowledged, commenting on the discovery of at least 60,000 violations of China's statistics law in 2001, there are 'widespread flaws in the system used to compile economic data'. Officials 'exaggerated, failed to report, refused to report, were ignorant of statistical processes or lacked sufficient training'.[8] Lies, damned lies and statistics, but in China it is mostly the first two.

So what is the truth behind the Chinese mirage? Which markets actually do exist, and how to reach them?

China as a Market

The painful fact that many foreign firms have tended to overlook is that although many of the markets they targeted for entry were indeed the world's biggest, they were also saturated and dominated by powerful local competitors, the best of whom already had long-standing foreign partners.

Take, for example, household appliances. Surely, the reasoning went, a good proportion of this 1.3 billion population needs a refrigerator, a washing machine or a television, and surely they know that the West can supply the best. Well actually, no, since there stands Haier, the king of the Chinese appliance market. In terms of sales, Haier is the world's ninth largest appliance maker, with factories in 13 countries, even entering the US market with its refrigerators, produced in South Carolina and sold in Wal-Mart stores.

The experience of the US-based white goods manufacturer, Whirlpool demonstrates perfectly the gulf between optimistic projections and the realities of building a position on the ground.[9] It entered the Chinese market in the washing machine, microwave oven, air conditioner and refrigerator sectors to make a 'strategic footprint' in Asia. A Gallup survey found 36% of Chinese owned a washing machine and 25% a fridge, most locally made and low-tech, so Whirlpool felt it had a good chance. However, the national statistics hid the real pattern of ownership. In the rich urban areas, almost 90% of the population owned a washing machine and 60% a fridge. The average was brought down by the 15% owning washing machines in the countryside. Also, there were, it emerged, over 650 white goods manufacturers in China, the two strongest by the mid-1990s being Haier and Kelon, and a large price differential between local and imported appliances, due to 50% tariffs.

Whirlpool entered via four joint ventures in 1994 with a $300 million investment, aiming to achieve a 10% market share within ten years and breakeven point by 1997. Instead, in 1997 it pulled out of its fridge and air conditioner ventures, defeated by, among other things, overcapacity, price wars, its failure to build a distribution channel and a 'Buy Chinese' campaign. 'The revenue streams just didn't come in as we expected', the company explained. This was perhaps not surprising given that, in its eagerness, Whirlpool had distributed products without having received payments, so that within a year, its debtors were Rmb70 million in arrears. Subsequently, it readjusted its strategy for microwave ovens, based on the lessons it had learned, and began again.

What about the PC market, projected to be the world's second largest by 2003? Surely all those 'little emperors' need a computer to play games on? Well sadly, blocking the way there is Legend Holdings, another powerful local competitor. In 1995, *The Economist* predicted that the then market leaders Compaq, IBM and HP would increase their 50% market share to 80% by 2000.[10] Unfortunately, as so often in China, the prediction was wrong. A year later, Legend became number one in PC sales in China. By 2000, it had 29% of the desktop PC market with two other local players at 9% and 5% in second and third position. The total market share of the multinationals had dropped to 20%. Although players such as Dell and Hewlett-Packard have since fought back strongly, Legend is firmly established, albeit in a market where growth is slowing.

In the personal products sector, Unilever benefited from a long-standing presence in the market, resuming production in the 1990s at the same factory it had been forced to leave in 1949 at the time of the Communist takeover. When its products were relaunched on the market, its managers realised they had completely underestimated both the demand and purchasing power but, for once, in a positive direction. Its Chinese subsidiary broke all records for the fastest roll-out of products and sales were 'off the graph' compared with every other country.

By 2000, Unilever brands dominated most categories in which they were offered; Pond's cold cream, a well-remembered favourite, was a runaway success; Lipton's black tea had over 80% of its market, and Wall's ice cream was again far ahead of the pack. It was also busy acquiring local Chinese brands, such as the number one toothpaste brand, Zonghua. But even Unilever was looking nervously over its shoulder at local rivals who were producing copycat items as quickly as possible and offering them to consumers who, as the glamour of Western brands wore off, were reluctant to pay premium prices.

Telecoms has been another market where investors, carried away by optimistic forecasts, paid a high entry price. Part one of the story in the 1990s saw Alcatel, Ericsson and Nortel all competing keenly, offering technology and localising production. But the profits never materialised and, instead, they discovered that they had fallen into the usual trap seemingly laid for foreign entrants. Having been lured in by the magnet of a huge market, their capital and technology were used to build up strong domestic players who quickly helped push prices down.

Part two started in 2000 with great excitement about the mobile phone market, forecast to rise from 121 to 370 million users by 2005. Unfortunately, disappointment was again the outcome as average revenues per user for 2001 were down by 35%. In June 2003, sales were hit by the SARS outbreak and by the time the market picked up, foreign firms realised that the Chinese electronics firm, TCL, had moved into third place. King of the television market, TCL had leveraged its TV stores to sell its jewel encrusted hand phones. Though mocked at first by foreign firms, this model was positioned to be a symbol of social status and success – and its sales demonstrated TCL's truer insight into Chinese culture and psychology. Within a year TCL was the most profitable local handset manufacturer in China. At the annual Geneva Telecoms Exhibition in 2003, the leading Chinese telecoms firms such as Huawei Technologies (recently sued by Cisco for copying software and violating patents and forced to withdraw from the US market) and ZTE were highly prominent, taking up the largest space with their stands. Alcatel, which had been affected by the slump, did not attend.

As with telecoms, China's beer market also saw two waves of competition. In 2003, its reputation as the fastest growing and second largest in the world led to the entry or re-entry of all the main international brewers. The return of SABMiller, Anheuser-Busch, Interbrew, Fosters, Bass, Heineken and Carlsberg once more demonstrated China's irresistible pull, since many of them had suffered embarrasing failures during their first foray into this most fragmented and overcrowded of markets in the 1990s. Then they had built expensive plants for a premium market that failed to materialise so that after sustaining heavy losses, they were finally forced to retire and leave the field to local brewers.

Pharmaceuticals has been another industry with great expectations from a market expected to be the largest in the world by the middle of the twenty-first century. Since pharmaceutical companies naturally think long term, waiting was no problem. By 1998, most of the leading players were present in the market, having invested $2 billion and set up around 1,700 Sino-foreign joint ventures.[11] But although they produced 40 of the 50 most popular drugs, they still only had a 20–30% share of market, and even this was at risk through sudden price caps, medicine price cuts and complex distribution chains.

In China, perhaps more than in other parts of the world, markets are hard to control and difficult to predict. Under the force of the competition they attract they can go from opportunity and rapid growth to overcapacity, bitter price wars and collapse in a short time, so flexibility and vigilance are vital. In many of them, for example household appliances, the easy money has already been made and with profit margins declining, things can only get harder. So how to find a market in which you might stand a chance of making some money – at least for a while?

A few hints

1. Don't look just at the often saturated markets of the coastal areas and special economic zones. China is a big place – so look at the more remote areas. The central government fears rural unrest as these areas are left behind, and may favour firms setting up operations to offer employment there and stop the drift to the cities. Being further from Beijing and less favoured, these provinces are more likely to offer you a better deal and give you support, as they are keen to attract foreign investment. Also, the local competition may be less fierce so, with luck, the market may turn out to be a winner. ATG, a three-way auto components joint venture between a UK firm, a Japanese one and a Chinese ex-SOE located in Anqing, got fast and favoured treatment from local officials in order to set up its venture and build a new factory. Within five years, it was number one in its market.

2. Clear your mind of all the hype about a billion consumers. Instead, go back to basics and do a classic marketing strategy exercise. Look at the external and internal environments, list the threats and opportunities, your strengths and weaknesses. Ask every question you can think of. Can we be competitive? Can the product be competitive? Will it make money? Is

anyone making any money? Study the local competition. Who are they? Would any of them make a good partner? Remember, it might be easier to sell a service than a product, since services are more difficult to copy.

3. Based on this, don't go for a blanket market approach; try to identify a segment with unfulfilled needs. The more tightly defined the segment, the better your chance of success. Try segmenting by age, gender, household income and size, education or occupation, or by the three Rs – religion, race and region. Remember, over two-thirds of the population live in the countryside, and still have a 'collective' mentality.

There are three distinct generations in China, each with different needs and lifestyles: the old Socialist generation that lived through the Mao years; the lost generation of the Cultural Revolution; and the little emperors, offspring of the one-child policy. And don't forget the future generation; China adds the equivalent of Australia (20 million) to its population every year. Maybe your key market hasn't even been born yet.

4. Remember your four Ps – price is still the main determining purchasing factor, not convenience or quality. However, a survey in 2001[12] found that brand awareness was growing to be the next most important factor for the richer segments, followed by price, packaging, advertising and promotion. For the moment, huge outside hoardings are the main advertising avenue in China, and still unregulated. However, check that your advert is visible. Chongqing boasted the world's biggest advertising hoarding but, unfortunately, it turned out to be 'surrounded by fog all the year round and not easily seen'.

5. If you missed out on a market the first time around, how about considering the replacement market? When many consumers bought their TVs, washing machines, refrigerators and so on, it was a novelty actually to own one. But next time round there may be particular pluses that could be attractive, such as flat screens, power consumption or noise on which you might compete.

Which industry might the government be looking to foster? Get in first if you have an advantage, in order to benefit from preferential conditions such as tax breaks or cheap land deals. But guard your advantage, especially if it is technological.

Taiwanese chip manufacturers, not normally the most welcome entrants to mainland markets, have found their expertise greatly in demand to feed the growth of China's semiconductor industry. Foreign firms are trading their technology for access to a market growing at 30% a year in 2002, fuelled by demand for mobile phone, computing and communications equipment manufacturers. But to guard their advantage, they are only transferring mature technology. Similarly, the retail firm Carrefour used logistics and back-office superiority to build up a lead and become the only profitable supermarket chain in China.

6. Start small and build according to demand (not the hockey stick forecasts supplied by local managers) to avoid being left with a warehouse full of unwanted products. In the absence of a mass passenger car market, Honda has found a profitable niche selling small volumes of high-priced Accord models to senior managers in large companies with foreign investment. Honda began slowly in 1998, importing cars via Hong Kong in order to establish its brand in booming southern China. During that time, it created a network of distributors and service centres so that when it bought out Peugeot's Guangzhou (southern China) plant, it already had the basics in place. Honda then negotiated with Beijing the right to set up its own dealer network – previously denied to foreign firms – in return for a cap on production.

Once it had sold the first production run and compiled a four-month waiting list, it applied for increased limits. In April 2002, Honda was producing its second model and planning a further increase in production by 2003.

7. Make exports part of your strategy. China can be an excellent location for low-cost export production; however, be sure to identify your markets before building a plant.

8. A market for premium priced goods does exist, usually for any products or service used by party officials or factory bosses. In 2000, Cartier, for example, sold more than US$13 million worth of jewellery, lighters and perfume in China, and planned to open six more stores in 2001 to meet demand. In October 2003, Lacoste said it expected China to be its top market within the decade, although it warned that there were over 100 brand counterfeiters operating in China.

So what does the future hold? Will China be the Eldorado of multinationals' dreams or the grave of investors' hopes when, as some analysts predict, spectacular growth ends in an overheated economy and boom gives way to bust? Can the 'Workshop of the World' continue to grow apace and still maintain harmonious relations with the US, the EU and other trading partners? And for foreign firms, will the attraction again prove fatal, or will they be successful the second time around and actually begin to make profits in China?

Whatever happens, you can bet that companies will continue to be pulled into its markets, however many times they read about treacherous partners who see alliances solely in terms of expediency, about corporate accounts that bear little relation to reality, about the pitfalls of operating in diverse markets where local competitors indulge in savage price wars, about delays and interference from local and central government, about the difficulties of repatriating profits and where whatever problems arise, turning to the judicial system for help or redress is not an option. China's banking system, for example, is widely acknowledged to be technically insolvent and riven with corruption and fraud. Yet HSBC and Citibank recently entered the sector which of course, the government says it is committed to overhauling so … the fatal attraction continues. But while foreign firms are busy trying to find ways to crack the China markets, they shouldn't forget to watch what the big Chinese firms are doing in overseas markets. Companies such as Haier, Legend and TCL are moving fast, and could soon be taking your domestic market share.

At the end of 2003, foreign companies were turning their investment attention to the Chinese hinterland, encouraged by a central government concerned to close the widening gap between the rich coastal and the poorer inland regions of the north-east and west of China. Whirlpool, Intel and perhaps most surprisingly, Gucci, all announced moves into the western province of Sichuan, 'Go West young man' seems to be the best advice for continued growth. Next stop Tibet? Now there's a challenge.

Key Lessons

■ Remember that there is no such thing as 'the Chinese market'. China is a series of regions and potential markets, each deserving of its own market entry strategy.

■ All procedures in China take time, patience and money.

■ Start small, target your segment and adapt your offering to its needs. Never underestimate the power of local competitors. Remember, an effective distribution and sales network is critical to success, but also very, very difficult to build.

■ If you discover that you have the wrong partner, if management clashes make the relationship one long battle or if the partner turns out to be useless, it is better to abandon ship than try to make it work.

■ Moderate your expectations. Don't be hypnotised by the hype, but concentrate on the reality.

Notes

1 *EIU Business China*, 'China: The good, the bad and the ugly', 29 April, 2002.

2 Ibid.

3 *Financial Times*, 'M&A in Asia falls 12.6% in value', 6 January, 2003, p17.

4 Taken from 'China's Haier Group: Growth through Acquisitions', case study by Robert Crawford, Ming Zeng and Hellmut Schutte, 2000 INSEAD-EAC.

5 *Financial Times*, Comment and Analysis, 25 August, 2003, p11.

6 *Financial Times*, 'Toyota loses China lawsuit on copyright', 25 November, 2003, p15.

7 *China's Foreign Trade*, no 320, 'How far can China's motors drive in the international market?', September, 2003, pp16–18.

8 *Financial Times*, 'China's data chief "confident" about statistics', 1 March 2002, p7.

9 Taken from 'Whirlpool in China, (A-C)', case studies by Deborah Clyde-Smith and Professor Peter Williamson, 2001, INSEAD-EAC Singapore.

10 *The Economist*, 'Leave it to the locals', 13 April, 2002, p63.

11 *EIU Business China*, 'Drug-induced', 7 January, 2002, pp5–6.

12 ChinaOnline, 27 March, 2001.

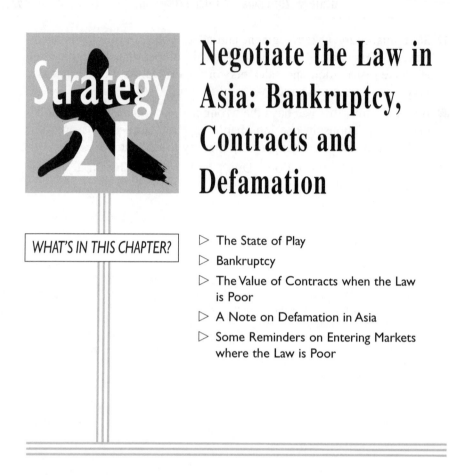

Negotiate the Law in Asia: Bankruptcy, Contracts and Defamation

The State of Play

There are crooks in business all over the world. The reason why there are fewer in the West than in Asia is not because of culture or tradition but simply because they can be taken to court in the West. The legal system also works well in Singapore and so its citizens are generally law-abiding. The threat of punishment has the same effect the world over.

A basic prerequisite for any developed country is an effective rule of law and that means an enforceable judicial regime to which every individual and every institution is subject. Political leaders, hereditary leaders and anyone else in a high position must be subject to the same constraints of the law as anyone else. The law should not exist merely to allow rulers to impose their whims on everyone else, no matter how benevolent. Rule by law is not the same thing as the rule of law, although in Asia the two are commonly confused.

One essential aspect of an effective rule of law is that legal codes should be written in plain language. They should also be clear as to their intent and thus minimise the opportunity for interpretation and discretion. If they do not do this, they invite corruption and favouritism. They also allow people to operate 'within the law' but nonetheless in a manner that is clearly 'wrong'.

The agencies charged with administering the law should also be as streamlined as possible. Approvals processes are best centralised within one arm of government for consistency, timeliness and to reduce the opportunities for discretion among far-flung and diverse bureaucrats. On this measure, Vietnam followed by India, then China, Thailand, Indonesia and the Philippines routinely top surveys of businessmen as the worst economies in which to operate when it comes to red tape. Hong Kong, Singapore and Australia rate as the best.

Good laws are essential for establishing and enforcing property rights and property rights are essential for good and transparent markets. Peruvian economist and writer Hernando de Soto writes:

> Imagine a country where nobody can identify who owns what ... addresses cannot be easily verified, people cannot be made to pay their debts, resources cannot conveniently be turned into money, ownership cannot be divided into shares, descriptions of assets are not standardised and cannot be easily compared and the rules that govern property vary from neighbourhood to neighbourhood or even from street to street. You have just put yourself into the life of a developing country or former communist nation.[1]

In Asia, de Soto's excellent description applies in varying degrees to Indonesia, China, Vietnam, Myanmar, the Philippines, Thailand, Cambodia, Laos, Bangladesh, Pakistan, Nepal and even India. De Soto points out that one reason why the poor stay poor in the developing world is that while they might often have assets, particularly land, they cannot adequately demonstrate title to the point where they can sell them. Most businesses are started with borrowed money, but how can you mortgage an asset which you cannot prove that you own? Houses and shops with no titles, crops with no deeds and businesses with no statutes of incorporation inhibit individuals' abilities to borrow against these assets and sell them. And when they do, they or the buyers risk attracting claims from others who also claim ownership.

Problems with property rights are not restricted to the poor. Asia's governments were advised by the IMF to privatise state-owned assets in the wake of the 1997–98 economic crisis. But how do you privatise an asset over which even the state's title is unclear? This is just the problem that the Indonesian government faced when it wanted to ready parts of Jakarta's international airport for privatisation in 2000. It was not clear that the government had title to all the land on which the airport had been built. Months were lost while consultants and lawyers sought to determine who owned the land on which the hangers and cargo sheds stood.

Arbitration is the most common form of commercial and labour dispute resolution in China. The China International Economic and Trade Arbitration Commission (CIETAC) is the usual body that mediates in disputes over commercial contracts which involve foreign parties. If the local party refuses to go to the CIETAC, the dispute must go to a local arbitration commission. Arbitration in commercial cases in China is usually a last resort and signals an irretrievable breakdown between the parties.

As rich as Japan is, it still has an inadequate legal system. It is understaffed and underresourced, judges are given skimpy budgets, and too little is spent on training lawyers and the judiciary. Most importantly, there are too few lawyers. There are about 17,000 lawyers in all Japan, most of whom do not practise commercial law. But there are more than 60,000 lawyers listed at the New York bar alone and as many as 150,000 law graduates in China. There is only one state-sanctioned law school, the Legal Training and Research Institute. Undergraduate law students face one of the toughest bar exams in the world. It takes the average student five attempts to succeed and only one attempt a year is allowed. Lawyers' fees are outrageously high owing to the shortage of lawyers.

The problem with the law in Asia is not only enforcement. The laws themselves are often poorly drafted. Sometimes they are vague to the point where it is unclear what is within the law and what is not. Consumer protection laws are weak in most of Asia and so too are competition laws. Companies can merge with their competitors to dominate a market, or use predatory pricing to force competitors out of the market, often with little legal repercussion.

Bankruptcy

High numbers of bankruptcies are a sign of a well-functioning economy and not a sick one. Too few bankruptcies are not a sign of a healthy economy, but rather of a poorly functioning legal environment. A World Bank report published in 2001 found that among 37 countries surveyed, the countries with a greater than average ratio of bankruptcies to total firms throughout the 1990s were all OECD countries, bar two, South Africa and Singapore.[2]

In Asia, bankruptcy law as it is written and applied works relatively well in Taiwan, Hong Kong, Singapore, South Korea, and Japan. The main criticism, though, particularly in respect of Korea and Japan, is that procedures are too rigid and slow. Part of the problem in Japan is the insufficient number of lawyers. Elsewhere in Asia, forcing debtors into bankruptcy can be more trouble than it is worth.

Enforcement is the main issue but the laws themselves require fine-tuning. Indonesia's new bankruptcy laws, introduced in 1998, allow single creditors to petition for the involuntary bankruptcy of apparent bad debtors. This means that the existence of one unpaid debt could bring about a bankruptcy even though the debt might well be the subject of a bona fide dispute between the debtor and the petitioning creditor. Bankruptcy in such circumstances is not warranted. The condition of bankruptcy requires that the debtor is generally unable to pay its debts to several or more of its creditors. Bankruptcy laws need to reflect this.

In Thailand, Indonesia and the Philippines creditors still prefer to go through voluntary debt work outs rather than risk costly and unpredictable court proceedings. Only 37 cases were filed with Thailand's new Central Bankruptcy Court in the first month after it opened in 1999, for example. This was way below the expected number. Indonesia's new bankruptcy court, established in 1998, attracted only 38 applications in its first five months. By way of comparison, there were approximately 1,000 similar applications in Australia for the same period, and Australia had not just been through an economic crisis. Many of the applications in Thailand and Indonesia were in relation to small debts and then fewer than half led to bankruptcies. Meanwhile, huge segments of the local business scene were obviously technically bankrupt.

China has bankruptcy procedures and these can function relatively well until they need to be enforced. Even state-owned entities have trouble here. The head of China's state-owned China Construction Bank has said that between 1998 and 2000 his bank took 1,300 of its corporate bad debtors, many of which are other state-owned companies, to court. It won judgments against 98% of them but the bank was still unable to get much of its money back because China's courts are so ineffective at enforcing civil judgments, especially against state-owned companies.[3] If this is so for an important state-owned bank, then what hope do foreigners have in China?

The Value of Contracts when the Law is Poor

If the law and its enforcement is poor, of what value are contracts? The answer is that they are essential, particularly if large sums of money are at stake. While contracts may not always be enforced, sometimes they are.

The best approach to Asia's more difficult markets is to have a range of measures to cover all contingencies, and a contract is one of them. In more developed markets, a contract might be a necessary and sufficient requirement but in others, contracts are merely necessary. Many companies opt to have contracts drawn up in jurisdictions with sound legal systems such as Singapore and Hong Kong, although the value of such documents in third countries such as Indonesia or Vietnam is questionable.

The value of contracts in Asia can be enhanced according to how they are presented. Contracts and other legal documents should be written as simply as possible using plain English and then translated into the local language. They should be explained clause by clause to the local party and each clause should be agreed on separately before discussion moves on to the next clause. If the local side is not given the opportunity to fully understand it, they might sign it anyway to save face. This will only lead to problems later on. If the local party does not understand the contract but signs anyway, they will be tempted to renegotiate it later on. Indeed, as any sort of serious negotiations progress in Asia, confirmation of whatever is agreed should always be sought in writing. Verbal confirmation might often mean confirmation that the matter will be considered rather than has been agreed to.

Contracts dwelling on penalties and dealing with relationship problems and exit clauses might prove detrimental to your relationship with your partner if presented at an early stage in the relationship-building process. 'We're still getting to know one another and already you're thinking about what to do if we bust up?' might be the surprised response.

Getting a local partner to sign a contract might prove difficult. Signing contracts might be routine in the West, but for some in Asia, the practice might be unusual and thus cause uncertainty. One Western businessman interviewed by the authors commented that in India:

> often contracts are not worth the paper they're written on. Often they won't sign any formal agreement before business begins. They want to see how business goes first and then they'll commit to signing a contract. It's as if a contract is not the precursor to business but rather a signal that it can continue to proceed.

It is a sentiment that applies throughout Asia.

Who draws up the contracts, joint venture agreements, articles of association and whatever else local laws dictate as being necessary is important. The foreign company might find it useful to offer to pay all the legal costs itself, if this means it can choose the law firm to do this. Otherwise, the local side might be tempted to choose a law firm on the basis that someone's cousin works there and so on. Law firms need to be chosen for the quality of their expertise and not because of personal connections. There are limits to the useful application of personal connections.

Often contracts are not seen in Asia as fixed for all time as they are in the West. They are viewed as a statement of principles which reflect current conditions. Should these shift unexpectedly, don't be surprised if the local side wants to repudiate the contract, pleading that it is no longer 'fair' that it should be enforced. It needs to be emphasised at the negotiating stage that the contract is fixed. When Asia's currencies plummeted in 1997, borrowers saw this as an excuse unilaterally to ignore their loan agreements, even if they still had the capability to service their loans. This was most evident in Thailand, where many large corporate borrowers felt that they should no longer have to meet their loan obligations. The 'fairness' of transferring their losses onto their creditors did not come into it.

Asia is home to some spectacular cases of contract repudiations caused because things did not work out as planned. The debacle that was Enron Corporation's US$3 billion Dabhol Power development in the Indian state of Maharashta is one example. The plant was the largest single foreign investment in India ever and when the demand for electricity in the state did not rise as forecast, the state government refused to buy all the power it had contracted to buy. It then stopped buying power from the project altogether. These difficulties contributed to Enron's collapse in late 2001.

A similar problem arose in Indonesia in 2000 between Indonesia's state-owned power company PLN and foreign investors who had been invited in to build power plants. Economic conditions had changed and so PLN felt this should allow it to repudiate its contracts. That same year disputes arose between the state-owned telephone company PT Telekomunikasi Indonesia (PT Telkom) and five foreign operating partners, including NTT of Japan, Telstra of Australia, Cable & Wireless of the United Kingdom and AT&T of the United States. The five partners accused the state company of breaching its contracts with them when it failed to lift telephone tariffs in accordance with a contracted formula and to cede management control to the five.

Arbitration: Arbitration can be sought in such circumstances but even this may not lead to the desired results for the outside party. If the local party will not meet its obligations under a contract, why would it comply with an unfavourable arbitration award? US energy company Karaha Bodas Co. sought compensation from the Indonesian state-owned oil company Pertamina after the Indonesian Government suspended the company's geothermal power generation project in West Java in 1997. Pertamina had been the contractee. The dispute went to a Swiss arbitration panel in 2000 which awarded Karaha Bodas US$261 million. Pertamina refused to pay and so Karaha Bodas then applied to seize Pertamina's assets in the United States. Payments for oil and gas produced by Pertamina and its partners are often made to trustee and escrow accounts in the United States and Karaha Bodas sought judicial access in the United States to these accounts so that it could collect the arbitration award.

One of the five international partners of PT Telkom, the AriaWest consortium in which AT&T had a 35% stake, signalled its desire to sell its business in Indonesia in September 2000 after PT Telkom ignored its contractual obligations. It demanded that PT Telkom pay US$735 million for the fixed line network that it had already laid down. Telekom refused, saying it was worth only US$280 million. AriaWest then filed a US$1.3 billion arbitration claim against PT Telkom in Geneva in May 2001. Perhaps mindful of Karaha Bodas's troubles in obtaining its arbitrated settlement in Indonesia, AriaWest's owners agreed to sell it to PT Telkom in March 2002 for between US$320 million and US$350 million.

The main centres in the world for arbitration are London, Hong Kong, Paris, Kuala Lumpur and Sydney. Singapore is attempting to position itself as an international arbitration centre too. In 2002, more than 60 international arbitration cases were registered in Singapore. The actual number probably was higher as not all cases are registered. The Singapore International Arbitration Centre (SIAC) cut its fees for case management and appointment fees by almost half in mid-2003 to further position Singapore as an international arbitration centre.

A Note on Defamation in Asia

Businesspeople in Asia typically do not sue for defamation or libel. This is partly due to the insufficient appreciation for intangibles. Paying service providers such as lawyers is almost an anathema for many in Asia. To pay them to protect something as intangible as one's reputation compounds the apparent folly. The smart ones are more likely to respond to an article or book about them that they don't like by simply claiming that 'not everything is correct'. Precisely what is not correct is left unsaid, so that the entire article or book is held in question – a clever tactic.

Having said that, the use of defamation action is growing in some Asian countries. Nowhere is this more so than in Malaysia, where sums sought for alleged damages have escalated dramatically. The 1994 award of M$10 million (currently about US$2.6 million) to Vincent Tan, the founder of Malaysia's Berjaya conglomerate, against a local freelance business journalist was a turning point.

Tan has since sued others for defamation, including a Malaysian academic for remarks printed in the *Asian Wall Street Journal*, the journal itself and a Malaysian journalist now based in Sydney for comments circulated by e-mail.

In 2000, Prime Minister Mahathir's son Mirzan sued the Malaysian printer of the *Asian Wall Street Journal* for remarks carried in the journal about his business interests. He sought M$150 million from the printer, notwithstanding the fact that the printer had no editorial control whatsoever over what was published. The matter was settled out of court. Separately, Mirzan also settled out of court the previous January with two Malaysian dailies in relation to allegedly defamatory comments they had published.

Later that year, the CEO of a listed Malaysian company claimed that he was defamed by his own company and two of its other managers when they proposed, without giving reasons, that he should be removed from his position. He claimed that the inference was that he had done something wrong. He claimed he had not and sought M$60 million for the alleged damage to his reputation.

Two Malaysian companies commenced proceedings against an *Asian Wall Street Journal* reporter in Malaysia around the same time for comments attributed to him but which he claimed he never made. The damages sought were M$40 million. In February 2001, Malaysia's largest private television station was ordered by a judge to pay M$100 million in damages to a little heard of local businessman. And later that year another Malaysian businessman filed suits against nine local newspapers claiming a total of M$1.3 billion in damages for their remarks about his business methods.

Outside Malaysia, Asia's businesspeople might be quick to threaten litigation for defamation or libel but rarely do they follow through, even in Singapore. The intention is more to threaten and discourage further exposure of their affairs. Many in Asian business do not appreciate that with defamation proceedings comes the process of discovery, whereby the court can compel the plaintiff to table all sorts of documents relating to their private business affairs, thus exposing them to even more scrutiny. The threat of discovery is one means of heading off defamation threats from proceeding to court.

Some reminders on entering markets where the law is poor

- Insist on a contract or similar document regardless of where in Asia you intend to operate. Contracts are necessary but not sufficient in markets where the law is poor. They become one of the modes of self-defence rather than the only mode in such countries.

- Make sure that contracts are written in plain language. English is the second, not the first, language for most people in Asia, so if they are to be presented with contracts in English it is far better that they are not loaded with archaic terms such as 'herewith' and 'thereupon'.

- The parties need to sit down and discuss proposed contracts clause by clause so that each clause is fully understood and individually agreed upon.

- Contracts in Asia are likely to be better received if they are not heavy on penalties for this or that breach.

- Offer to pay the legal bill to ensure that you can to choose the legal team that will draw up contracts and other legal documents.

- Arbitration is the most usual and preferred means of solving commercial disputes in Asia. Outside parties need to understand local arbitration mechanisms before they enter into contracts of any substance in Asia.

- Bankruptcy is still not a viable option in much of Asia for creditors attempting to recover debts. Creditors need to prepare for often drawn out negotiated debt work outs.

Notes

1   De Soto, H., 'Why capitalism works in the West but not elsewhere', *International Herald Tribune*, 5 January, 2001.
2   World Bank, 'Bankruptcy around the world: Explanations of its relative use', background paper, 2001.
3   *Asian Wall Street Journal*, 'Asia banking-reform efforts losing steam, bankers warn', 11 September, 2001.

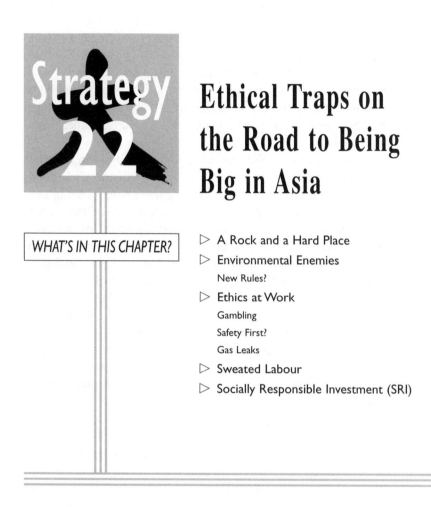

Ethical Traps on the Road to Being Big in Asia

A Rock and a Hard Place

Asia has generally had a bad press when it comes to ethical issues; corruption, counterfeiting, intellectual property rights and so on have all been well publicised. In these cases, Western firms generally class themselves as the victims. But there is another set of ethical issues where they themselves run the risk of being seen as the guilty parties, and these concern their responsibility for the damage to the natural and human resources of the region.

In recent years, many foreign firms have faced unwelcome publicity brought by Western or local pressure groups and NGOs (non-governmental organisations) over issues including the use of 'sweated' labour, environmental damage from mining or logging activities, or from investing in other projects considered environmentally unsound. Schemes such as China's massive Three Gorges project faced scrutiny and several Western firms have been forced to pull out by pressure groups protesting at the displacement of up to two million people that it will cause. Investment in Myanmar with its poor human and labour rights record is another perennial target for criticism.

The senior management of Western companies involved in scandals have often claimed to be unaware that the factories producing their goods were in effect sweatshops, or that illegal logging was taking place in their forest concessions, unaware, that is, until they opened their local newspaper or saw a headline in *Business Week* pillorying them for unethical behaviour. More recently, Western companies have tried to protect themselves by contributing to organisations investigating working conditions, only to find that this too has failed to save them from attack, not just in their home countries but in Asia as well. Frequently, they are caught between powerful Western lobbies and increasingly vocal local critics and organisations in the countries where they are operating. Doomsday forecasts have increased awareness in the region about the scale of the problem. An Asian Development Bank report has warned that Asia is on the 'brink of environmental catastrophe' and that 'environmental degradation in the region is pervasive, accelerating and unabated'.[1]

For any company accused of unethical behaviour, the consequences can be highly damaging, not only financially but, more crucially, in terms of the company's reputation. The growth of the Internet means that allegations and evidence can be made available the world over cheaply and quickly. Protestations of innocence can appear very flimsy against the power of emotive statements and petitions. And such accusations tend to linger in the collective memory for a long time, as Nestlé and Shell have discovered to their cost.

This chapter examines some of the most frequent ethical traps which companies risk falling into in Asia, and the choices open to them if the worst happens and they wake up to find themselves public enemy number one.

Environmental Enemies

Using the region's natural resources, whether it is prospecting for oil, mining coal or metals, or logging timber, can be a very risky business. Western firms dealing in certain industries – timber, paper, or furniture making – are open to accusations of environmental abuse, even in countries where, until recently, the emphasis on sustainable resources was not a government priority. But forewarned is forearmed, and the only real weapon for such companies is to prepare carefully for any attack that might come and have all the necessary evidence ready to refute any charge of poor practice or damage to the environment as soon as it occurs. After that, the only remaining alternative is withdrawal.

This worked in the case of the UK group, Inchcape plc, which was in the middle of a media exercise to reposition the company as a focused, international marketing and services company, when it woke up to a huge spread in the UK's *Sunday Times* taking it to task for poor management of its logging activities in Borneo.[2] The newspaper's 'Insight' investigative team had produced an emotive article entitled 'Log 'em and leave 'em.' It was potentially highly damaging to Inchcape's prospects for a successful relaunch. However, its corporate affairs department was very quick off the mark and able to refute fully all the accusations. This worked as a short-term measure but the company knew that this particular business, although profitable, would always be a potential source of trouble, and so finally took the decision to sell it off.

Companies in other environmentally sensitive businesses have come to the same conclusion, faced with the unrelenting attacks of pressure groups. For example, the energy firm Cogentrix set up in Mangalore, a region of India deemed of environmental concern. After eight years of negotiation, three revisions of its power purchase agreement and an investment of US$27 million, its power project had still not got off the ground, but remained blocked in the courts by environmentalist suits. Cogentrix decided to withdraw.

One company that is perennially accused of all sorts of transgressions in its operations in Asia is the US company, Freeport-McMoRan Copper & Gold. Since it began mining operations in Indonesia's Irian Jaya province in 1973, it has been accused of causing massive destruction to one of the world's richest and least explored environments. In May 2000, not for the first time, the government threatened to suspend its operations after a rock-waste storage facility collapsed, causing flooding and leaving four workers dead. Under intense pressure, Freeport has spent $40 million annually on environmental monitoring and funded a comprehensive survey of the region's biological diversity and richness. However, it remains a target for environmental activists and NGOs.

Perhaps surprisingly, local firms too can have their businesses threatened by accusations of damaging the environment, although in these cases the motive may be as much political and commercial – one *guanxi* network outdoing another, weaker one – as environmental. In such cases, however, the environmental card can be a very strong one to play, as the case of PT Indorayon demonstrates.

In 1989, the ethnic Chinese owner of Indonesia's Raja Garuda Mas Group (RGM) completed the building of a state-of-the-art pulp mill, PT Indorayon, in Porsea in northern Sumatra.[3] Later, a rayon mill was built at the same site. Since the plant involved chemical processes, the company was well aware that some pollution was inevitable, but had tried to minimise the damage by working with Scandinavian consultants to procure and install equipment conforming to the highest environmental standards. It also had an agreement with the Ministries of Environment, Research and Technology and Industry specifying permitted levels of effluent, the volume and concentration of chemicals, how many days of aeration were necessary and so on. According to Indorayon's calculations, pollution from the mill would be below normal government standards. It also had a comprehensive nursery and replanting programme to replace deforested areas.

During a trial run of the water treatment plant, however, the lagoon through which water passed for bacteriological treatment collapsed. In fact, there was no waste water in the lagoon at the time, only rain water, but this ran out towards the river, washing away some shacks lying in its path. However, the incident quickly became a hot political issue locally and then in Jakarta, where it was reported that the waste water had poisoned the river and the whole surrounding area.

Lacking any experience in PR, the company failed to rebut the stories firmly enough. Although aware of how important environmental concerns could be, the owner believed that having the best Scandinavian equipment in place, and a state-of-the-art computerised control system, would be protection enough. Unfortunately, this did not turn out to be true. Scenting a good story, the national press moved in. In lieu of statements from the beleaguered Indorayon, the journalists had a field day with stories of pollution, itching skins and dead fish, allegedly stirred up further by managers from a hydroelectric plant upstream who had opposed the project from the start. Eventually a team of six ministers from Jakarta inspected the site. The water was tested, fish put back into the river and seen to survive. At a press conference, the ministers announced that the mill fulfilled every environmental requirement and, eventually, the story died down.

But that was not the end of the matter. A second dam burst four years later and this renewed the criticism, but an environmental audit by the US firm Labat Andersen again largely cleared the company. In 1998, local pressure caused the temporary closure of the plant on the grounds that Indorayon's operations had caused 'not only serious environmental problems, but also economic, social, cultural, legal and political problems in north Sumatra'.[4] Few local firms could fight such a comprehensive list of accusations and although negotiations continued, in 2000 the rayon operations were closed down completely by the government of former President Wahid, although the pulp and paper plant was allowed to restart. The story is a sobering lesson for Western investors. If a powerful local firm is unable to run such operations and appease local and national pressure groups in Indonesia, despite taking so many precautions to ensure it is acting responsibly, then what chance would a foreign investor have?

New Rules?

Governments are tightening the rules relating to forest management and downstream emissions. Under pressure, Indonesia has trialled open tendering for forestry concessions. In the past, concessions were handed out on the basis of cronyism, corruption and nepotism. Many concession holders were responsible for driving out indigenous people and using slash and burn techniques, which destroyed valuable forests and eventually led to the forest fires that engulfed much of Southeast Asia in choking smog during 1997. Theoretically, there will be much more rigorous checks on the expertise of companies granted the concessions, who will also be required to share profits with the local community and grant part of the land to a local village cooperative. There are also proposals for a certification process such as the one operated by the Forest Stewardship Council, an international environmental organisation which certifies wood products.

Such moves may give Western companies, with their better developed environmental systems, more of a chance to enter these industries. However, despite the growing awareness, enforcement will probably continue to be lax and left to local governments, making it easy for local companies to flout the rules. A January 2003 report on Indonesia by the Anglo-American environmental group, the Environmental Investigation Agency concluded that 'the processes under way to tackle illegal logging' had 'very little chance of success', hampered as they were by rampant corruption.[5] Any Western firm entering this arena should therefore remain extremely vigilant – if their own lobbies don't catch them, the locals probably will. And there will be a high price to pay.

Ethics at Work

Gambling

One little-reported issue that Western managers often face in the betting-mad Chinese environment is that of gambling on work sites: do they try to stop it or turn a blind eye? One expatriate in Thailand was informed by one of his supervisors that an illegal lottery was being run on the factory site. He decided to ignore it after further investigation revealed that the supervisor was only motivated to complain because the lottery was affecting the takings from his own gambling activities. Companies can choose either to ignore or prohibit it – either way, it is worth having a policy on gambling before it becomes an issue, so that when a response is required, it is not ad hoc and made on the run.

Safety First?

A more serious issue is that of safety standards, which are rudimentary in many parts of Asia. Most Western managers are shocked by their first experience of safety practices in many parts of Asia, and the total lack of precautions taken by workers clambering up swaying scaffolding or working with electric equipment. One veteran construction manager, sent out from Europe to head a team building a factory in Indonesia, was shocked on his first day on the site to see workers hanging upside down from bamboo scaffolding, wielding blow torches with no sign of goggles, safety hats or shoes. Further on, he saw his foreman hammering in rivets using a home-made hammer, his bare toes curled over the scaffolding as he hung down, hardly able to see where the blows were going. On the ground, barefoot workers – male and female – in jeans and T-shirts worked in deep muddy trenches pulling cables, surrounded by moving machinery and unstable scaffolding.

However, within a few weeks the same manager had become inured to the risks, having realised that when he insisted on safety clothing, it caused more accidents than it prevented. Few of the local workers, for example, wore shoes habitually and so were used to clinging on barefoot. They found the heavy safety boots a hindrance which made them clumsy and more likely to fall, apart from the fact that finding the right size to fit their slender feet was a big problem. The same was true of the hard hats he gave out, which they usually left at home, along with the shoes, for their children to play with. They found the masks uncomfortable in the hot and humid weather but the goggles were accepted, although, again, size was often a problem and workers complained that they caused headaches. 'It's amazing', he concluded, 'every second guy is doing something wrong but considering the risks, they don't often hurt themselves.'

Another manager working in Thailand, spent months organising safety lectures for his employees, and was gratified one day to see a worker wearing a safety harness as he worked high up on a gantry. His pleasure did not last long, however, as a second later he realised that the harness was not actually attached to anything. He also noted how, when he toured the site, workers would disappear into doorways and then ostentatiously reappear carrying pieces of safety equipment. But rarely did he see them put them on. The Western manager of a chemical plant received a safety report that noted happily how 'Nobody was smoking on site, and almost all personnel were wearing hard hats'. Fire drills, he discovered, were a novelty that caused much merriment.

In fact, most Western firms try to put safety rules and procedures into practice in the plants they run in Asia, aiming to have the same standards throughout their global operations. A key post in any post-merger plan is usually that of safety officer. However, finding a qualified person to fill it can be difficult, if not impossible. One multinational attracted many applicants when it advertised for a safety officer, but none of them actually had any experience or formal qualifications for the job. Usually, the only way to find one is to poach them from another company. Choosing a likely candidate and sending them for training is another option, but it is odds-on that they in turn will soon be poached. One multinational found the ideal safety officer, then lost him two days later when he accepted the same job at another company. The difference was in the job title, the second firm called him the safety manager – albeit on a lower salary.

Currently, safety and labour rights are receiving a great deal of attention in the Western press, and these concerns are spilling over into Asia-Pacific. Consumer movements, the media and NGOs are investigating safety standards around the world, and it also tends to be one of the subjects CEOs enjoying writing about in annual reports – statistics about the excellent safety record are always non-controversial and an occasion for self-congratulation. Consequently, many expatriate managers find themselves under greater pressure to impose Western safety standards in their Asian operations. Some companies issue safety charters as part of a corporate-wide drive for better health, safety and environmental standards. These standards are often reinforced by guidelines and local workplace procedures based on best practices. Special pleading on the grounds of different cultural attitudes is no longer accepted. But should safety standards be universal? How far should Westerners impose their standards on other cultures, especially if the result is to cause more accidents, not fewer?

In reality, most experienced managers working in the region concentrate on what is possible, and take a step-by-step approach to inculcate new safety habits. 'Safety', observed one, 'is a way of life. It's a long-term process of education and training. You can't expect it from people who have never been taught it.' Therefore companies might begin by concentrating on maintaining a clean environment on the factory site – no spilt oil, no empty drums rolling round loose, machinery kept clean – these are all important tasks which managers can focus on, leading to an improved safety record. Following up after accidents and putting up notices around the factory with large illustrations showing the effect of bad practices can further reinforce the message. By setting an example and getting their managers to follow them, company heads are more likely to succeed. Once the managers are committed and begin to enforce the rules, then safe behaviour may spread to other areas such as the use of safety equipment. Acting in this way and setting aside time to drill and teach basic behaviours is usually far more effective than trying – and failing – to impose strict Western standards.

Gas Leaks

Another perennial threat for those operating in industries involving chemicals is the danger of leaks – gas, chlorine or other toxic substances. The chemicals industry has a high profile in Europe, where pressure groups are quick to demonise any company thought to be neglecting safety issues. Equally, in Asia leaks are a safety hazard that Western managers must treat very seriously on two fronts, the operational and the emotional. Dealing with the source of the problem is likely to be a matter of automatically activated systems but what they must deal with equally promptly is the local media in order to avoid bad publicity. Nobody wants the tag 'Another Bhopal' attached to their company name.

One manager found how damaging this issue can be when he received a call from one of his supervisors at the factory site in an industrial park outside Jakarta.[6] He learned that during his absence on a one-day training course in Jakarta, there had been a chlorine leak from one of the chemical storage tanks. The leak was not due to any breakdown, but had been caused by an operator, who had only been with the company a few months, taking a short cut when carrying out a manoeuvre instead of following procedures. Luckily, the technology installed in the plant had triggered an immediate shutdown and of the 15 tons of chlorine stored on site, only one kilo escaped. According to the supervisor, this low concentration meant that there was no danger to any personnel on site, and everyone present had been accounted for.

His next decision turned out to be vital; should he return to the site at once, or rely on his professional, qualified staff as he would in, for example, Europe? In the end, the manager stayed put, but he had forgotten one vital cultural trait that might have made him change his mind. In Indonesia, as elsewhere in Southeast Asia, nobody likes to make their superior feel uncomfortable by reporting bad news. How bad was the spill really? Had all the bad news been reported and had it been reported accurately? It turned out that the real problem was not the leak itself but the perception of it by the local media. As is often forgotten in Asia, the crisis had two elements – the physical one and the public relations element. The former was adequately dealt with, whereas the local media greatly exaggerated the leak and its effects, in what had been, in reality, a minor episode. The lesson is clear; whatever the incident, however apparently innocuous the emission, be on the spot to give your interpretation and, above all, to show concern for the community as a responsible investor.

Sweated Labour

Perhaps one of the greatest public relations disasters that can befall a Western company in Asia is to be accused of breaking a country's labour laws and, even worse, employing child labour via the contractors and suppliers that work for you. Increasingly, this has been happening, despite all their attempts to have clean hands. The Asian Monitor Resource Centre, which monitors working conditions in China, reported in 1999 that workers making Disney products were being forced to work up to 16 hours a day, seven days a week with almost no overtime pay. A second report on toys named four factories, which were subcontractors to Mattel, the world's largest toy maker, with similar sweatshop conditions.[7] Yet both companies had done a great deal to improve working conditions in their Asian factories and both had codes of conduct; Disney carried out 10,000 inspections. Some observers believed that the allegations were false, either based on unchecked allegations or maybe by people with a grudge. Whatever the truth, the damage was done.

Ikea, the Swedish retailing group, was another company caught out by accusations of child labour. It was unprepared to meet the allegations and its excuse of 'We didn't know the situation at our suppliers' was considered inadequate. Ignorance is no longer a defence, given the well-publicised cases in some Asian countries and the growth over the last decade in the number of pressure groups watching out for such abuses.

Social Accountability International (SAI), for example, designs and oversees the SA8000 factory conditions standard. Launched in 1998 by a coalition of US activists and multinationals including Toys R Us, Avon and the food company, Dole, the SAI sets standards and appoints inspectors to fight the sweatshop war, especially in China. It limits workers to 48 hours of regular shifts a week, with 12 hours overtime. Wages must be enough to meet basic needs, and the factories are scheduled for inspection twice a year.

Some companies, such as Levi, have made an ethical stance the core of their company. The company pulled out of China in protest at human rights abuses in the late 1980s and long before other companies, Levi's global sourcing task force created guidelines designed to hold its overseas contractors to the highest possible standards of labour practices. Wal-Mart has been asking its suppliers to sign a code of basic labour standards since 1992, and hired outside auditing firms to inspect supplier factories. Nike, Reebok and Gap have set up similar procedures.

Yet despite all this, still the horror stories come out; guards beating up workers, illegal deposits to cover food and lodging in the factory dormitory, workers handling toxic glues and solvents without gloves, and factories burning to the ground after an explosion, with the workers still inside. Despite the inspections, real change is slow in coming. Many suppliers and contractors to Western firms either fail to implement promised reforms, or simply close their factories down, open them up under new names and go on producing the same goods with the same people.

Perhaps the company that has suffered the worst publicity in this context has been Nike, which has subcontractors in 700 factories in 50 countries. There was global coverage of the notorious e-mail asking for 'sweatshop' to be printed on the side of one of its running shoes, and a BBC documentary on child labour in Cambodia that showed children hand stitching footballs for Nike. In response, Nike plus Gap and other vulnerable companies set up the Global Alliance for Workers and Communities to report on sweatshop conditions in Indonesia, Vietnam and Thailand. Nike is also a member of a US-based group, the Fair Labor Association, a coalition of clothing and footwear companies such as Levi-Strauss, Adidas-Salomon, Phillips-Van Heusen, Reebok and Liz Claiborne. Founded in 2001, it sends in external monitors to audit factories round the world and publishes detailed tracking charts of progress in improving working conditions. Such transparency is designed to encourage brands to take corrective action when abuses are uncovered. Although much of the emphasis on sweatshops and labour abuses has so far been on the garment and footwear industries, campaigners are now turning their attention to conditions in the IT and electronic industries which are similarly vulnerable.

Such moves have been greeted by accusations of hypocrisy and being little more than a cosmetic exercise to stave off criticism. After all, it is not easy to change attitudes and practices unless people genuinely want to change, or are convinced that the alternative is more profitable. Moreover, if you are going to continue to earn the high profit margins commensurate with having your products made in low-wage countries, you cannot expect to get away unscathed. Those who play with fire are liable at least to feel some heat.

Socially Responsible Investment (SRI)

The fact that ethical issues are becoming more prominent is demonstrated by the emergence of socially responsible investment funds in Asia, which follows the rapid growth of this industry in Europe and North America. In the US, the total size of these funds doubled to US$2.2 trillion in two years, showing that it has become an important issue. Increasingly, companies in the West have begun to realise that they cannot afford to ignore these funds, and this pressure has increased the impetus for maintaining high environmental and safety standards throughout their global operations.

In February 2001, the Association for Sustainable and Responsible Investment in Asia (Asria) was set up with the backing of a group of mainly Western-based fund management companies. Its aim was to build a regional research base to allow socially responsible funds to be set up. Companies will increasingly be asked questions about their safety records, how they treat potentially dangerous emissions from their plants, how environmentally friendly their products are, where they are made and by whom.

Early in 2002, CalPERS, the Californian pension fund, announced it was pulling out of three Asian markets on mainly ethical grounds. Such moves send a powerful signal.

The same year saw a different but equally strong warning delivered via a landmark case in the US, where a judge ordered the oil giant, Unocal Corp. to stand trial for alleged human rights abuses committed by the Myanmar government, Unocal's partner in the development of a gas field. Exxon Mobil found itself under similar attack over abuses by Indonesian security forces protecting its natural gas fields in Aceh. Such developments threaten US multinationals with a new and potentially very expensive risk in their foreign operations, and one that may be picked up in other countries.

Myanmar has, of course, long been on the blacklist of countries which ethical investors avoid and the focus of much lobbying over its human rights record. Heineken withdrew as early as 1996 in response to international pressure over human rights, followed by the Danish brewer Carlsberg and Pepsi-Cola. In March 2002, Triumph, the German-owned lingerie firm, joined a long queue of firms pulling out, partly in response to the 'Clean Clothes Campaign'.

Between 2000 and 2003, over 40 US firms joined a boycott of products from Myanmar, prompted by the US government which, in September 2003, banned all imports from the country. The last two British firms to withdraw were Premier Oil and BAT, the latter in November 2003 at the request of the British government. However, the downside of such actions is that they invariably do more harm than good to the workers involved. One European executive described how the government took over the factory after his firm's departure and, he assumed, the plant was now operating without the safeguards for the workers or the environment that they had insisted on. Similarly, the boycott by US clothing retailers such as Saks Inc. and others led to the collapse of the garments industry, one of the country's main sources of employment.

The Kingsway Group, which launched an Asian SRI programme in 2000, believes that companies will come to see that a focus on ethics can reduce the risk of being named and shamed in the press, with the resultant negative consequences on share prices. Increasingly, being seen to behave in a principled and ethical manner has real, tangible pay-offs.

Whatever you do, in the long term you probably cannot win – at least not totally. Adverse situations can be moderated but rarely eliminated. The poor working conditions of subcontractors can be influenced only so much, for example. Outside companies may have to accept that they will be in a permanent state of issues management and damage limitation in this area – to an extent they are held hostage by circumstances beyond their control. Operating in Asia means being exposed to a whole range of ethical traps. The key – as always – is to develop policies that anticipate problems before they arise, rather than rushing to develop responses as they occur. It is not the ethical traps that are the problem – they are unavoidable – but how companies respond to them.

Notes

1   *Financial Times*, 'Asia propelled to 'brink of environmental catastrophe', 19 June, 2001, p8.
2   'Managers & Mantras: One Company's Search for Simplicity', by Charlotte Butler and John Keary, Wiley & Sons (Asia) Pte Ltd. 2000, p103.
3   Taken from 'PT Inti Indorayon Utama' (A-D), set of case studies by Charlotte Butler and Professor Philippe Lasserre, 1991 INSEAD-EAC.
4   *The Jakarta Post*, 'Experts back new audit of Indorayon', September, 1998.
5   *Financial Times*, 'Graft mars crackdown on illegal logging', 14 January, 2003, p4.
6   Taken from 'A Difficult Start', case study by Charlotte Butler and Professor Henri-Claude de Bettignies, 1997 INSEAD-EAC.
7   *The Economist*, 'Sweatshop wars', 27 February, 1999, p66.

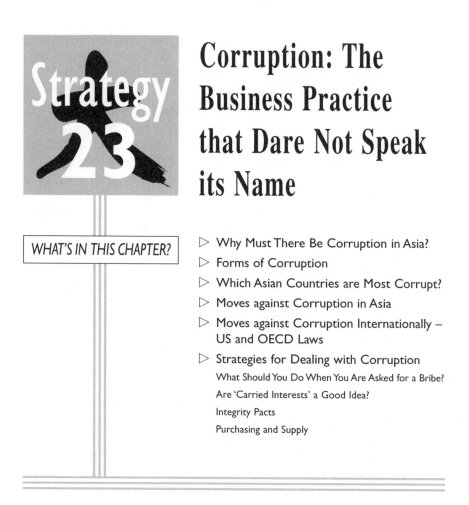

Corruption: The Business Practice that Dare Not Speak its Name

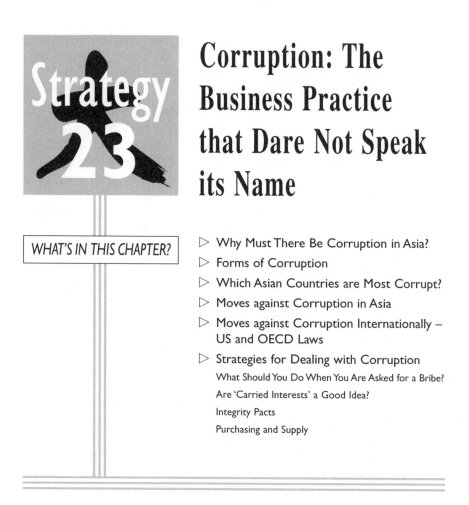
Why Must There Be Corruption in Asia?

An African infrastructure minister calls on one of his Asian counterparts. The African asks the Asian infrastructure minister, 'Your house is magnificent! How can you afford to have such a large house?' The Asian minister takes his visitor over to the window and points to a newly built bridge that crosses a nearby river.

'See that bridge. 50% went to me.'

A few months later, it is the Asian minister who calls on his African counterpart and it is his turn to be impressed.

'This house is fantastic. How can you afford it?'

The African minister takes his visitor over to a window and points to a river.

'See that bridge?'

The Asian minister shakes his head. 'No, I don't see a bridge.'

'I know', says the African. '100% of it went to me.'

Not all of Asia is corrupt and nor is corruption unique to Asia. There is a genuine desire on the part of most officials in Asia to get things done despite corrupt practices. There does seem to be a sense even among the corrupt that corruption does need to be balanced with the national interest. So things in Asia are not hopeless when it comes to corruption; those with a genuine desire to fight it do have something to work with.

Corruption is bad. It is unfair at best and severely damaging to an economy at worst. Corruption is not an acceptable practice in Asia, neither is it an intrinsic part of any of Asia's cultures. The sanctions – legal and social – that apply in respect of it might differ but there is not a single culture in Asia that sees corruption as a 'good' thing or even as acceptable. It causes embarrassment to the perpetrators whenever it is exposed. Everyone who engages in it in Asia is aware that they are doing something wrong.

China increasingly influences perceptions of corruption in Asia as its economy grows and becomes important and more open, relative to the rest of Asia. Corruption statistics show an alarming increase in recorded corruption in China, although that need not mean that actual corruption has increased. Nonetheless, anecdotal evidence from foreign businesspeople who do business there is that China's new generation of businesspeople is ruthless, intensely driven to succeed and prepared to do almost anything to reach its goals. Elsewhere, if rules and laws are lacking as a means of constraint on private actions, social and religious constraints can help to fill the gap. But not in China. The current generation is, after all, the generation that is the product of Communist ideology during its formative years and the Cultural Revolution, with its repudiation of religion and parental authority.

Confucianism is often blamed in part for the prevalence of corruption in Asia, particularly in Korea and China. Confucian principles dictate that honesty is a relative concept and can be traded away for the sake of loyalty. Officials who use their positions to help friends and relatives are seen as corrupt but also loyal, and loyalty in Confucian eyes is a mitigating factor. But it is more of an excuse than a sensible explanation. Confucian but corruption-free Singapore provides an excellent counter-example. Indeed, Singapore is something of an embarrassment to the rest of Asia. It shows that when it comes to corruption, culture is no excuse. At the end of the day, the real victims of corruption in Asia are not outsiders but Asians.

Forms of Corruption

Petty Corruption

Civil servants in countries such as Indonesia, China, the Philippines, Thailand and Myanmar routinely ask for small payments to do their jobs – to hand over forms, process them, provide statistics and undertake the minutiae of bureaucracy. Payments such as these help to speed up bureaucratic processes. They are a form of user pays, even a form of tax that is used to top up bureaucrats' meagre salaries. The amounts paid are typically trivial – a few dollars – and amount to paying civil servants to do their jobs rather than influencing them to do something that they otherwise would not do.

Examples of such payments are the 'fees' that might need to be paid to staff at the Central Bureau of Statistics in Jakarta to get hold of publicly available data on imports, or payments made to immigration officials in the Philippines to get visas processed in a timely fashion. Depositors at state banks in Myanmar have found that they need to pay small processing fees even to withdraw their *own* money from their bank accounts, otherwise a five-minute transaction can take half a day. In Vietnam, the relevant agency or ministry might even collect all the unofficial payments together, pool them and then divide them among all the staff on a regular basis.

Other ways in which small payments might be extracted are from the sale of items such as stickers, pens and calendars for employees' welfare funds and the like. Contributions are usually 'voluntary' in the same way that civil servants can choose to handle your requirements either slowly or quickly.

Such payments are small compared with the hassle and costs that can be imposed by not making them and foreign businessmen should not be too bothered when asked to pay them. They are an irritant and in their own small way do little for transparency but payments such as these are not properly considered bribery and rarely are they treated as such.

Some aid agencies have even formalised the process whereby part of their project budgets are allocated to topping up the salaries of local officials. This ensures that the local officials actually implement the aid programmes rather than pilfer from them. It has been estimated that foreign donors pay as much as 53% of all government wages in Cambodia, often through this means.[1] Western aid agencies which have chosen not to go down this route have found that their programmes may be completely obstructed, leading to money being spent but no aid being delivered. Their choice is stark – either be pragmatic or stay away.

Serious Corruption

Serious corruption – payments in cash or in kind – to secure significant advantage that cannot be guaranteed using fair and regular methods is reported to be widespread across Asia. Sometimes the payments are so regularised that negotiations are not necessary. They might even be non-negotiable. It is widely believed that the current flat 'fee' for getting a project approved in Manila is US$50,000. Perhaps almost all such projects would be approved anyway. But that does not make such payments any less corrupt. Their size, for one, ensures that they are. Cutting senior officials and their families in on a deal to ensure approval is another means of overt corruption. Sometimes this can be disguised as a 'carried interest', which is discussed later.

Kickbacks to ensure that supply tenders are won are another form of corruption. Famous instances of this type of corruption abound. The Lockheed scandal in Japan is perhaps the most famous but is only the tip of the iceberg. Also in Japan, the Tanaka faction of the Liberal Democrat Party always ensured that one of its members was appointed construction minister. This wasn't out of the faction's abiding interest in national development, but rather to ensure that it took a mandatory 3% on all major infrastructure projects and thereby earned itself tens of millions of dollars. The Bofors corruption scandal in India is another example. But more mundane purchases by government almost inevitably seem to require a kickback to someone somewhere in most of Asia, be they the provision of new computers for schools or cleaning contracts for government offices.

Kickbacks and commissions are hardly unique to the government sector. One businessman from a Western country interviewed by the authors tells the story of how he lost the business that he was doing in India because he refused to pay 'commissions' to the new purchasing manager of a large company that had been buying his products. He describes how he was 'character assassinated' by the purchasing manager, causing him to lose the business which he had so carefully cultivated, and how the senior managers in the company were unwilling to properly investigate the matter – he suspected because they too were to be cut in on the 'commissions'.

Taxation revenues are way down on what they could be in much of Asia due to corruption. Probably most local and many foreign companies in Indonesia 'negotiate' their tax obligations with the Ministry of Finance. Partly they do this because ministry officials expect it. Pay them a bribe and they will come up with a sensible assessment. Don't and they might hit you with something extraordinary. But corruption is not restricted to income tax collection. One more example comes from tax and excise stamps and labels that are overprinted from Indonesia to Vietnam and Myanmar. They are sold to alcohol and tobacco producers at discount prices; the proceeds being pocketed by the officials.

Asia needs fewer civil servants who are paid more, rather than more who are paid less. But, in the wake of Asia's economic crisis of 1997–98, countries in the region following the IMF's remedies of cutting government spending opted for cutting civil servants' salaries. South Korea, for example, announced pay cuts for its almost one million civil servants in early 1998 of 20% for those at vice-ministerial level and above and 10% for the rest.

Which Asian Countries are Most Corrupt?

Corruption by its nature is impossible to measure. But it is well known in which countries it is greatest and where it is least. Similarly, it is hard to know the costs of corruption, although as a rule of thumb about a third of all government procurement budgets in Indonesia, the Philippines, Vietnam, Cambodia and Thailand are thought to be lost through misappropriation, fraud and other forms of corruption. A similar proportion is probably lost in India, Pakistan, Bangladesh and Nepal.

Perceptions are the best way we have to measure corruption. But perceptions come through a mixture of reality and myth. It also depends on whom you ask. Malaysia is seen by many Westerners as corrupt. But the perception might come more from Westerners being uncomfortable with past policies in Malaysia which called for the selection of indigenous businessmen for contracts and privatisations rather than from any real corruption. Ask a Filipino or a Thai if Malaysia is corrupt and the response is often one of genuine surprise. 'Our country is corrupt, but not Malaysia. That is why Malaysia is rich', is a typical response.

Transparency International, the Berlin-based NGO, attempts to assess countries' relative corruption. Each year it surveys businesspeople, academics, officials and journalists on their perceptions about relative corruption levels in a range of countries. Table 23.1 shows the results of Transparency International's surveys for 1998–2003 for all the Asian countries that it considers. The rankings for Australia, the United States and the United Kingdom have been provided for comparison.

It is Indonesia that is the clear and persistent winner in Asia in the perceived corruption stakes. Corruption is not seen as 'right' in Indonesia as it is not anywhere else, but it is widely accepted and tolerated. There are few social sanctions against it. Those who become rich through corruption are actually accorded respect on account of their wealth even though it might be widely known how the riches were accrued. Legislative sanctions on the corrupt are lax and even then are hardly enforced. Quite a few high-profile arrests for corruption were made in 2002 but these were still small relative to the amount of corruption that exists. They were almost certainly politically motivated too.

Officially, corruption in Indonesia is only considered as such under law if it causes damages to the finances of the economy or the state. Thus, stealing state funds is corrupt by law, but receiving a bribe may not be. Each of the high-profile arrests in 2002 related to missing state funds – quite a narrow subset of the universe of sins inflicted upon the Indonesian people by government officials.

Table 23.1 Ranks of countries according to perceived levels of corruption

	1998 (85 countries considered)	1999 (99 countries)	2000 (90 countries)	2001 (91 countries)	2002 (102 countries)	2003 (133 countries)
China	equal 52	equal 58	equal 63	equal 57	equal 59	equal 66
Hong Kong	16	equal 15	equal 15	14	14	equal 14
India	66	equal 72	equal 69	equal 71	equal 71	equal 83
Indonesia	80	equal 96	equal 85	equal 88	equal 96	equal 122
Japan	25	equal 25	equal 23	21	equal 20	equal 21
Korea	equal 43	equal 50	48	equal 42	equal 40	equal 50
Malaysia	equal 29	equal 32	36	36	equal 33	equal 37
Pakistan	71	equal 87	n.a.	equal 79	equal 77	equal 92
Philippines	55	equal 54	equal 69	equal 65	equal 77	equal 92
Singapore	7	7	equal 6	equal 4	equal 5	5
Taiwan	equal 29	28	equal 28	27	equal 29	equal 30
Thailand	61	equal 68	equal 60	61	equal 64	equal 70
Vietnam	74	equal 75	equal 76	equal 75	equal 85	equal 100
***	***	***	***	***	***	***
Australia	equal 11	12	13	11	11	equal 8
United Kingdom	equal 11	13	10	13	10	equal 11
United States	equal 17	18	14	16	16	equal 18

Source: Transparency International, www.transparency.org. The higher the rank, the more corrupt a country is perceived to be.

That Indonesia is seen as Asia's most corrupt country and one of the most corrupt in the world is not a judgment that comes only from outside. One of its finance ministers admitted in 1999 that a full crackdown on corruption would not be possible because economic activity would 'grind to a halt' and 'most businesspeople' would end up in jail. The defence minister had only just explained that it would be 'impossible' to end corruption in the Indonesian military because its needs far exceed its official budget allocation.[2] The then Attorney General referred at a conference at around the same time to the 'massive commercial fraud that took place [in Indonesia] in the last 10–15 years'.[3] His replacement entered office claiming that corruption in Indonesia's courts was so deeply ingrained that it might take 'more than two decades' to clean up. There is much corruption in Indonesia and it will stay that way for a long time. It is an issue that all companies must face if they wish to operate there – as they will if they want to operate in China, India, the Philippines, Korea and Thailand. The key is to have a strategy to deal with this eventuality before it arises rather than rushing to deal with the issue at the time that it does.

Moves against Corruption in Asia

All governments in Asia recognise that corruption is a problem, but not all are serious in tackling it. China today has the most onerous sanctions against corruption. Large numbers of officials found to be corrupt have been executed. The first comprehensive statutes on criminal law were adopted in 1979, which included allowing for officials who took advantage of their office to be jailed or in serious cases, executed. Revised regulations were issued in 1997, which sct out in more detail the types of instance that could be considered corruption. Included was a more detailed scale of punishments. Cases of corruption involving Rmb5,000–50,000 now lead to jail terms of 1–5 years. Cases involving Rmb50,000–100,000 earn 5–10 years in jail, and those involving more than Rmb100,000 earn ten years to life imprisonment. Finally, there is the death penalty and the confiscation of property for especially serious cases. And yet corruption remains a huge problem in China. The highest number of convictions not surprisingly are in economic hotspots such as Shenzhen, Guangzhou and Shanghai.

Some Asian countries have established national anti-corruption bodies. These differ widely in their powers. Asia's two most powerful corruption fighting agencies are Hong Kong's Independent Commission Against Corruption (ICAC) and Singapore's Corrupt Practices Investigation Bureau

(CPIB). These are also the two countries in Asia that happen to score the best in Transparency International's perceptions of corruption index.

Hong Kong in the early 1970s was a hotbed of corruption. Today, instances of overt corruption are infrequent and the civil service and the police are regarded as highly professional. This is partly due to the rise in civil service and police salaries, but the setting up of the ICAC in 1974 was especially important. It was given the powers of investigation, arrest and detention. It was also empowered to embark on a community education programme about the evils of corruption. It used radio, television and print media advertisements to publicise its work and tell the public how to report instances of officials' corruption. It even sponsored television dramas with anti-corruption themes. The ICAC is very well resourced and has a massive staff of 1,400.

Hong Kong's Law on Bribery Prohibition and the rules that govern the conduct of civil servants have also been important. Together, they mean that civil servants are not allowed to receive cash, gifts and entertainment of any substantial nature without the permission of the chief executive. Loans from friends must not be more than HK$2,000 and must be repaid within two weeks. Measures such as these are strictly enforced.

Singapore has had its Prevention of Corruption Act for many decades. The CPIB operates under the Act. The prime minister appoints the head of the Bureau although the Bureau itself is independent. It can arrest any suspects without a warrant. It comprises 49 officials, including 41 special investigators, which is relatively small but it cooperates closely with other government agencies.

Thailand introduced a new constitution in 1997 and with it came the National Counter Corruption Commission. The Commission has shown itself to have teeth, although to date it has largely concerned itself with determining the eligibility of politicians to remain in parliament. It comprises nine commissioners who are appointed for nine-year terms. One of its biggest 'successes' involved Sanan Kajornprasart, a deputy prime minister and minister who was convicted in 2000 of concealing his assets and forced to relinquish his government positions. 'I love Petrus', he was quoted as saying two years later, referring to a Bordeaux wine that sells for US$1,000 a bottle or more for a good vintage, 'I drink about a bottle a week.'[4] Sanan might not have been all that repentant but at least he was no longer in office.

South Korea has the Board of Audit and Inspection as its corruption watchdog. The Board does not have powers of investigation though and must refer cases to the public prosecutor. It has 800 staff, although this number might still be insufficient. The Board is not as powerful as Hong Kong's ICAC or Singapore's CPIB but it still has some teeth. For example, it referred the cases of 100 people to the Prosecutor General's Office in December 2001 pending further investigation. All were banned from going overseas in the meantime.

The government of President Kim Dae Jung introduced a Citizen Ombudsman System in 1999, whereby citizens can force an investigation into corruption of a particular government agency or body if they request one in sufficient numbers. One thousand requests must be received with regard to a central ministry and 500 for a provincial body. No doubt it was a move designed to appeal to the electorate but surely a single citizen's well-founded allegation of government corruption is worthy of investigation.

Moves against Corruption Internationally – US and OECD Laws

Investigations by the US Securities and Exchange Commission (SEC) in the mid-1970s found that more than 400 US companies admitted making questionable or illegal payments worth in excess of $300 million to foreign government officials, politicians, and political parties. The US Congress passed the Foreign Corrupt Practices Act (FCPA) in 1977 in response to these findings. The Act makes it illegal for US citizens and companies to bribe foreign officials to obtain or maintain business or to have third parties do so on their behalf.

An amendment to the Act in 1988 removed the illegality on making 'facilitating payments' for 'routine governmental action' such as payments to obtain permits, licences or other official documents; processing official documents, such as visas and work orders; providing police protection, mail pick-up and delivery; providing phone service, power and water supply, loading and unloading cargo, or protecting perishable products; and scheduling inspections associated with contract performance or transit of goods across a country. Thus these types of petty corruption would no longer be caught by the Act.

Other countries followed the US's anti-bribery stance via the OECD's Convention on Combating Bribery of Foreign Public Officials in International Business Transactions. It was unveiled on 21 November 1997 and was modelled on the principles of the Foreign Corrupt Practices Act. Thirty OECD members and four non-members were signatories. Almost all signatories have since ratified the Convention and introduced legislation into their national parliaments to make it a criminal offence for their companies and their citizens to bribe foreign public officials to obtain or retain international business. Among the signatories who have brought in such laws are the US, Canada, Sweden, Australia, Italy, the Netherlands, New Zealand, Spain, France, Germany, the United Kingdom, Ireland and Japan.

The Convention obliges its members to make it an offence for its citizens, companies and other legal entities to offer, promise or give 'any undue pecuniary or other advantage'. It is also an offence to use intermediaries to do the same, nor does the form of the bribe matter, be it cash or gifts – 'or other advantage' is a very broad, catch-all caveat. Authorising bribes is also an offence.

Companies and employees will be charged if they pay or offer bribes, not only to procure contracts but to obtain permits or influence taxation, customs, judicial or legislative proceedings. The Convention also calls for bribery to be an extraditable offence.

The legislation introduced by the Australian Government subsequent to its ratification of the Convention is typical. It allows for jail terms of ten years and a fine for bribing foreign officials. It specifies that in determining whether a pecuniary advantage or benefit was 'undue', regard must be given to the following:

- the fact that the benefit may be customary, or perceived to be customary, in the situation
- the value of the benefit
- any official tolerance of the benefit.

The Australian legislation includes within the definition of 'foreign public official' employees of international organisations and individuals who perform work for such organisations under contract. Thus a bribe paid to a UN official or even to a consultant to the UN would be caught by the legislation.

Thus, laws on bribing foreign officials are now uniform across much of the West and even beyond it. No longer can American companies complain that they are at a disadvantage in foreign markets compared with their competitors because laws at home prevent them from offering bribes to officials. If companies believe that their competitors have won contracts overseas through bribery, they should report it to the winning company's home government.

Strategies for Dealing with Corruption

Companies once believed that, rather than pay a bribe in cash, they could not be found to be behaving corruptly if they entertained an official and his wife on foreign shopping trips and so on. However, the OECD Convention and the resultant national laws now catch inducements such as these.

Some foreign companies now offer trips back to the head office for 'research and training' for officials, ostensibly so that they can achieve a better understanding of the company's capabilities and thus make a more informed decision when it comes to allocating contracts and tenders. Inducements such as these are in more of a grey area and may still be caught under the terms of the OECD Convention, depending on how local legislatures have interpreted their obligations under the Convention. Any sort of travel or similar benefits for officials paid for by companies is open to question.

Gift-giving and entertainment are a part of many Asian cultures. But at what point does this become corrupt? It all depends on whether it is 'excessive'. Companies doing business in Asia need comprehensive and clearly worded policies on bribery and corruption, which detail the limits and the consequences if they are not followed. Some Western companies now do not allow their employees to have meals bought for them. What is your company's policy on giving and receiving entertainment?

What Should You Do When You Are Asked for a Bribe?

- If you are an employee of a foreign company, explain that laws at home prevent you and the company from offering such payments in any form. Explain that it is a criminal offence and that the company could receive a massive fine, your government could jail and fine you and you would almost certainly lose your job.

- Alternatively, explain that you are not authorised to make such a payment. If you were to seek authorisation from your superiors and they agreed, they would be putting themselves at risk of possible extradition and criminal penalties, including fines and jail. You too could face prosecution for conspiracy to corrupt.

- Offer an alternative. Are there any good works projects the officials are interested in which could be funded by your company instead? Perhaps your company could show its commitment locally by offering to fund scholarships for local schools or contributing to the cost of local playgrounds.

- Remember that projects come and go but once a bribe is given it is always there to be unearthed – by investigators, competitors and the media.

- Should companies pay to secure meetings in Asia with senior officials and politicians? Preferably not, but then access is everything. Professional lobbyists in the United States and elsewhere are well paid for the access that they have. The important thing is that companies should adopt clear guidelines on this, whether they decide that this practice is acceptable or not.

Are 'Carried Interests' a Good Idea?

Another way to acquire influence in some Asian countries has been to cut local officials, politicians and their families into projects by allocating them equity in the project under consideration. The equity is not given to them, as that would run foul of the OECD Convention and the US FCPA, but instead is provided in the form of a loan, which is paid back from earnings from the project. The manoeuvre is known as providing a 'carried interest'. The effect is the same as a bribe even if technically such equity transfers cannot be deemed as such.

'Carried interests' are not without their problems. One large US company gave 15% of its Indonesian venture to a company owned by a relative of the then President Soeharto. That company contributed no cash for its stake – the deal was structured whereby the American company 'lent' the Indonesian side the sum for its stake. After Soeharto was removed from office, the deal fell apart and questions were asked about its efficacy. The American company conducted an 'internal inquiry' in 1999 which found that everything was above board. But the media fallout didn't look good. The conduct of the American company was criticised in a number of newspaper columns, articles and editorials. 'Carried interests' have their dangers.

Integrity Pacts

Transparency International has developed what it calls Integrity Pacts for Transparency in Public Procurement Procedures, processes that interested companies might consider suggesting to agencies for consideration when they call for tenders for projects. These Pacts involve a commitment on the part of all bidders, and the agency overseeing the bidding process, not to give or accept bribes, or collude with other bidders, to disclose all payments, and to report any violation of the Integrity Pact by other bidders during the bidding or the execution of the service. In the event of a breach of the Pact, sanctions come into force against bidders and officials, including liability for damages and blacklisting from future tenders.

Transparency International monitored such a Pact used in combination with a least cost selection method tender in Pakistan in February 2002 to select a consultant to design the Greater Karachi Water Supply Scheme (K-III Project). It did this in cooperation with the Karachi Water and Sewerage Board. The Board had set aside the equivalent of US$4.2 million for the tender, but the process led to a winning bid of just US$1.04 million, leading to a saving of 75% on what the Board expected it would have to spend. Transparency International believes that the bulk of the savings was due to the openness of the process brought about by the Integrity Pact. It recommends the use of such Pacts elsewhere and to date has overseen around 100 similar Integrity Pacts worldwide.

Purchasing and Supply

Purchasing and supply are huge areas for potential corruption in Asia. Kickbacks are so commonplace in many countries as to be practically routine. Companies doing business in Asia must protect themselves against corrupt practices when they buy their own supplies. They must scrutinise all purchasing officers in Asia carefully. They need to be on the lookout for:

- unnecessary purchases
- family connections between purchasing staff and suppliers
- unexplained wealth of purchasing staff which might suggest significant kickbacks have been received
- a lack of preparedness on the part of purchasing staff to be active in seeking out new and cheaper suppliers
- stationery and stores cupboards that are filled to the point of lavishness
- purchases from suppliers that seem inconvenient when more convenient options are available, for example meeting rooms are booked in hotels on the other side of town when more convenient venues are nearby
- monogrammed gifts from suppliers – purchasing staff on low salaries can attach great importance even to gifts as minor as cheap wristwatches, mugs and shoulder bags. Monitor the importance that staff attach to such things
- Just as it is wise practice to change internal accounting staff occasionally, it may be prudent occasionally to change staff who are responsible for purchasing, in order to guard against long-term cosy relationships between the staff and suppliers.

Notes

1   *Wall Street Journal*, 'Aid agencies often spend money on paying civil servants' salaries', 8 February, 2002.
2   As quoted in 'Kwik cites dangers of Indonesian cleanup', *Asian Wall Street Journal*, 9 December, 1999.
3   Backman, M., 'The New Order Conglomerates' in *Perspectives on Chinese Indonesians*, Godfrey, M. and Lloyd, G. (eds) 2001, Crawford House, Belair (Australia).
4   *Asian Wall Street Journal*, 'Label-obsessed Asians flaunt big-name wine', 22 March, 2002.

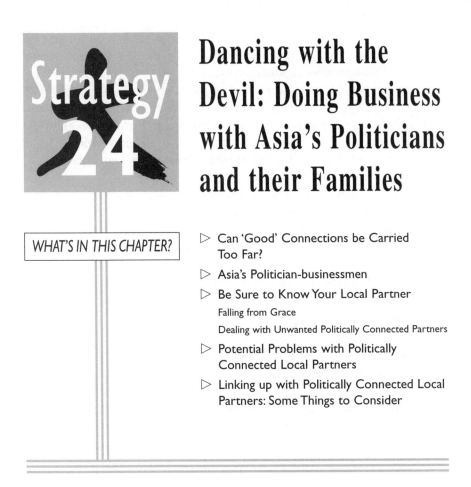

Dancing with the Devil: Doing Business with Asia's Politicians and their Families

Can 'Good' Connections be Carried Too Far?

Relationships and connections matter a great deal in Asia, and the weaker the local legal system, the more they matter. But how far do you go? A good local partner is one who can open doors and keep them open, smooth things over with the authorities and help to get approvals in a timely matter. But does this mean that the local authorities themselves make even better local partners? What about senior bureaucrats, the military or even senior politicians and their families? Instead of trying to win approvals from senior politicians, might it not be better simply to make them or their families your local partner, so that the approvals will be guaranteed?

The answer is fairly simple. The ideal local partner can do a range of things, including managing the relationship with government. If you choose the family of a local politician as a local partner, typically handling the relationship with the government is about all the local partner will manage, unless they are already successful in business and can bring some genuine local business attributes to the relationship. Partners who already are in business and have a good understanding of dealing with the local bureaucracy and the government typically make the better partner, if indeed one is needed.

Politically connected partners might bring connections to the table but they might also bring unwanted intrusion, stigma and, ultimately, risk, if they fall from grace. Rarely will they bring capital. 'The mountains are high and the Emperor is far away' is one maxim that's commonly heard to explain why China's southeastern provinces have done so well compared with the rest of the country. Proximity to power is not always a good thing.

Asia's Politician-businessmen

Politicians all over Asia have shown a tendency to want to get into business. Very often, they use their political positions to enrich themselves and their families. Foreign investors with cash are one source of funds for such politician-businessmen. Sometimes, the families of political leaders simply want a passive stake in new enterprises, perhaps in a nominee arrangement. This was the preferred mode of the Marcos family of the Philippines. They wanted riches without the responsibility. Other politicians and their families want to be directly involved in business themselves. They see themselves as entrepreneurs and have a genuine and active commitment to their enterprises.

It is not just Asia's politicians who seek corporate advancement from their official positions, but also civil servants and the military. Among civil servants, it is senior officials of state-owned enterprises who are most likely to have a personal involvement in business. Many set up private companies which become suppliers to the state-owned enterprise.

The military's involvement in business in Asia generally comes from its need for off-budget financing. Governments in many Asian countries give the military less funding than required and, in any event, many generals want to develop a separate source of funds to ensure some measure of financial independence from government and politicians. Thus, the defence forces of Indonesia, Thailand, Myanmar, China and the Philippines have direct involvement in running and managing businesses. These are among the most opaque of all businesses in Asia. It is difficult to appreciate the importance of the military's involvement in business. Little is published, military-backed companies rarely list on stock exchanges and rarely file corporate records or results.

Sons and daughters of government officials who use their parents' positions or names to go into business are another variation on the theme. In China, they are called the princelings or *taizi*, and they include the sons and daughters of senior Communist Party officials or senior officials with China's many state-owned enterprises. Some foreign investors in China seek out the *taizi* as partners on the assumption that they can open doors and help to protect their investments. This might prove to be true, but since the mid-1990s senior officials and their families have fallen in and out of favour in China with increasing regularity, often in the wake of embezzlement and corruption scandals. Officials in China have been known to be very senior one day and executed or imprisoned for life the next. Silent partners are one thing, dead partners are quite another.

Using one's official position to financially benefit oneself and one's family is expected in Indonesia. There is a story – possibly true – that one of former President Soeharto's ministers came to him and said he could no longer live on his ministerial salary and would it be possible for a pay rise? Soeharto was incredulous. 'You have been a minister in charge of a large department all these years. What on earth have you been doing?' said Soeharto or words to that effect. Soeharto used his position to enrich his family and he expected all other officials to do the same.

When Soeharto stepped down as president, his family had interests in at least 1,251 separate companies in Indonesia alone.[1] Many ventures were with foreign investors who saw linking up with the family of the president as one way to have investment approvals fast-tracked and potentially obstructive bureaucrats frightened out of the way. But Soeharto was not alone in the practice. Many of his ministers arrived in office with little but left with a conglomerate. Soeharto expected this of his ministers and other senior officials – indeed he wanted them to behave like this. It saved the need to remunerate senior officials properly and provided a better context for the nepotism of his own family.

Be Sure to Know Your Local Partner

The flip side of selecting a well-connected local partner is that occasionally they present themselves but do so without fully disclosing who they are or with whom they are connected. This can lead to later embarrassment for the foreign investor.

Business development managers of one Western firm eager to sign up a local partner in Indonesia in the mid-1990s did so with what they believed to be a company backed by several former senior military figures. In their haste they did insufficient due diligence and, some months later, found out that their new partner was in fact one of the more odious members of the Soeharto family.

One American producer appointed a local company in Myanmar as the distributor for its products. It ended the relationship in 1998 as part of an informal international boycott against Myanmar for human rights abuses. But the end also came after it was disclosed that the local company was the private investment vehicle of one of Asia's most infamous drug lords.

Mistakes like these can be averted with more thorough research. It is obviously far better to determine as much about a prospective partner before, rather than after, a deal is signed. One problem with signing up politically influential partners is that unsigning them can prove difficult. What was supposed to be a business development move might end up closing doors rather than opening them. Signing up the prime minister's younger brother might seem like a good idea, but firing him as a partner could prove devastating.

Falling from Grace

Choosing a local partner because of his current high political connections is a dangerous thing if for no reason other than that power and influence are rarely permanent. The family of President Soeharto is a case in point. Since Soeharto left office most of his close relatives have been investigated for corruption and related matters and several have been arrested and imprisoned, including his youngest son Tommy Suharto who was jailed for fifteen years in 2002. Foreign investors find that local partners whom people once queued to see are now *persona non grata*. On top of that, they are left with the public stigma of being linked to a partner who might now be openly acknowledged to have been corrupt and nepotistic, or worse.

Dealing with Unwanted Politically Connected Partners

Sometimes, foreign or outside investors do not choose to go into business with politically connected parties. Instead, the politically connected choose them. When Soeharto was president, he personally approved almost all foreign investment projects in Indonesia. Thus he had close knowledge of who wanted to invest in what and where. From this it is thought that various members of his family were tipped off about promising projects and they would then present themselves as 'partners'. Foreign investors found themselves in a position in which they had to choose between having the Soehartos as their partner or not proceeding with the project at all.

The best advice for outsiders in such situations in whatever country is that they should resist such entreaties as far as they possibly can. If they can stall for as long as possible, hopefully the local party that is attempting to inject itself into the new venture will give up. But if it does not and it becomes clear that the project will not proceed unless the local 'partner' is taken on board, the investor must decide whether to proceed at all, or how the unwanted party can best be accommodated, keeping in mind the future risk that political circumstances might change and the local partner might suddenly fall from grace.

Potential Problems with Politically Connected Local Partners

- Politically connected partners are subject to sharp reversals of fortune either due to politics or policy. Well-connected partners one day might be an anathema and a liability the next.

- Getting information on prospective politically connected local partners can prove difficult. Their proximity to power might mean that they can avoid all the corporate filings and declarations that lesser-connected parties are obliged to make. Many Soeharto-backed companies in Indonesia simply never bothered to lodge articles of association, for example. A powerful local partner might mean having one that is opaque, even by Asian standards.

- The military is short of cash everywhere, and this is often why it goes into business. The military will bring almost no business expertise, no capital and will be more interested in what it can take out of a venture compared with what it can put in. Other local businesspeople may be loath to do business with your venture because of its military links.

- Business is not the main attribute of politically connected partners and rarely is business their main occupation or skill. In such circumstances, rarely will such local parties be in a position to contribute their ascribed share of capital to the venture.

- Linking up with the powerful so that their power can be utilised is a risky business. If there's a falling out, that power can be turned against you. James Peng, an Australian businessman of Chinese descent, discovered this in the early 1990s. He formed a business relationship with Deng's niece, Ding Peng. The two fell out and, as a consequence, he lost control of Shenzhen Fountain, the company he founded. It was seized by Ding Peng, and he was kidnapped from a Macau hotel room, spirited across the border to mainland China, put on trial for embezzlement and jailed for 18 years. He was released in November 1999 after six years' imprisonment, following the intervention of the Australian Government.

Linking up with politically connected local partners Some things to consider

1. Will the form of the partnership have any implications under the US Foreign Corrupt Practices Act or similar legislation?

2. Can the prospective partner genuinely bring anything to the venture other than political connections?

3. What arrangements are there for either party to exit the relationship?

4. How secure are the prospective partners' links to power?

5. Should opposition forces come to power, how will that affect your business?

6. Will your prospective partner be in a position to threaten your business or your staff should the relationship flounder?

7. What other partnerships does your prospective partner have with outside business interests and how have they been treated?

Note

1 Backman, M., *Asian Eclipse: Exposing the Dark Side of Business in Asia*, John Wiley & Sons, 1999, 2001.

Strategy 25

When Things Go Wrong

History Repeats Itself

Disappointment and even disasters are more frequent than success for most foreign firms investing in Asia. These are often associated with the break-up of joint venture relationships and the consequent deterioration of the company's investment. Sometimes the break-up is reasonably amicable, sometimes it can end in a protracted court case. An acquisition, too, is more likely to disappoint than prosper, and can be even more expensive if a firm paid a premium for what it thought was a rising star, only to discover it was a black hole. In many cases, Western companies decide to cut their losses and withdraw, but those who do often return to the region later, unable to resist the lure of those untapped markets, only to make similar mistakes. History repeats itself because few people listen sufficiently the first time around, and rarely are mistakes dissected. People are normally too busy ducking for cover.

The following true stories illustrate some of the most common reasons why attempts to be Big in Asia all too often lead to a retreat from Asia.

Chinese Takeaway

A typical disaster was that experienced by Asimco, a Beijing-based investment company set up in 1993 with three US majority shareholders; TCW Capital Investment Co., Dean Witter Capital and General Electric.[1] By 1999, it was one of the biggest investors in China, having put US$450 million into 15 auto-related joint ventures and two breweries.

In the auto industry, its strategy was to take majority stakes in promising Chinese component makers and provide them with management expertise and new technology. In 1996, it paid US$7.5 million for a 60% stake in a Chinese company, CAC Brake Ltd, run by a Guangdong entrepreneur. The company produced auto brake components and clutch disks, and appeared to have a healthy order book, so the investors simply put in a financial manager and left the entrepreneur (who was vice-chairman of the board) and his team of deputy general managers to run the company.

Subsequent events would have come as no surprise to those with experience in China. The entrepreneur proceeded to strip the company of as much money as possible via a series of simple but effective frauds. For example, employee housing which remained under CAC's control was rented to the joint venture, with the proceeds going to the entrepreneur. Another ruse was to raise mortgages from a local bank for two new buildings, supposedly for additional factory space even though the existing space was ample. Although they were actually built, the shoddy workmanship and low ceilings made them unsuitable for use as factories but the entrepreneur was able to take his cut anyway. As a grand finale, the entrepreneur opened up letters of credit (LCs) to pay for non-existent equipment and, in the last few months before he left town, stopped paying vendors and took the cash himself. In December 1996, he disappeared during a business trip to the US, having looted the company of over US$6 million.

Moral: Don't run your joint venture at arm's length. Make sure that you keep a firm eye on what is happening, put in your own senior finance people and check the books.

The rescue: Asimco finally sent in an experienced auto man to run CAC, and recruited a financial manager. It also sued the local bank, arguing that there must have been some collusion and the bank should have realised that the LCs were fraudulent. Not surprisingly, the local city court ruled against Asimco, which then took its appeal to the provincial court in Guangzhou. From there the case went to the national court in Beijing where nothing happened for two years, despite pressure from the US embassy.

In the meantime, the two new managers turned the company around by improving production and introducing stricter controls. Wastage was cut and quality standards raised, enabling CAC to win an ISO9002 qualification. A key move was to cut the number of products from 400 to 100. More units of lesser variety allowed for greater economies of scale and this led to greater productivity. Taking advantage of being in a buyer's market, the US manager negotiated discounts and an extension of payment terms from 30 to 60 or 90 days, and to cut fraud instituted a strict purchase control system.

Salesmen were paid on a commission-only basis, and travel expenses were phased out. Distribution was improved by using CAC's own trucks to take stock to a warehouse, from where it went by rail to three distribution points and then on to customers by truck. Export sales were increased to account for 45% of revenues, the rest coming from original equipment manufacturers (OEM) auto makers and the after-sales market.

As a result, CAC stayed in business and, despite a setback in 1998 due to the economic downturn, broke even. Financing remained a problem. In the short term, CAC employees were given a bond, which was redeemable at the end of the year for a month's salary plus 8%, in lieu of a month's salary. In the longer term, the plan was to cut the labour force and win more OEM contracts.

Indian Soap Opera

The Indian subsidiary of Unilever, Hindustan Lever (HLL), one of the largest private sector firms in the country, fell victim to a different sort of disaster – the rise of a new local competitor who proceeded to revolutionise the market for detergents which HLL had dominated for years.[2]

HLL had a long and highly respected presence in India; the first crates of soap were unloaded in Calcutta in 1888 and HLL soon emerged as the market leader in soaps, detergents and personal products, as well as food and beverages. Unilever gave its subsidiaries great autonomy, and in India this was reinforced by HLL's reputation for successful innovation and effective local management. For ambitious young Indians, joining HLL was the first step in a successful career as a professional manager – the right to wear an HLL tie spoke for itself. They were an elite corps serving an elite company.

India was one of the largest fabric wash markets in the world and HLL had played a great part in developing it, as customers graduated from using laundry soaps to detergent powders. Its leading product, Surf, led both in terms of value and volume and, with a 67% market share, was unbeatable. By the late 1970s, the industry was marked by an almost feudal structure with HLL presiding majestically over what was known as the organised sector for detergents, as opposed to the vast unorganised sector that still used cheaper laundry soap. HLL felt secure in the knowledge that, given the range of international brands it could call on from the parent company, it had nothing to fear in the future. HLL managers had made the rules of the game; they took it for granted they would continue to win.

This complacency was rudely shattered in the late 1970s by the eruption into the industry of one small cottage firm, armed with little packets of yellow soap powder labelled Nirma. It was the creation of an ambitious entrepreneur, Karsanbhai Patel, who set up a business in 1969 with the firm intention of making his brand the biggest in the world. His belief in the principle of 'develop a good product and there will be a market for it' was absolute.

Production of the brand that, within a decade would become one of the largest in the world, began in a small shed in a suburb of Ahmedabad. The detergent powder, made from materials bought locally and dumped on the shed floor, was hand-mixed in batches by Mr Patel and packed into polythene bags which he stapled together. He then loaded the packets in gunny sacks onto his bike, and sold them through house-to-house rounds of the city.

During the next decade, Mr Patel barely diverged from this simple approach to the four Ps – product, price, packaging and promotion. Although refined and enlarged according to market circumstances, the formula remained essentially the same, enabling him to run an efficient operation at a fraction of the cost incurred by HLL and other big firms. The simple Nirma chain of distribution, for example, contrasted starkly with the complex HLL machine and won him great loyalty from the distributors. They discovered that lower trade margins were compensated for by larger volumes and quick rotation, and refused to desert him even under pressure from rivals. His greatest extravagance was in advertising.

At first young women were hired to visit shops asking for Nirma. Later, he offered prize draws, and Nirma was the only Indian advertiser at the 1980 Moscow Olympics, apart from the state bank. Hoardings blazoned the Nirma message and its catchy jingle, 'Nirma washes whiter than white', punctuated every radio programme.

As sales grew, Patel took his relatives into partnership and methodically extended his operation to adjoining districts, provinces and then the whole of western and northern India. By 1977, HLL wrote to a branch manager in Ahmedabad asking for information on this brand called Nirma. The reply was dismissive: 'You can't expect me to know about every junk product coming out of Ahmedabad.'

But between 1977 and 1985, Nirma sales grew at a compound rate of 45%, and by 1980 was outselling Surf by 3 to 1. It had also spread into southern and eastern India and, with a market share of 58% to Surf's 8.4%, was one of the largest selling detergent powder brands in the world. HLL finally woke up to the fact that it was losing a war it didn't even know it was fighting.

Moral: Never underestimate an Asian entrepreneur.

The rescue: Nirma's greatest success had been to convert the unorganised soap market in urban areas and, more importantly, in rural India to detergent powders, all under HLL's nose. The realisation forced HLL to alter its strategy and mindset in order to regain its market position. Its response came in stages; it began selling Surf in polybags instead of the more expensive cartons; changed its advertising message to show that Surf represented value for money; and launched another soap powder to match Nirma directly on price. These were successful in shoring up Surf's market share. By then Mr Patel was moving into the toothpaste and toilet soap markets to offer a full range of Nirma products.

In the longer term, HLL implemented a 'stop Nirma' campaign code-named STING (Strategy To Inhibit Nirma Growth). This campaign led HLL to rethink its attitudes to quality, financial management and production methods. The whole episode had a traumatic effect on HLL's management; in the future their watchword would be 'edge' – competitive edge through marketing, distribution and technology. But a decade later, Nirma dominated the low-end market for detergents, and had a 35% share of the overall detergent market to HLL's 30%. Mr Patel was planning an attack on the premium detergent market, and said to be contemplating the Chinese market.

The Thais That (Don't) Bind

Ferodo Thailand Ltd (FTL) was another company which fell into many of the well-documented traps associated with a joint venture relationship.[3] What made this particular failure all the more interesting was the fact that the three partners were all well known to each other, and had successfully cooperated for many years. Yet within a few years of forming a joint venture, the relationship between two of the partners had irretrievably broken down. The three-way split was between Ferodo Ltd (the friction materials subsidiary of the UK-based auto components group, T&N) its long-time associate, the Japanese brake manufacturer, Japan Brake International (JBI) and the Thai Boonpong Group.

Like most Thai trading companies, Thai Boonpong Co. Ltd was a family firm, founded in 1949, initially as a bus company and maintenance operation, specialising in brake and clutch systems. The son of the founding entrepreneur, who took over in 1977, decided to concentrate on distributing brake and other automobile parts, mainly for passenger cars, and from its early days Boonpong sold imported Ferodo products, which had a worldwide reputation for quality. These were marketed under the Boonpong name, since the Ferodo brand was not well known in the Thai market. In 1995, Boonpong had total assets worth Bt1.3 billion and employed 367 people.

In 1985 Mr Subhawat, grandson of Boonpong's founder and a graduate in medical technology and an MBA, succeeded as managing director of Boonpong. Within two years he came to the conclusion that Boonpong should stop importing and instead produce brake pads in Thailand. Following a visit to the Ferodo headquarters in the UK, he decided to build the Ferodo brand name in Thailand and, on his return, launched a marketing campaign to increase the visibility of the brand. He invested between Bt40–50 million in advertising on buses and radio announcements, sponsored racing events, and even offered clients a Ferodo discount card.

However, although he could supply brake pads in high volumes to European cars, the complexity of the Ferodo production system meant there could be a time lag of up to two years before parts for Japanese models could be supplied from the UK. This caused some impatience among Boonpong's customers. Eventually, Subhawat decided that the only solution would be for Boonpong to manufacture these models themselves. He therefore invested in a factory and new machinery and, in 1992, approached Ferodo Ltd for a manufacturing licence. Since Ferodo was then setting up several joint ventures in Southeast Asia, it readily agreed.

Boonpong paid Ferodo Ltd Bt5 million for the transfer of the necessary technology to start up the factory, and agreed to pay Ferodo UK an annual 4% royalty on sales volume. After 18 months of successful production, Ferodo Ltd and Boonpong began discussions to turn the licence into a joint venture.

The move came at a time of rapid growth in the Southeast Asian automobile industry in general, and in Thailand particularly. For Ferodo Ltd, which supplied brake parts to all the main auto manufacturers, expansion into the region was of major strategic importance. This opening in Thailand seemed a golden opportunity to manufacture brake pads cheaply, since Boonpong's factory was already producing a variety of Ferodo models. It would be relatively simple to increase production there, and in time use Thailand as a hub to supply the rest of the region at lower cost. The prospects for success seemed dazzling, given that, in 1996, the Thai automotive industry was valued at US$12 billion, accounting for 6% of GDP and 2% of the country's exports (valued at almost US$1.3 billion).

However, T&N Group, the holding company to which Ferodo Ltd belonged, required that if technology was being transferred to a joint venture then T&N must remain the majority shareholder. For Subhawat, this meant giving up the independence of his family-run firm, but he was loath to miss this opportunity and more importantly, given the long relationship with the UK team, he believed that Ferodo Ltd's management respected him. As he recalled: 'When I went to the UK, it seemed we were all one family.' Ferodo Thailand Ltd (FTL), the new company, was capitalised at Bt80 million. T&N's shareholding was 51%, Boonpong's 49%. Later, the shareholding was revised with the entry of JBI, which took a 9% stake at the expense of Boonpong. As an original equipment specialist, entry into the rapidly growing Thai component market was a strategic necessity for JBI, with whom T&N had a long-standing cross-licensing agreement.

Unusually for Ferodo, the terms of the joint venture agreement applied only to the manufacturing side of the business and excluded sales, marketing and distribution. Sales and marketing for the domestic market were exclusively Boonpong's preserve, leaving the export market to Ferodo Ltd. It was also agreed that brake pads manufactured by FTL would be sold to the joint venture partner at cost plus 15%, to ensure that the company would be profitable, again an unusually high margin. Because the majority shareholder was British, the Thai Board of Investment regarded FTL as a foreign company. This meant it was required to export at least 60% of the product during the first five years, for which Ferodo Ltd took responsibility. At the time Ferodo Ltd was confident that its sister company, Ferodo Australia, would pick up the 60% export quota for the export market.

However, within a year of the joint venture being signed, things began to go downhill. The deteriorating relationship between Subhawat and the new Ferodo managing director for joint ventures and licences, Ken Lambert, bedevilled the first year. On his first visit to Thailand in 1996, Lambert identified a number of problems; quality defects, low production volumes and, most disturbing, huge stockpiles of unsold products. A series of complaints from Ferodo Australia, FTL's chief export customer, confirmed the production defects. To make matters worse, he realised that the terms of the joint venture agreement gave him little latitude to change the way things were being done. His views were clearly communicated to both the factory management and Subhawat, who had not begun to repay the huge debt owed to Ferodo for equipment supplied or kept up with royalty payments.

Lambert did not make a good impression on Subhawat, who was not prepared for what he considered to be the tougher and more aggressive way of working adopted by Lambert and his boss Sam Thomas. He believed that:

> They didn't have any respect for me … Ken had his ideas, and was going to put them into place. I have six companies in my group, and would never be disrespectful to middle management. But Lambert interfered with middle management … He and Sam Thomas just cleared out everyone who didn't perform well or listen to them, and brought in new people from the UK. Some of them had a bad attitude to the Thai people.

Lambert introduced weekly reporting systems. He kept in close contact and asked for reports more often than before. The relationship between Boonpong and its dealer network he also found incredible. In Thailand, typically, dealers expected to be treated royally, for example receiving presents of gold bars as a bonus, winning rich raffle prizes or being sent on luxury weekend holidays with their families. To Lambert, this was a waste of scarce financial resources which could have been put to much better use.

Another issue concerned the potentially profitable motorcycle after-market, which was larger than the automobile market. Lambert wanted Boonpong to go after this but, due to the terms of the contract, was unable to exert the influence he wished. He also suggested to Subhawat that the 15% margin should be lowered to be more competitive. Subhawat refused. Subsequently, when Boonpong failed to make any inroads on the market, he claimed the failure was due to poor quality. Lambert disagreed and told the Boonpong management it could not sell the stock because it was priced too high. The pads were returned to FTL and stockpiled. Tensions rose.

FTL was also having difficulty in filling the orders from Ferodo Australia and, consequently, a backlog was developing. There were also problems with the quality of the exported parts that needed sorting out urgently. Again and again, Lambert pointed out all these problems to Subhawat, underlining how FTL had to increase market share so that it would be ahead of the game when the competition arrived. His blunt way of explaining these and other facts did not go down well with Subhawat. The rows finally culminated in the dramatic resignation of Subhawat, not only as chairman of the board but also as director of FTL, in December 1996. Announcing that he had 'better things to do than sit in boardrooms with high-ego people', Subhawat swept out of the room. Subhawat's resignation took Lambert by surprise. He had realised he was not popular with the Boonpong team but thought that, given the discoveries he had made on his arrival, he had been very gentle with them.

All these tussles were having their effect on Worawut, the Thai deputy director of the factory and an old school friend of Subhawat. He felt more and more unhappy as the situation deteriorated: 'Ken Lambert quarrelled with Mr Subhawat about the non-payment. They were both wrong. I felt like I was in the middle. There was no trust between anyone.' When FTL's managing director moved to Ferodo South Africa, Lambert appointed Worawut in his place. But this put him under great pressure, made worse when the technical and control manager also resigned. For Worawut, it was all too much. The next day he sent a fax to Ken Lambert, resigning. As he explained:

> I am ashamed of the problems we had during the first two years of production. I blame myself. But I spent too much time filling in forms and reports, and solving problems. There was not enough time for everything. The factory is semi automated and you could triple the output with no problem. All it needed was the standardisation of the systems between T&N and Boonpong.
>
> It is difficult to lead and motivate people when they do not feel part of a winning team. They are a young workforce here, and sixty is a small number of employees for a factory. If they see capacity being underused, they will lose heart. They need to see the factory expanding, to feel they have career, promotion and training prospects. This is where T&N could help, to project leadership and vision, and motivate the workforce.

This was the last straw for Ken Lambert. It left him with a factory that was not running to capacity, quality complaints, stockpiles of goods destined for the domestic market on the one hand and unfulfilled export orders on the other, and a huge gap in the management structure. This was before taking into consideration the failure to meet the BOI 60% export quota. Morale had already been low before Worawut's resignation – now it would reach rock bottom. In addition, Thailand was about to be hit by a major currency crisis, whose effect on business was unknown at the time. How on earth was he going to put the joint venture back on track?

Moral: The story illustrates many of the points covered in previous chapters. A relationship can still go badly wrong, even when it is founded on a long-term knowledge of each other and a good record of cooperation. Having formed a closer partnership, it turned out that they were in the same bed but dreaming different dreams. The way the agreement was drawn up built in difficulties which could not be overcome, given that their strategic goals were not aligned, there was not enough technical standardisation, and that there were the final exacerbating factors of cultural clashes and different management styles.

The rescue: The story had a happy ending. Lambert sent in two veteran managers from Ferodo's South African subsidiary to be managing director and marketing manager respectively. Together, they turned the company around, despite the Asian crisis, sorting out the backlog and extracting payment from Subhawat. The key move was finding a new market in the after-market for older cars. This was identified by the marketing manager who, after studying the statistics, realised that as cars in Bangkok braked about every 70 metres on average, new brake pads were going to be a regular must. By 2000, FTL had the potential to expand, its workforce was highly skilled and motivated, and working towards an ISO/QS9000 award. Its problems were not over, but it was on the right path. Ken Lambert oversaw the changes and then retired.

Rising Sum[4]

In 1998, the US-based Merrill Lynch International entered the Japanese market for the second time with high hopes. The memory of the 1980s disaster, when it had set up a small retail operation of six retail branches which, on closure in 1993, boasted only five or six customers apiece, had dimmed. This time it moved in via the 33 rented branch offices and 2,000 salespeople it had bought from Yamaichi Securities Co. for $300 million. Yamaichi, Japan's fourth largest brokerage, had collapsed to the tune of ¥3.2 trillion ($25 billion), the biggest bankruptcy in Japanese history. The chairman of Merrill Lynch had spotted an opportunity to be first into the market and moved quickly so that, almost overnight, the company had become the first Western concern with an independent brokerage network in Japan, staffed by experienced locals.

Its nearest rivals were Japan's big three, Nomura, Daiwa and Nikko, but Merrill Lynch believed that its US business model could not fail to attract customers. Japanese customers are conservative savers, preferring to put 94% of their savings in the post office, despite earning less than 1% in annual interest. The lure of these ¥242 trillion in savings, together with the 1998 deregulation of the broking industry, was an irresistible target Merrill Lynch felt it could crack. It aimed to transform the Yamaichi brokers into US-style financial advisors, where commitment to clients and integrity would be paramount. What could possibly go wrong this time?

Merrill Lynch Japanese Securities opened for business on 1 July 1998. The market was not favourable, given an economy that, by then, had been flat for years. Ominously, from the beginning revenue failed to meet expectations, with a loss of ¥25 billion in the first nine months. A forecast revision pushed the venture's breakeven point out by another two years to 2002.

Perhaps even more unfortunately, the US-style business approach unsettled both employees and customers. The former did not take to the new merit-based reward system, while the retraining programme foundered on the branch managers' dislike of being required to read instructions in English. Dress-down Friday was another cultural hurdle few Japanese could cross: many arrived in suits and changed in the office washrooms. As one explained: 'If I left home in casual clothes, my wife would think I was having an affair.'

The US business approach also upset customers, for whom trust in a relationship was an important element. Merrill's request for customers to fill in forms asking for family and financial details was deemed intrusive in Japan. It also offered unfamiliar products and stressed long-term buy and hold investing, which was not common in Japan. Merrill also broke a local custom whereby Japanese brokerages frequently covered the losses of favoured clients. Understandably, Merrill refused to do this but it didn't endear it to the big end of town.

Its advertising campaign, costing tens of millions of dollars, also backfired. The ads and Merrill's shop fronts featured the company's trademark bull. One possibly apocryphal story had it that a Japanese mistook a Merrill branch for a Korean barbecue restaurant. Such instances of the lack of awareness and understanding of the Merrill brand took the US management by surprise. It finally realised that 'Our market research was too simple'.

Nevertheless, the chairman persisted in his belief that it was just taking a while for the Japanese to adjust to the cultural change and, in the first year, brokers were told not to worry about missing asset targets. However, when results failed to improve in the second year, hundreds were dismissed and more followed in succeeding years. Merrill reorganised its business, closed branches, cut staff and concentrated on big account holders. Still the retail venture lost about $600 million in three years.

Moral: As Merrill's chief financial officer reportedly observed: 'What works in one place won't necessarily work in another. It sometimes looks easier than it is when you get into someone else's back yard.'

The rescue: There was none. In November 2001, the operation became part of major, worldwide cutbacks at Merrill. Most of the 28 retail branches left were closed by early 2002, and about 700 financial consultants, three-quarters of the sales force, were dismissed. Merrill took a $2.2 billion fourth quarter charge in 2001 to cover the cost of the job cuts and other measures. Still, third time lucky?

Star Wars

In 1993, Rupert Murdoch acquired the pan-Asian broadcaster Star TV for US$950 million. With it, he hoped to achieve his aim of breaking into the Chinese market. However, over the next nine years it failed to live up to its profit potential, despite continued investment. In April 2002, it finally came out of the red, announcing an operating profit of $2.4 million in the third quarter of its fiscal year ending June 2002. That year also saw it opening in China, where it launched a 24-hour Mandarin language channel offering light entertainment. The channel was aimed at the growing young *nouveau riche* segment in Guangdong.

For Murdoch, this represented the fruits of nine years' hard labour to correct the effects of a disastrous after-dinner speech in London when he noted how modern telecommunications had 'proved an unambiguous threat to totalitarian regimes everywhere'. Satellite television in particular, he observed, made it possible for 'information-hungry residents of many closed societies to bypass state-controlled television channels'.[5] In response, Beijing enforced a ban on the reception of foreign satellite television in China.

In the intervening years, Murdoch slowly inched back into favour with the Beijing government. Star TV stopped showing BBC news. Control of

Hong Kong's *South China Morning Post* was sold to an ethnic Chinese tycoon perceived as sympathetic to Beijing. He also pulled out of a book contract with Chris Patten, the last governor of Hong Kong. As he said at the time: 'We're trying to set up in China, why should we upset them?'

The first signs of rehabilitation dawned in 1999, when News Corp., Murdoch's media group, was allowed to open a representative office in Beijing, the only major foreign media company granted that privilege. President Jiang Zemin praised Murdoch for 'presenting China objectively and cooperating with the Chinese press'. Murdoch single-mindedly continued his campaign. There was a venture to archive the Chinese newspaper, the *People's Daily*, and a documentary about Tibet made under Beijing's direction, which cost $450,000 but made only $175,000 in its first year of release. Murdoch's new wife, a mainland Chinese, also contributed – she was reported to be working on 'special projects' for the company in China.

The pay-off came in March 2002 when Xing Kong Wei Shi (Starry Sky Satellite TV) began broadcasting for the first time. One of the programmes, 'Wanted', was produced in collaboration with the Chinese Ministry of Security.

Moral: You can probably work it out for yourself.

A Learning Process

Many multinationals admit to having made mistakes in their approach to their Asian joint ventures and acquisitions, but did they learn from them? And, if not, how can they avoid falling into the same traps the next time?

These are good questions that usually remain unanswered. Few companies have the time or the processes to capture vital information about the evolution of their relationships with the companies they have acquired, or their partners, and describe what happened and what changes were made. Although successes may be celebrated by graphs showing production outputs and profit rises, failure and the reasons for it are usually quickly forgotten. Yet documenting this failure could help to build up valuable expertise at the centre, which could then be transmitted to those about to be sent out to take over and continue the work in progress, or run new investments. Unfortunately, the present habit of rotating expatriate managers every three years, which has become the norm, militates against any long-term database of local knowledge and experience. The maxim that managers feel lost for the first year of their posting, come to grips with it during the second and only truly perform in the third, holds for many. It is a pity then that after that one good year, they are sent back home or on a cross-posting. The experience they carry in their heads is often lost.

However, if this knowledge was recorded, it could be used to brief those just setting out, or to give presentations within the company. Inchcape of the UK, for example, developed a series of case studies that gave a picture of the company's operations, and these were given to new managers to read and learn from.[6] Cemex, the Mexican cement group, keeps an archive of documents on the PMI process for different acquisitions which is used as a reference for new acquisitions.

Unfortunately, such forethought is rare. If, instead of burying mistakes, companies were able to analyse what went wrong and why, it might prevent heavy, unnecessary losses in the future, or enable companies to work faster in turning round a new acquisition. It might even prevent a second disaster.

Notes

1   *EIU Business China*, 'Back from the brink', 15 February, 1999, pp1–2.
2   Taken from 'Hindustan Lever Limited: Levers for Change', a case study by Charlotte Butler and Professor Sumantra Ghoshal, LBS-INSEAD-EAC.
3   Taken from 'Ferodo (Thailand) Ltd.' (A) and (B), case studies Charlotte Butler, Anne-Marie Cagna and Professor Henri-Claude de Bettignies, 2001 INSEAD-EAC.
4   Taken from 'Bull Run', case study by Ted Chan and Professor Gordon Redding, INSEAD-EAC and *Asiamoney*, 'The Fair Weather Friend', by Fiona Haddock, December 2001–January 2002, **12**(10).
5   *Far Eastern Economic Review*, 'Star Crossed', 27 July, 2000, pp30–2.
6   See 'Managers & Mantras: One Company's Search for Simplicity' by Charlotte Butler and John Keary, Wiley & Sons (Asia) Pte Ltd. 2000.

Acknowledgements

WHO DO WE THANK?

This book would not have been written if Robyn Flemming, who edited both our previous books, had not detected the fact that the two authors had a similar approach to writing and so should at least meet. Meet they did and over a long lunch opposite the Paris Bourse, the outline for this book evolved. As Robyn herself remarked, most 'good' ideas developed over a long lunch evaporate as soon as the bonhomie induced by the wine wears off. But that was not the case for us. We ended up with a contract with Palgrave Macmillan.

And so it is the folks at Palgrave Macmillan who must also receive our thanks. Their enthusiasm and hard work in producing the book, especially Stephen Rutt who was our first contact with the company, and Jacky Kippenberger who was always a cheerful voice at the end of the phone, has been greatly appreciated.

Separately, Michael Backman would like to thank businessman and gourmet Jeffrey Tan of Melbourne for his many valuable insights on the practicalities of doing business across Asia, and also the many readers of his columns who have written to him with firsthand accounts of their own experiences.

Charlotte Butler would like to put on record her thanks to the Euro-Asia Centre and its director, Ben Bensaou, who encouraged the writing of this book and gave her the time to work on it. She would also like to thank all the Euro-Asia Centre faculty with whom she has worked over the last twelve years to produce the case studies that provide vivid illustrations for many of its chapters. Such a varied (in terms of nationalities, characters and expertise) team of colleagues has made for a rewarding, enjoyable and certainly never dull experience. Also at the Centre, she would like to thank Keeley Wilson and Ted Chan, who took the time to read the early chapters and make valuable suggestions for their improvement, whilst in the EAC library, Mary Boldrini was a tremendous help in tracking down sources. Joan Lewis, as ever, was a great supporter and friend.

London and Paris

Index